T0334119

"China sits at the heart of global manufacturing – and its innovations in logistics are an important reason why it's likely to stay that way. In this important new book, Clifford and Logan offer a rich and timely appraisal of the complex webs that define China's deep web of supply chains and provide essential strategic guidance for industry professionals."

> – **Dr. Parag Khanna**, Founder & CEO of AlphaGeo and internationally bestselling author of *Connectography* and *The Future Is Asian*

"China's logistics industry has experienced the stages of traditional logistics and modern logistics, and is now entering the era of intelligent and green logistics… My friend Paul [Clifford] has participated deeply in the reform process of transforming…many Chinese logistics enterprises, and has become a witness to this history. This book is his unique observation [in which] he has extracted many important conclusions, such as [on] the huge impact of Chinese government policies, on the Belt and Road Initiative and e-commerce logistics…This book deserves attention from readers who are interested in the development of Chinese logistics."

> – **Dr. Wu Youxi**, Executive Director of China Logistics Society, Vice Chairman of Expert Committee of China Warehousing and Distribution Association, Visiting Professor at the Ministry of Commerce and at Beijing Jiaotong University.

"In an increasingly volatile and complex global supply chain environment, an understanding of how China has emerged as a world leader in logistics is crucial. Clifford and Logan not only provide the reader with insight on the market's development but deliver a clear 'horizon scan' of potential risks in an uncertain future."

> – **Professor John Manners-Bell**, Founder, Foundation for Future Supply Chain and Author of 'The Death of Globalization'

"It's impossible to understand global supply chains and logistics without understanding China's evolving role, strategies, and tactics. *China Logistics* analyzes drivers and dynamics, from geopolitics and trade networks to the role of technology in improving efficiency and sustainability. This book will help readers to think clearly about the obvious, probable "gray rhino" challenges across China's logistics landscape."

> – **Michele Wucker**, Author of The Gray Rhino

China's Logistics

Exploring an underreported subject with global ramifications, this book sheds much-needed light on the rapid development of China's logistics industry over the past several decades and puts it into historical context.

Though still lagging behind global logistics leaders overall, China has invested heavily in logistics infrastructure and technology to become a vital link in global supply chains and is forging ahead in e-commerce logistics. This timely book analyzes the key policies, infrastructure projects, technologies, and companies that have transformed China's domestic logistics capabilities and enabled it to become deeply intertwined with the worldwide supply chain. As the world enters a new era of geopolitics and confronts the possibility of US-China decoupling, it is more critical than ever to understand China's logistics system to navigate uncertain times — and with their decades of experience, these authors are the very best guides.

Business leaders, policymakers, and logistics and supply chain professionals will benefit from this comprehensive and readable book's insights into how and why China's logistics system developed as it has, what that means for businesses and nations connected to China, and where we go from here.

Dr. Paul G. Clifford is a Senior Fellow, Harvard Kennedy School and the author of *The China Paradox: At the Front Line of Economic Transformation*. He worked in China in banking, consulting, and technology. He advised Chinese logistics clients and was Executive Director, China Federation of Logistics & Purchasing. He was educated at SOAS University of London and Peking University.

Christopher Logan is the President of LOGISTEED International and Chief International Business Officer of LOGISTEED Ltd. Previously with Accenture, Livingston, Agility, and Oliver Wyman in Beijing where he advised logistics clients. Educated at Ivey Business School, Western University, with further executive training at Harvard, Yale, and the Lee Kuan Yew School.

China's Logistics

From Laggard to Innovator

Paul G. Clifford and
Christopher Logan

Routledge
Taylor & Francis Group

NEW YORK AND LONDON

Designed cover image: Alamy

First published 2025
by Routledge
605 Third Avenue, New York, NY 10158

and by Routledge
4 Park Square, Milton Park, Abingdon, Oxon, OX14 4RN

Routledge is an imprint of the Taylor & Francis Group, an informa business

© 2025 Paul G. Clifford and Christopher Logan

Library of Congress Cataloging-in-Publication Data
Names: Clifford, Paul Gilmore, author. | Logan, Christopher
(Management consultant), author.
Title: China's logistics : from laggard to innovator / Paul Clifford
and Christopher Logan.
Description: New York, NY : Routledge, 2025. | Includes
bibliographical references and index. |
Identifiers: LCCN 2024032613 (print) | LCCN 2024032614
(ebook) | ISBN 9781032787077 (hardback) | ISBN
9781032771076 (paperback) | ISBN 9781003489115 (ebook)
Subjects: LCSH: Physical distribution of goods—China. |
Shipment of goods—China. | Business logistics—China. |
China—Commerce.
Classification: LCC HF5780.C6 C55 2025 (print) | LCC HF5780.
C6 (ebook) | DDC 658.7/880951—dc23/eng/20240912
LC record available at https://lccn.loc.gov/2024032613
LC ebook record available at https://lccn.loc.gov/2024032614

ISBN: 9781032787077 (hbk)
ISBN: 9781032771076 (pbk)
ISBN: 9781003489115 (ebk)

DOI: 10.4324/9781003489115

Typeset in Times New Roman
by codeMantra

This book is dedicated to
(From Paul) Miriam, Jasper, Hugo and Zoë
(From Christopher) Kirsten, Ellis and Fionn

Contents

Acknowledgments

We would like to acknowledge and thank not only those who have contributed ideas and provided encouragement as we planned and wrote this book but also those who over decades of work in China helped shape our knowledge and insights.

We are grateful for the support and guidance provided by Prof. Anthony Saich and Prof. Edward Cunningham at the Harvard Kennedy School and by Prof. William Kirby and Prof. Meg Rithmire at the Harvard Business School. Thanks also to Dr. Wu Youxi of the China Logistics Society, one of China's leading logistics experts with whom we have enjoyed a most fruitful exchange of ideas and knowledge. We are grateful to Ding Junfa, of the China Federation of Logistics and Purchasing whose advice and written work have guided us over the years.

Below, in alphabetical order, we wish to thank many more.

David Aikman, Nitin Ahuja, Mohammed Akoojee, Craig Allen, Larry Alberts, Alexander B. Alexiev, Holger Altvater, Morten Andersen, Sal Arora, Ehab Aziz, Manuel Baeuml, Amit Bagga, Sarah Banks, Roger Baugher, Alan Beacham, Benn Bekic, Borhene Ben Mena, Caroline Berube, Mike Bible, Steve Bishop, Michael Blaufuss, Marco Bloemen, Bunty Bohra, David Bovet, Kerry Brown, Peter Brown, Chen Xiangming, Ding Junfa, Cao Dong, Cao Mengqiu, Liam Casey, Kher Tean Chen, Harvey Cheung, Ruuchi Chhabra, Deven Chhaya, Esben Christensen, Lee Clair, John Clancey, Roy Coburn, Craig Conway, Andrew Collier, Remi Cornubert, Jim Cox, Andrew Craig-Bennett, Thomas Crampton, Ron Crompton, Roger Crook, George Dallas, Rob Denious, Joris D'Inca, Jim Down, Bill Driegert, John Drzik, Cyril Dumon, Toby Edwards, Michael J. Enright, Mohammed Esa, Thomas Escott, Elliott Etheredge, Stephane Ethier, Herman Evert, Mark Fagan, Vasco Fernandes, Stephan Feuchtwang, Greg Fishbein, Mariam Al Foudery, William Flynn, Jeremy Foxon, Lance Fritz, Spring Fu, James Gagne, Gao Weijie, Sam Geall, Greg Gilligan, John Gittings, Matt Goodman, Ben Gordon, Roddie Gow, Richard T. Griffiths, Oliver Gritz, Yu Gu, He Dengcai, He Liming, Mike Hanson, Bill Harsh, Bernie Hart, Carl Hemus, Edwin Hewitt, Carla Hills, Ghim Siew Ho, Sum Ho, John Holden, James Hollis, Henry Hillman, Rima Hochman,

Wolfgang Hollermann, Ellen Hu, Eddie Huang, Huang Yiping, Marc Iampieri, Ron Jackson, Gert-Jan Jansen, Kenneth Jarrett, Robert Jessing, Bernard Jiang, Jiang Kai, Parag Khanna, Koji Kawakita, Jiang Xingquan, Mark Kadar, Joan Kaufman, Ryan Keyrouse, Thomas Knudsen, Kenneth Ko, Greg Kovacic, Yuichi Kuroume, James Kynge, Ma Xiaodong, Peter Lacy, Paul Lam, Nick Lardy, Justin Yifu Lin, Mykell Lee, Wolfgang Lehmacher, Ian Leong, Ron Lentz, Kelvin Leung, Frank Leung, Peggy Liu, Qian Liu, Borje Ljunggren, Luo Kaifu, Lu Feng, Kevin Lu, Gary Lynch, Winston Ma, Stephen Markscheid, Ma Zehua, Gheorghe Magheru, George Magnus, John Manners-Bell, Christopher Marquis, Kazuya Matsui, Mark Millar, Jim McAdam, Jett McCandless, Ross McCullough, Valentin de Miguel, Todd Miller, Lisa Minoura, Rana Mitter, Suv Mohapatra, Kerry Mok, Dan Mongeon, Jon Monroe, James Chin Moody, Simone Morandi, Beatrix Morath, Chris Munro, Chris Murck, Yasuo Nakatani, Jeff Nankivell, Raju Narisetti, Kazushige Natori, Henrik Naujoks, John Negroponte, Eddy Ng, Steve Orlins, Mei Pang, Sharad Parashar, Charlie Parton, John Pattullo, William Payson, Ted Perlman, Stephen Perry, Ryan Peterson, Christopher Pollard, Oliver Plogmann, Mitch Presnick, Steve Preston, Chris Price, Scott Price, Kevin Prokop, Suhail Qureshi, Robert Reiter, Bill Rennicke, Edwin Ritchken, Nevino Rocco, Gerry Romanelli, Cobus Rossouw, Daniel Rosen, Andrew Rothman, Gilles Roucolle, Bill Russo, Anoop Sagoo, Essa Al Saleh, Henadi Al Saleh, David Saperstein, Anton Scheepers, Raphael Schoentgen, Klaus Schwab, Jen Zhu Scott, Vishal Sharma, Willie Shih, Shiv Shivaraman, Issac Shongwe, David Schulingkamp, Lutfey Siddiqi, Sam Sidiqi, Beat Simon, Sachu Simon, Rashad Sinokrot, Harriet Skipworth, Robert Smith, Tim Stratford, Peter Stokes, Tarek Sultan, Dorjee Sun, Sun Jiakang, Sun Yueying, Philip Sweens, Scott Szwast, Tao Suyun, Chin Hwee Tan, Yinglan Tan, Donald Tang, Sue Anne Tay, Hua Fung Teh, Derek Thomas, Jim Thompson, Tomas Tichy, Raymond Tsang, Steve Tsang, Fabio Vacirca, Carl Van Dyke, Georges Vialle, Stephane Vidal, Lianne Xiong, Wang Hui, Simon Wang, Tina Wang, Wang Zuo, Xin Jin, Wang Jian, Kevin Wang, Mei Wang, John Watling, Stephan Weber, Paul ter Weeme, Wolfgang Weidner, Wei Jiadong, Wei Jiafu, Gabriel Wildau, Ben Williams, Niklas Wilmking, Alain Wilson, Peishan Wong, Chris Woodward, Jonathan Wright, Mark Wu, Michele Wucker, Yang Dongming, Yang Ting, Frank Yao, Yao Yang, Ye Ping, Ye Weilong, Yen Shan, Mark Young, Yu Jianmin, Yu Lai Boon, Michael Zea, Douglas Zhihua Zeng, Zha Daojiong, Zhang Hong, Zhang Jianwei, Zhao Yumin, Zheng Yongnian, Cliff Zhou, Jie Zhou, Levin Zhu, Richard Zhu, Zhu Shaoding, Zhu Yulan, and David Zou.

Our thanks also to our publisher Routledge who were quick to sign us up and have moved things along smoothly. It has been a pleasure working with their highly professional team: senior editor Meredith Norwich, editorial assistant Bethany Nelson, editorial director Catherine Bernard, production editor Hannah Rayner and codemantra project manager Dhivya Lakshmi.

Of course, we should hasten to add that we alone bear responsibility for the contents of this book. Any errors or omissions should be laid firmly at our door.

Introduction

Framing the issues

China's logistics is an under-reported story with massive implications not only for China's economy, business, and society but also for the world at large. The subtitle *From Laggard to Innovator* is purposefully ambiguous since it captures two key elements. Firstly, it describes the enormous progress China has made from the status of laggard to a new situation where it is outpacing the rest of the world. Secondly, it also explains that today China's logistics still have serious weaknesses, so that the current situation ranges from dire backwardness to major technological advances.

China's economic reforms after 1978 were combined with the "open-door policy" under which foreign direct investment was welcomed, albeit with many restrictions. In that early period, foreign firms that took the plunge and put factories in China were faced with many challenges. One key issue that came as a surprise to many investors, as they drafted the feasibility study for their China project, was China's totally inadequate logistics system. It was hard to get raw materials to the factory or to get finished products out to the market. China's transportation was poor: inefficient railways, no superhighways for long haul, no locally produced heavy trucks, and little or no air cargo. Warehousing was substandard, often with leaking roofs and not secure from theft. There were no local firms that, as a *Third-Party Logistics* (3PL) provider, could offer the modern outsourced integrated logistics upon which the rest of the world already relied to bring the transportation and storage together into a seamless service.

At the turn of the century, we worked closely with the China Federation of Logistics and Procurement to conduct a survey of the China 3PL market and we served as advisors to China's largest logistics companies to help them restructure their organizations and rethink their strategies so that they could address the needs of the market. What we found was that during the first two decades of the reforms, that is through the 1980s and 1990s as China's economy boomed, its outsourced logistics industry had failed to make its own transition and remained woefully incapable of meeting the needs of the burgeoning industry and commerce. Fortunately, this was a wake-up call, and,

DOI: 10.4324/9781003489115-1

with strong impetus provided by China's reform-minded political leadership, that transformation of China's logistics began in earnest.

The positive theme is that, over the last 25 years, transformation has taken many forms whether in the massively improved transportation system as the backbone for logistics or in the emergence of large Chinese 3PLs. Among the China 3PLs, we have seen not only transformed state-owned firms that have achieved world-class performance, but also the extraordinary flourishing of privately owned e-commerce and express delivery firms whose development and adoption of technology qualify them as innovators who are outpacing the rest of the world.

The negative theme is the industry's continued monumental underperformance and inefficiency. "Large but not strong (da er buqiang)": this was how, in late 2022,[1] the Chinese government roundly and candidly criticized the state of its logistics industry, pointing out that it was not competitive by global standards. These strong words were brutally frank and remarkable coming from officials that are more used to beautifying harsh truths.

China's leaders attach a very high priority to addressing the weaknesses of China's logistics since doing so brings major benefits across six dimensions, by:

- Increasing economic efficiency and thus driving toward a "better GDP."
- Playing a critical role in helping China achieve its green agenda to reduce greenhouse gas emissions.
- Contributing to China's long-standing goal of enhanced economic and political integration.
- Through local-level initiatives such as logistics parks and hubs, attracting and stimulating broader-based development in manufacturing and service industry.
- Improving social well-being and living standards, as way to address the economic and wealth disparity between the developed and less developed parts of China.
- Through e-commerce down to the smaller cities and rural areas, incorporating less-developed regions into the economy and in so doing moving toward a consumption-driven economy, as an alternative to one driven by government stimulus measures.

This brings us to another major strand of our narrative. If we had room for a second subtitle to this book it could be "*From Government Tailwinds to Geopolitical Headwinds.*"

The tailwinds are the positive supportive role played by China's government, at the central and local (mainly city) levels in fostering the upgrading of China's logistics. This is the predictable outcome of the six dimensions set out above. In China, the role of government in logistics is a central and determining factor that far transcends what we see in advanced Western economies. This is a core theme that appears throughout our work.

The headwinds that China's logistics face are the geopolitical tensions and trends that not only bring into question the future of the globalized economy but also, with the risk of Taiwan crisis, present the possibility of a massive disruption of world trade and of the logistics that power it. These are already manifesting themselves in punitive tariffs imposed on Chinese goods and in restrictions put on semiconductor exports to China. In examining these tensions, we highlight China's methods of mitigating these risks through its developing nations play (the Belt & Road Initiative) and with that the China-Europe land bridge (railway links).

The reader may well ask what "do we mean by logistics?" Later, we delve more deeply into the thorny question of its definition and the special terminology surrounding it. But, here it is useful to provide a simple explanation. We acknowledge two valid meanings of "logistics." In the broadest sense, logistics covers the entire system whereby goods flow through the economy, encompassing transportation of all modes, and the warehousing where goods are stored during that process. In the narrowest sense, logistics refers to *modern outsourced logistics*. These are not handled by the shipper (usually the manufacturer) in-house but are outsourced, or contracted out, to a 3PL. The 3PLs are also often relatively asset-light, with few or no transportation or warehouse assets of their own. These services are integrated through technology which in many cases is still just through email plus Excel spreadsheets but when it comes to the most advanced, logistics firms are further optimized through IT platforms that harness the power of the Internet of Things (IoT) and Artificial Intelligence (AI).

By carefully addressing the definition of logistics, we aim to clarify and demystify this sector and help make this subject accessible to the general reader. This in turn feeds into our desire to ensure that what might otherwise be an overly dry and technical topic becomes a vivid and gripping narrative. We seek to highlight the aspects of the story that might be counter-intuitive – elements that may come as a surprise to the reader. That said we stay clear of hyperbole and remain rigorously fact-based.

Let us first revert to the two strands of our story – the backwardness and the newly found innovation. The statement above about "big but not strong" was made in China's five-year plan for logistics (2021–2025), which remarkably was the first time the nation had a comprehensive plan for logistics, indicating the extent to which this vital sector had not received the priority it deserved.

Two decades earlier, in 2002, a veteran Chinese expert on logistics had already sounded the alarm, writing with both honesty and poetic flourish:

Logistics is strange and mysterious to many people. In fact, it is everywhere and at every moment. Countries cannot do without logistics: markets cannot; enterprises cannot; and consumers cannot. Developing our logistics is not an easy thing to do since our comprehensive level is still backward over 20 years compared to the developed countries.[2]

He provided a number of most telling metrics of just how backward China's logistics were. Logistics costs were 20% of GDP compared to 9.9% in the US and represented 30%–40% of product cost – "unimaginable in developed, market-oriented economies," he commented.[3]

What is striking is that, two decades later, in many respects, China's logistics are still hugely underperforming. In 2020, logistics accounted for 14.7% of GDP, still twice the 7.4% recorded in the US. By 2023, it had fallen slightly to 14.4%.[4]

However, this may not be an exact apples-to-apples comparison. China has much more primary (process) industry and secondary manufacturing, which might imply more logistics costs, compared to other countries. But other ways of assessing logistics efficiency, such as cost per ton/km or per capita cold storage area also reveal that China's performance in logistics falls far short of that of developed nations.[5]

Recently, a senior Chinese official expanded on the issues, stating that Chinese logistics "face the problems of unbalanced, insufficient and imperfect, which results in it being large but not strong, coarse and not refined, integrated but not unified."[6]

However, when we consider the upside, there is ample space for rapid improvement and, with that, significant business opportunity. Back in 2002, the Chinese market for 3PL services was tiny, at around US$ 4.8 BN, but growing at an annual rate of about 25%.[7] The reason the market was so small back then was simply that few shippers or manufacturers were willing to outsource their logistics. The China 3PL market was in its infancy. But two decades later in 2023, the China logistics market was RMB 18.2 Trillion (US$ 2.6 Trillion). Of this, transportation, storage (warehousing), and administration accounted for RMB 9.8, 6.1, and 2.3 Trillion, respectively.[8]

But, the total market number may be deceptive and should be treated with caution. We need to be healthily wary of statements about "enormous market opportunities." The true business opportunity, the actual addressable market for any given logistics provider, is of course very different from this aggregated figure. Foreign and large Chinese 3PLs are simply not competitive in huge swathes of a price-driven, poorly regulated market. Also, even Chinese 3PLs need to focus on the needs of specific segments of the market. That said, if the target client segment is carefully defined and the offering is a highly differentiated value proposition, then opportunities can be unlocked. Given the fast growth and increased sophistication of the demand for logistics in China, Chinese and foreign firms are energetically pursuing opportunities through deploying state-of-the-art technology. A new segment of Chinese players, those in e-commerce, has exploded into action and is in fact leapfrogging the rest of the world in their logistics. During the period 2015–2021, the number e-commerce items handled rose from 5.7 BN to 100 BN, making China the largest e-commerce market for eight consecutive years.

To guide the reader, we have broken the book into four sections.

Section 1, The Context: From Geography to Politics, is a vital building block for our narrative. Our goal is to avoid a glib or one-dimensional snapshot of China's logistics at this moment in time. We eschew the language of business journalism which focuses on the "winners and losers" of the day. Our approach is to carefully place the current state of China's logistics in its historical and political context, so that we can understand its origins, better assess what is driving it today and provide guidance on where it is heading. We look at China's logistics not in isolation but as a product of the nation's overall trajectory and ambitions.

To explain the backwardness, we delve into China's modern history since the 19th century and in particular the long and troublesome legacy of the now dismantled Soviet-style centrally planned economy.

To shed light on the foundations over which China's logistics run, we explain the geography that is destiny and the comprehensively transformed gleaming new transportation network. We put China's logistics in its broader context of economic development and political goals, explaining firmly how they serve to enhance national integration – how they have tracked China's development from the coastal plains in the East to the remote areas in the West.

In this section, and throughout the book, we highlight the absolutely critical role that the Chinese government (the party-state) has played in China's logistics, at central and local levels.

In *Section 2, Challenges and Goals; From Backward to World Class*, we drill down more deeply into how China's logistics are evolving.

We first focus on the enormous challenges faced by the industry. How does the low level of outsourcing to 3PLs hold China back? For the logistics firms, how can they escape a world of fragmentation, intense competition, and poor profitability?

We then move on to the inspiring story of China's logistics whereby they are not only catching up but, in some cases, leapfrogging the rest of the world. How is the trend toward specialization in logistics playing out, for instance in building out China's cold-chain capability?

We devote a chapter to information technology (IT) that lies at the very heart of the transformation of China's logistics. How are China's 3PLs rapidly deploying mobile internet/IoT and AI? How is technology being harnessed to match trucks to loads, thus reducing the dreaded "empty backhaul"? How are robots, automation, and drones being deployed? Why are autonomous trucks becoming a reality in China faster than cars?

China is making enormous progress in achieving China's logistics greener, as a key element of the agenda to create a better, not just a larger, GDP. How is this policy direction being translated into action by China's logistics firms, whether through using electric vehicles (EVs) for ground transportation or through container ships being fueled by methanol?

In several chapters, we comprehensively address China's massive role in international logistics. What will be the impact on logistics of the efforts to unwind globalization and decouple the US and China? How critical is China's Belt and Road Initiative, its trade, and investment push globally, to the continued growth in China's logistics industry? How is China catching up through investing more heavily in air cargo or in overseas ports management? How do we see Chinese rapid growth in China-Europe rail links further evolving? We examine in some depth the potentially catastrophic impact that conflict or blockades over Taiwan would have on global logistics.

Section 3, The Key Players: Profiles and Case Studies, is devoted to the logistics firms themselves, the true actors in our drama, the businesses that make logistics work, that make sure the goods flow smoothly and efficiently from the factory to the consumer.

For the Chinese firms, we provide profiles of the large state-owned firms and of the recently arrived e-commerce and express delivery private firms. How have these different players adapted or emerged? How do they interact with the Chinese government? As Chinese firms grow and improve, are they able to capture business from large Multinational Corporations (MNCs)? How are Chinese e-commerce firms, which are selling Chinese goods in the US, storming the market?

The narrative then turns to foreign logistics firms in China. Why was China so slow to welcome them in? Why have these foreign firms succeeded in cross-border logistics but struggled to compete profitably in the intra-China logistics market?

In *Section 4, Conclusions,* we begin by setting out potential scenarios based on geopolitics and economic trends. Against this background, we explore the strategic implications of China's logistics, both their impact on China's domestic economic trajectory and their role in global trade. We provide the reader with a clear foundation and road map for viewing the future and for evaluating the new developments and transitions in logistics, as they emerge.

Notes

1 State Council of the PRC, *"shisiwu" xiandai wuliu fazhan guihua ("14th Five-Year Plan" Modern Logistics Development Plan),* Dec 15, 2022.
2 Ding Junfa, *zhongguo wuliu (China's Logistics),* China Logistics Publishing House, Mar 2002.
3 Ding Junfa, *zhongguo wuliu (China's Logistics),* China Logistics Publishing House, Mar 2002.
4 *2023 Nian quanguo wuliu yunxing qingkuang tongbao,* issued by the NDRC and the China Federation of Logistics and Procurement. On *China Logistics Information Centre,* Feb 7, 2024.
5 Wu Youxi, *Wuliu gaozhiliang fazhan ying ruhe tuijin,* on *jingjiwang,* June 21, 2023.

6 He Dengcai, *Cong ronghe youxiao xuqiu deng wufangmian jianshe xiandai wuliu tixi* (Build a Modern Logistics System from Five Aspects, Including Integrating Efficient Demand), on *Reminwang*, Mar 18, 2021.
7 Survey by Mercer Management Consulting (with China Federation of Logistics & Purchasing), *The State of Third Party Logistics in China*, 2002.
8 *2023 Nian quanguo wuliu yunxing qingkuang tongbao*, issued by the NDRC and the China Federation of Logistics and Procurement. On *China Logistics Information Centre*, Feb 7, 2024.

Section 1

The context

From geography to politics

Chapter 1

Unpacking logistics

Trade's backbone explained

The military origins of logistics

Throughout history, there was of course significant international trade, for instance in metals, grains, wool, spices, tea, and luxury goods. But most economic activity occurred close to the easily accessible local marketplace. Until the 19th century, the supply chain for a large proportion of manufacturing was not that complex since the factories or small-scale workshops were located near to both the raw materials they processed and the markets they served.

But when it comes to the military, it is easy to see why the logistics were much more strategic and complicated than those in the everyday civilian world. When nation-states fought foreign wars across vast tracks of land and ocean, the efficient and timely provision of food, transportation, weapons, and other supplies became a critical and highly complex element in successful campaigns. The term "logistics" dates from the mid-19th century when it entered the English language from a French term used in the military.

Military officer training academies such as West Point in the US and Sandhurst in the UK drill into their cadets the importance of logistics. They teach how, in ancient times, victories were tied to prowess in logistics. They look at how Hannibal (45–181 BC) and Alexander The Great (357–324 BC) integrated logistics management into their strategies. Alexander said: "My logisticians are a humorless lot. They know they are the first ones I will slay if my campaign fails."[1] Modern military tacticians and countless modern business advisors have found much to learn from in *The Art of War*, written in China by Sun Zi about 500 BC. In more recent times, logistics are credited with playing a decisive role in the Peninsula War (1807–1814) in Portugal which was fought under the leadership of the Duke of Wellington.

Equally, the failure of logistical support is seen as a key element in the defeat of armies that became overstretched. Notable were the ill-fated invasions of Russia first by Napoleon (1812) and then by Hitler (1941). But also worthy of mention is how in the 1860s, China's Taiping rebels, which came close to overthrowing the Qing Dynasty, completely botched their thrust from their powerbase

DOI: 10.4324/9781003489115-3

in central China up to the Beijing capital in North China in part because their logistics let them down, including in supplying those southern troops with rice, rather than the wheat that was more available in the North.

So, logistics is a term that has been widely used for a very long time in the military context. But in the civilian world, it is relatively new and has many meanings. Civilian logistics owes much to military logistics but differs from it in one major respect: unlike the military type that includes moving troops around, the civilian variety is essentially about just materials, goods, and products. The transportation of humans is typically discussed quite separately as passenger transportation.

Logistics versus supply chain management

Although there is plenty of overlap, logistics is not exactly the same as *Supply Chain Management (SCM)* and is really a subset of it. SCM encompasses a broader area. For an electric vehicle assembler, SCM would include establishing a reliable supply of battery producers and with it the issue of mitigating the supply chain disruption risk associated with raw materials that go into them such as lithium. Likewise, a designer of semiconductors spends much time finding ways to identify and qualify a wafer fab that is capable of manufacturing its chips and in the volumes it requires. In contrast, logistics is fundamentally about the movement of goods within the supply chain, their transportation, distribution, and storage.

Logistics versus plain transportation and warehousing

One useful way of getting to the meaning of "logistics" is to say what logistics is and what it is not. Firstly, what it is. Logistics encompass the movement of goods through society and internationally, through various modes of transportation, through warehousing and storage, plus the overall management, facilitated by IT systems, of these processes and flows. This is coupled with various kinds of *value-added services (VAS)* provided during the passage of goods through the system, such as break-bulk, consolidation, palletization, packaging, labeling, and even further processing such as chemical formulation. For the logistics provider, these VAS can help ensure better pricing and customer loyalty.

Secondly what it is not. It is sometimes the case that commentators and policymakers treat plain transportation or plain warehousing alone as logistics. But that is not how we intend to define modern logistics. By the same token, slapping the name XYZ Logistics Solutions on a truck does not make it a modern logistics firm. What is needed to make it modern logistics is for the service to include the integrated management of the overall broader goods flow.

The Chinese language term for logistics is *wuliu* (物流) is an abbreviation of the term *wuzhi liutong* (物质流通) which means "the circulation of materials" or in other words the "flow of goods." Linguistically that is more accessible than "logistics." Within the term logistics or *wuliu*, the Chinese government distinguishes three key elements: transportation, warehousing, and administration.

There is also a much narrower definition of logistics, which is often called *Third-Party Logistics (3PL)* and within that *Contract Logistics*. All these definitions are valid. But we are careful to distinguish between them.

A working definition

Much of traditional logistics was in the past not even called logistics. Transportation or warehousing was provided with a focus on the core assets such as trucks and buildings. The management of these assets and the services they provided were relatively simple and often highly fragmented, the very antithesis of the modern integrated supply chain to which we aspire today.

In a way, civilian logistics might be seen as a part of the economy which was neglected and forgotten, to the point where it became a severe bottleneck in industrial and commercial development, especially as the world entered a new phase of globalization where raw materials, factories, and markets were no longer local but more often than not located on the other side of the world.

In recent decades, new logistics concepts and new providers of these services have finally emerged to fill this gaping capability gap. The age of Modern Integrated Logistics began. A US professional association devoted to this industry has defined logistics management (as opposed to the broader SCM) as:

> ...that part of supply chain management that plans, implements, and controls the efficient, effective forward and reverse flow and storage of goods, services and related information between the point of origin and the point of consumption in order to meet customers' requirements.[2]

It then goes on to explain that logistics includes: "inbound and outbound transportation management, fleet management, warehousing, materials handling, order fulfillment, logistics network design, inventory management, supply/demand planning."[3] A key element of the definition provided is the heavy emphasis on how logistics is integrated into business strategy:

> It is involved in all levels of planning and execution--strategic, operational and tactical. Logistics management is an integrating function, which coordinates and optimizes all logistics activities, as well as integrates logistics activities with other functions including marketing, sales manufacturing, finance, and information technology.[4]

We endorse this as a sound and comprehensive definition of logistics management which informs and underpins our narrative.

Who does the logistics? In-house or contract out?
The emergence of the 3PL

Whether in the past or today, industrial manufacturers or service providers (which are typically called *shippers*, that is those who ship the goods) have, at least in market economies, had the choice of handling their own logistics, known as *in-house logistics*, or contracting them out to a *logistics service provider*, typically referred to as *3PL* provider. By the third party, we mean that the firm running the logistics is neither the shipper nor the end-user/recipient of the goods. In other words, we are talking about logistics that are outsourced to a third party. We refer to market economies, since in China things were different. Under Soviet-style central planning until the 1980s, factories lived in a system under which they had no control over their inbound or outbound logistics or over their domestic or international customer relationships, all of which was handled by other government agencies located in separate government stove pipes, or silo-like bureaucracies. This presented a huge barrier to China sorting out its backward and wasteful logistics, as it forged ahead with its economic reforms. We discuss this baleful legacy in Chapter 2.

Today some Western firms have left their logistics in-house. The retailer Walmart built its low-price retail business by running its own highly efficient and optimized logistics operations, including trucks, which permitted it to reduce costs across the supply chain. E-commerce firm Amazon originally outsourced its *fulfillment* (delivery of products to the consumer) but has recently entered the ground logistics business, building its own network of regional warehouses, trucks, and vans in the US and elsewhere. In the US, when it faces capacity constraints with its in-house logistics, it is still happy to outsource to the United States Postal Service. So, it gets to have its cake and eat it too.

Chinese shippers have been slow to outsource their logistics, due in part to their ownership of legacy transportation fleets and in part due to a lack of confidence in the capabilities of Chinese 3PLs. But in the US and elsewhere, the trend has been strongly toward manufacturers and retailers outsourcing their logistics needs. Of course, much of the logistics outsourced still resembles the old-style transportation and warehousing. But the business model of Modern Integrated Logistics that has come to dominate is the 3PL.

The 3PL provider marks itself off from traditional transportation or warehousing providers in a number of ways. It typically works with its customers on a contract basis, maybe a year and often longer. This *contract logistics* is a radically different approach from the traditional spot, or short-term, one-off, purchasing of transportation or warehousing. The focus is on longer term customer relationships, seeking to move away from just price and toward the quality of service, and customized solutions.

Among 3PLs, there is a major distinction between those that own all or much of their transportation assets and those that are "asset-light." 3PLs often feel a need to own some transportation or warehousing assets in order to demonstrate a) that they fully understand the business, b) that they have "skin in the game," that is a commitment to the supply chain beyond just network design and the outsource assets, and c) have full control over the service quality at all points.

The asset intensity of a 3PL often has to do with a firm's origins. There are shipping lines such as Maersk and China's Cosco Shipping that have expanded into ground-based services while maintaining their container fleets. In the US, there are those such as Werner, J.B. Hunt, C.H. Robinson, and Ryder who still maintain their original trucking fleets. France's postal service La Poste has branched out with a 3PL called DPD which runs its own transportation fleet. Then, there are asset-light freight forwarders, such as Kuehne & Nagel and Schenker (now part of Germany railways) that have now become full-service 3PLs.

In the global express, delivery, and airfreight market, three massive firms, UPS, FedEx, and DHL (now owned by German Railways), are utterly dominant. Called "integrators," they have an "asset-intensive" approach, providing door-to-door pickup and delivery using their own planes, trucks, vans, sorting, and warehousing facilities. As we shall see, they have not been able to replicate that dominance in China's domestic market.

It is also useful to distinguish between basic logistics and more sophisticated integrated logistics, as described below[5]:

Integrated logistics

Contract manufacturing/ assembly

Fulfillment services

High-end packaging services

Inventory replenishment

Demand planning

Merge-in-transit

Order processing

Transportation and warehousing optimization

Basic logistics

Freight forwarding

Warehouse management

Carrier selection

Fleet management

Direct transportation services

Packaging, labeling, kitting

Shipment consolidation

Cross-docking

Truck brokerage

Breaking down the term logistics

Logistics is typically broken up into several categories based on the stage it represents in the supply chain. *Inbound logistics* refers to the handling of raw materials, components, or other goods flowing into manufacturing facilities for further processing or assembly into a product. *Outbound logistics* refers to the handling of goods, either semi-finished goods bound for further manufacturing elsewhere or finished products going into the wholesale distribution system or direct to the retail outlet. Finally, there are *reverse logistics* whereby products are returned to the manufacturer or the distributor due to a defect and some other reason for customer rejection.

We shall use these terms throughout this book in the way explained above.

The key attributes of logistics. From efficiency and cost to specialization and customized solutions

Taking the above definitions as a basis, we can drill down to the main requisite attributes of logistics and how these are evolving and being added to.

Put simply, logistics was and remains essentially to do with the transportation and storage of goods throughout the entire supply chain, from raw materials to factories and out to the end user, domestically and internationally. Usually excluded from logistics is the handling of basic materials, parts and components, and finished products in the factory itself. Traditionally and globally, logistics has been around two-thirds of transportation cost and the remaining one-third being warehousing. In 2023, the Chinese government defined the nation's US$ 2.57 trillion logistics market (including cross-border logistics) as comprising 54% transportation, 33% storage, and 13% administration.[6]

As mentioned above, the traditional goals of "efficient, effective" remain at the core. *Effective* has to do with reliable, predictable, on-time delivery without damage to the goods. Decades ago, UK publishers faced horrific incidents of trucks overturning or getting stuck crossing the Alps in winter, as they carried books from the printers in Italy north to the rest of Europe. In that case, the logistics of that part of the supply chain were fragile and not "effective." With regard to warehousing, "effective" has to do with how well insulated it is from the heat and rain, rodent proof, and also safe from theft.

"Efficient" has to do with the cost of logistics, not just the cost compared to competing ways of transporting or storing but also relating to the proportion logistics represent in the total cost of a product and more broadly as a proportion of the total economy or GDP. We shall see that while in China this measure of efficiency has improved over recent decades, it still lags what is achieved in more developed markets. When we consider the impact on the shipper, when today we talk about warehousing, the costs include not only the fees charged but also the cost of capital locked up in the inventory being stored.

Now we can add to this by bringing onto the stage what is often referred to as *Modern Integrated Logistics* which is marked off from traditional logistics in a number of ways. As modern integrated logistics have emerged, the term logistics has itself become a buzzword. Even a traditional trucker with one vehicle may today plaster on his truck a flashy name and logo that exudes technology, modernity, and solutions to problems. But putting that aside, there is the true emergence of a new strategy for the delivery of logistics services, and within that a series of highly customized models to fit specialized needs.

Building on the discussion of "efficient, effective," there are other attributes of logistics that we see in modern logistics. There is a heavy emphasis on *visibility* throughout the process at all stages and preferably real time. *Track and trace*, using barcodes, radio frequency identification all seamlessly and real time (through the Internet of Things) integrated into the 3PL's IT platform is now an essential part of the process. Those shipping the goods or those waiting for them to arrive expect to be able to know at any time exactly where they are and not just when they will arrive. This has become a core competence of firms such as Amazon, UPS, and FedEx who provide the physical side of e-commerce. But, it has also become ubiquitous across most logistics providers.

There is a need for *flexibility*. Modern business strategy stresses a customer-driven approach. While in the past, there was basically a one-size-fits-all approach that addressed mainly the need for "efficiency" and cost reduction, today this is balanced against the need for a more *fluid* approach that supports solutions tailored to individual customers. This in turn feeds into a trend toward longer term contracts rather than the spot business and with that a focus less on the cost of the service but more on its quality. In the course of service delivery, customers may make changes to the final destination while the goods are in transit or may need to "break shipment" while it is in a distribution center. This also requires a flexible approach.

In response to customer needs, we have also seen the emergence of *specialization*, for instance in the chilled chain (that is chilled or refrigerated transportation and storage used from dairy products, meat, fish, and vegetables, and for pharmaceutical and other medical supplies), fast-moving consumer goods, electronics components (often air cargo), dangerous goods such as chemicals, auto (parts and finished vehicles), and large and bulky items of equipment. This specialization has for some time been taken for granted in the US and elsewhere. Not so in China where specialization has seriously lagged the needs of the market. Later we highlight how 3PLs have been required by fast food chains entering the China market to put *food safety*, which is closely tied to a resilient cold chain, as a key attribute of their logistics services.

There has been a big change in the kind of skills and assets needed to run a logistics firm. While in the past, the emphasis was on assets such as trucks and buildings, plus a largely poorly educated workforce, today things have moved dramatically toward fewer but *highly educated and trained professionals*.

Later, we devote Chapter 7 to the transformative role of technology, of digitalization, in China's logistics industry. Here, we simply note that IT has been an essential driver of integration in logistics, whether it is horizontally across the supply chain or vertically within the logistics firm and is acknowledged as a key element of its business strategy. IT has become the glue that holds everything together and creates the seamless approach that the shipper and end-customers demand today. The definition of logistics, quoted above, also includes the flow of "related information." Clear and complete information was always vital to the smooth handling of goods. But today, the digital revolution is transforming this aspect of modern logistics in countless respects.

Logistics earn their space in the "C Suite"

That brings us to how logistics are seen and valued. Logistics were always the poor relative, seen as an important but still lowly part of operations. But today, logistics are finally and decisively integrated in the strategic thinking of every successful manufacturing or service company. It is a key part of their strategic big picture and an essential element of risk management. Discussion of logistics is part of all aspects of corporate planning, from new product development, manufacturing processes and location, customer satisfaction and retention, human resources, working capital management, and business disruption risk.

Corning Incorporated, an upstate New York-based producer of specialty glass for consumer electronics which has a broad global manufacturing footprint including across China, is an excellent example of the integration of logistics into corporate strategy. The high degree of complexity of its businesses has led Corning to attach the highest priority to supply chain innovation. This is not only to drive efficiency and cost reduction but also to enhance customer experience and satisfaction through end-to-end visibility. It also deepens its relationships with a myriad of upstream suppliers. It is closely related to the fundamental imperative of mitigating supply chain disruption whether it be pandemic disease, a typhoon or issues with a trucking company. As Corning put it, "It is no longer acceptable to be as good as your competition in supply chain. We need to get ahead of them and deliver a competitive advantage for our business partners and customers."[7]

In recognition of the priority given to the supply chain, Corning has created the position of Chief Supply Chain Officer. Globally, it has three central supply chain hubs, in the US, Switzerland, and Singapore, plus secondary centers.

For Corning, with a complex supply chain involving cross-border shipping from production sites to customers, there were constant variations in import duties and practices at ports that have an impact on the price paid by the customers. These supply chain elements have to be carefully meshed with the sales function. Integrating logistics closely into the business permits these issues to be handled smoothly.

A heavy reliance on digitalization helps cement supply issues into the core of the firm's strategy. Corning has formed strategic partnerships with firms that provide software that can address different aspects of digitalization. One software vendor provides Corning with supply chain visibility through an online platform that integrates procurement, logistics, manufacturing, and inventory. Another provides data analytics using AI to anticipate and address supply chain disruption. Another firm provides software that Corning uses to automate and streamline payment processes.[8]

The key factor is that SCM and logistics are integrated into Corning's business from the corporate leadership down to the individual product line management. Corporate leadership directly manages a pool of supply chain resources that can be deployed globally, including in China. At the same time, each business group has its own set of supply chain resources embedded day-to-day into the business and product management teams.[9]

Reality and aspiration

Modern integrated logistics is a globalized business, in terms of both its guiding theory and strategy and of its practice and day-to-day operations. Therefore, as a starting point, we have delved into what this new form of logistics looks like in its most developed and advanced form.

Throughout the world, much of the logistics we see still falls far short of these aspirational goals. China is no exception and as it entered the period of economic reforms after 1978, it was much further behind due to the quirky unfolding of history and politics. In the next chapter, we examine the debilitating legacy which China's logistics had first to shake itself clear of, before it could begin to become an innovator.

Confucius, the ancient Chinese philosopher, regarded the "rectification of names" (*zhengming*), that is the careful definition of terms, as the prerequisite of an orderly society. Having followed his wise advice, we are now well equipped to dive into our narrative.

Notes

1 Attributed to Alexander The Great, *My Logisticians Are a Humorless Lot*, on *The Logistics of Logistics*, https://www.thelogisticsoflogistics.com/my-logisticians-are-a-humorless-lot/.
2 Council of Supply Chain Management Professionals, Supply Chain Management Definitions and Glossary.
3 Council of Supply Chain Management Professionals, Supply Chain Management Definitions and Glossary.
4 Council of Supply Chain Management Professionals, Supply Chain Management Definitions and Glossary.
5 The state of third-party logistics in China, survey by Mercer Management Consulting, 2002.

6 2023 Nian quanguo wuliu yunxing qingkuang tongbao, issued by the NDRC and the China Federation of Logistics and Procurement. On China Logistics Information Centre, Feb 7, 2024.

7 Scott Robinson, Corning's Director, Supply China Management Programs, quoted in Kay Zeman, Corning Incorporated, in Supply China World magazine.

8 Kay Zeman, Corning Incorporated, in Supply China World magazine.

9 Confidential interview with a retired Corning executive, Nov 27, 2023.

Chapter 2

How history and politics shape China's logistics

When China launched its economic reforms in 1978, its logistics, as with the rest of the economy, faced the challenge of dealing with the legacy of the Chinese Communist Party's (CCP) embrace of the dysfunctional Soviet-style "centrally planned" economy during the first three decades of the People's Republic. Fortunately, the new hybrid development model adopted post-1978 has provided a highly positive context for the development of China's logistics. It saw a move toward a rational and productive economic order within which logistics plays a strategic role as China seeks to move up the global economic ladder, and as it shifts from growth *per se* to a "better quality" GDP, based on productivity gains and on green sustainability.

The Republic of China (1912–1949)

Before addressing the legacy of the CCP's centrally planned economy, we shall briefly mention the previous Republican period (1912–1949). This is a brief mention not because we wish to dismiss the Republic of China as unworthy of consideration. It is because firstly the CCP, when it took power in 1949, did its utmost to erase all traces of the previous political and economic order. Secondly, it is the legacy of the PRC's first three decades which is the one that has weighed most heavily on the Chinese economy and its logistics.

Sun Yat-sen, who, after the Qing dynasty was overthrown, became the Republic of China's first president, was a strong advocate of developing China's transportation as a way to unify both the economy and the nation. He called for 10,000 miles of new roads and his "Railway Plan of China – 1921," envisaged an expansion of China's railways that would link all the provincial capitals. He urged China to emulate the US railway system.[1] However, the Republic soon fragmented into a series of warlord ministates. Some warlords worked hard to improve the road infrastructure in the areas they controlled, notably General Yan Xishan (in Shanxi) and Feng Yuxiang (in Gansu). Feng said, "we must have railroads and wagon roads and irrigation."[2] Warlord Wu Peifu built roads for military purposes in Henan and Hubei.

DOI: 10.4324/9781003489115-4

But it was not until the Republic of China's so-called Nanking (Nanjing) Decade (1928–1937), when China enjoyed relative stability and prosperity, that there was a concerted program to upgrade the nation's transportation infrastructure. Having taken on warlordism and largely united the nation, the government, based in Nanjing, Jiangsu Province, embarked on a variety of ambitious social and economic programs, among which was railway and road construction which contributed to a growing industrial and commercial integration of the nation. In the late 1930s, The China Development Finance Corporation[3] started the construction of railway lines between Shanghai and Hangzhou and Ningbo and between Chengdu and Chongqing, but this was not completed due to the Japanese invasion in 1937.

After the defeat of Japan in 1945, the Republican government returned to power but almost immediately found itself in a renewed civil war with the CCP. The Republic, weakened by the long war with Japan and sapped by corruption and economic mismanagement, was roundly defeated in 1949 by the CCP. The transportation system that the PRC inherited from the Republic had been heavily compromised by the decades of first invasion and then civil war.

The People's Republic and the centrally planned economy

During the Anti-Japanese War (1937–1945), the CCP had worked hard to claim the mantle of the true patriots who fought the Japanese, seeking to make a distinction between themselves and the Republic of China they sought to replace. Also, with the goal of contrasting themselves from the corruption and misgovernment of the Republic, the CCP was successful in generating broad-based popularity using their "New Democracy" program which, in retrospect, disingenuously promised a vital role for capitalists and intellectuals in the new "People's China." Chinese peasants who had flocked to the CCP armies had also been promised a bright new future in terms of land reform, a moderate "a land-to-the-tillers" program. However, in the early years of the People's Republic, these promises were not honored. The world had changed. The Korean War and the US talk of "rollback" or at least containment of the CCP threatened the existence of the new Chinese state. Moreover, China's leader, Mao Zedong, was keen to speed up China's "socialist transformation." Farmers were "encouraged" to give up their private plots and to form collectives. Capitalists were forced to agree to nationalization of their factories. Intellectuals, writers, and professors were forced to confess and bow to Party power. Foreign educators and doctors were driven out of China.

The CCP, borrowing from China's age-old tradition of totally negating the previous regime, dismantled and replaced the institutions of the pre-1949 Republic of China. Some vestiges of the previous order survived, including some of the industry and commerce, albeit transformed by the wave of "socialism." But the big picture was one of creating a *tabula rasa*, painting a bleak picture of a past order that was portrayed as irredeemably black. New institutions, bureaucratic structures, processes, and job titles were introduced. The entire fabric of society, down to the very lowest level including industry and commerce was transformed so that in every conceivable respect, it closely mimicked the society built by the Soviet Union under Joseph Stalin. China, finding itself isolated from the US and West, initiated the policy of "leaning to one side," that is forming a close alliance with the Soviet Union. In February 1950, the Sino-Soviet Treaty of Friendship, Alliance, and Mutual Support was signed. China received loans from the Soviet Union worth hundreds of millions of dollars. Thousands of Soviet experts, engineers, scientists, and other academics moved to China, to assist in the building of the new institutions and the establishment of a "Centrally Planned Economy." This included adopting the Soviet approaches to logistics, to transportation and warehousing.

After a period of recovery from the civil war and from the impact of the Korean War, in 1953, the CCP launched the nation's First Five-Year Plan (1953–1957) which set the goals for the planned economy. Written by the State Planning Commission, it was executed by the State Economic Commission and its local agencies. During that period, with the nationalization of industry, transportation, commerce, and logistics and the collectivization of agriculture, the government controlled all the levers that shaped the economy.

During the economic reforms that began in 1978, this planned economy was slowly and painfully dismantled to be replaced by an economic model in which market forces were allowed to prevail. That said, the post-reform Chinese economic model is a hybrid one in which these market forces are strongly complemented by the Chinese party-state through a large public sector and by state-owned banks that dictate the allocation of capital.

Notwithstanding, the continuing powerful role of the party-state to this day, the planning function has seen a fundamental change. Although China still has a five-year economic development plan (it is currently into its 14th – 2021–2025), it is more a tool to guide the economy rather than to rigidly or directly run it. We shall examine the current sub-plan on logistics later in Chapter 4.

Given the appalling outcome of Chinese central planning through the period of Mao's rule, its failure to deliver economic results and wealth for the Chinese people, it is easy to totally dismiss that model as inherently flawed and to mock its claim to be "scientific." That may be a little too harsh or conceited when we also consider the waste and anguish created by the boom-and-bust cycle of Western "advanced" capitalism.

When we read educational documents issued in the 1950s by Chinese planners to help Party officials understand how central planning operates, there is plenty of logic and sound process. In the explanation of "transportation planning" (The word logistics does not appear, and the focus is simply on transportation (*yunshu*)), the discussion is sensibly about matching transportation capabilities with social demand. In the selection of a mode of transportation, there is careful analysis of the trade-offs between speed and cost and also geographic coverage/distance. There is a clear preference for rail transportation, based on China's large geography and with a stated reference to Soviet practice.[4] This was a seemingly rational approach which might just as well as have come from a shipper or a 3PL in a Western capitalist economy. But, there were also some big and fundamental differences.

Firstly, the issue has to do with what was a central and bureaucratic approach rather than one geared to the fast-evolving market. The effort to create "scientifically" planned transportation services was handled at a national level and in a highly bureaucratic fashion. It is universally accepted across the globe that government plays a key role in planning and constructing the transportation infrastructure over which the logistics services can be provided. But China's attempt to provide an overarching plan for those services themselves was bereft of the flexibility and adaptability required. This was in stark contrast to logistics services designed and executed by commercial players today, be they shippers, manufacturers, or the logistics service providers, working together day-to-day on specific and fast-changing needs at the basic level.

The "central" in the centrally planned economy is a key to understanding its weakness. The way it worked was that the local (province and city) "bureaus" of government agencies in different parts of the supply chain (in manufacturing, transportation, etc.) would, on a biannual basis, go up the capital Beijing for meetings at which production output and the related transportation services and assets were agreed. This led to a system of mandatory targets and quotas that were then disseminated downwards and across the supply chain. Despite some occasional efforts to decentralize the system, the central nature of this planning – its bureaucratic nature (handled by officials divorced from the production-level reality) and its rigidity – made it ill-equipped to adapt to new and changing circumstances, such as an uptick in industrial or consumer demand, or regional differences and imbalances.

One result of this was that China's regions, its provinces and cities, created a way to mitigate this dysfunction. The work-around was to sidestep the risk of relying on central planning and to localize as much manufacturing as possible, creating an inefficient duplication of production without economies of scale. In turn, this led to a more fragmentation of transportation and logistics. The centrally planned economy ironically militated against a nationally integrated economy and undermined impetus to create efficient centers of industrial production.

The second great weakness of the centrally planned economy was how it arbitrarily broke the supply chain into bits, with each bit managed by a separate Ministry, each with a vertical chain of command, with a series of bureaus below it at the Province, City, and County levels. These structures created what is sometimes referred to as a "stovepipe" economy broken up into vertical structures that found it hard to talk to each other or to coordinate economic activity, especially at the local level where the industrial or commercial activity really occurs. These bureaus not only reported upwards to their Ministry but also horizontally to the local government, something referred to as "dual control." The relative influence of the center or the locality in this formula varied over time and in relation to how strategic the activity was considered. This complex web of linkages may have been portrayed by its creators as the apex of rational planning. But, in reality, it also had its roots in a Stalinist desire to create multiple levers and bureaucratic separation in order to avoid the emergence of alternative power centers and to permit the exercise of absolute control.

Under China's central planning, manufacturing industry was broken up into a series of ministries such as metallurgical, building materials, machine-building (seven separate ones!), light industry, and textile industry. Below these ministries at each level were arrayed the factories. The factories operated as lifeless entities required simply to fulfill government-set targets. They had little or no control over their business strategy or their finances. Contacts with their raw material suppliers or their customers were managed indirectly at arm's length through other government bureaucratic silos. This disabling of or the total absence of normal, healthy, and rational market relationships extended to the provision of logistics.

Some large manufacturers, especially those involved in process industry such as steel and cement, were involved in their own transportation and logistics. But, generally speaking, transportation and logistics were not handled by the factory but by a series of separate state-owned stovepipe verticals. While this may seem to superficially resemble the current embrace of outsourced logistics (3PLs), its bureaucratic nature meant that it was light years away from the modern integrated logistics of today.

Three major bureaucratic structures provided the logistics for China's manufacturers. One focused on in-bound raw materials and outbound heavy industrial goods. A second handled outbound distribution of finished consumer goods to wholesalers and retailers. A third handled the factories' relationships with the outside world. These three structures worked with the Ministry of Railways and with the Ministry of Communications (under which China's ocean cargo fleet operated).

Firstly, there was the *State Materials Bureau* (*guojia wuzhi ju*), which later became the Ministry of Materials. It handled inbound raw materials for steel, cement, glass, tar, soda, and other process industry. It also shipped a wide range of finished products to downstream manufacturers, such as auto parts, bearings, compressors, tires, pumps, electrical gear, and vehicle chassis. It worked closely with the local railway bureaus to get goods onto railcars. It also operated a wide range of local trucking companies, some dedicated to specialized products.

Second, there was the *Ministry of Commerce* (*Shangyebu*) (MOC) which at one stage was broken into two Ministries, one handling logistics for light industrial products and the other focused on basic agricultural products. The MOC was responsible for creating strategic reserves throughout the nation using warehousing to store grain, frozen pork, and other food commodities. It shipped processed goods from factories reporting to the Ministry of Light Industry, as well as produce from the collective farms (People's Communes) and state farms, to the wholesalers and retailers which it owned. It had separate distribution entities devoted to eggs, chicken, fish, beef, pork, grain, and edible oil.

The MOC also handled the distribution of nonfood products from factories under the Textile Ministry and the Ministry of Light Industry. This involved an array of specialized transportation and storage entities distributing "daily-use" (*riyong*) products (like cosmetics, soap, and toilet paper), "cultural" products (ink brushes, table tennis bats and balls, musical instruments) to both department stores and specialist stores, all owned by the MOC.

Finally, there was the ministry that handled China's foreign trade. Its name has changed over the years. For simplicity, we refer to it as the *Ministry of Foreign Economic Relations and Trade (duwai jingji maoyi bu) (MOFERT)*, its name as of 1983.

Under central planning, China's factories, in the same way that they had no direct contact with domestic customers, were not permitted to work directly with foreign suppliers or buyers. This had to be handled through MOFERT's foreign trade corporations (FTCs) specialized in areas such as minerals and metals, textiles, oil and petrochemicals, light industry, animal products, and publications. Foreigners negotiated not with the factories but with these FTCs, either at the biannual Guangzhou Trade Show or at MOFERT's bleak "Negotiations Building" (*Tanpanlou*) in Western Beijing. The logistics for cross-border trade, such as freight forwarding (comparable to the travel agency role in passenger travel) and customs clearance for cross-border shipments, was handled exclusively by a MOFERT entity call Sinotrans, which in recent times has transformed itself into one of China's leading logistics service providers (See Chapter 13).

As China entered its period of economic reforms and slowly dismantled central planning, the role of these ministries and their countless entities that provided logistics services either melted away or were transformed and reborn. In 1993, the Ministry of Materials merged with the MOC to form the *Ministry of Domestic Trade (MODT)* which itself was ultimately dissolved. It left behind many officials looking for jobs or being moved into government-owned and -led trade associations, such as the China Federation of Logistics & Purchasing.[5] It also left behind an over complex three-level distribution network that collapsed into something simpler and, in many instances, went from state-owned to private ownership.

This distribution network comprised a plethora of elements in the supply chain, not just sprawling low-grade warehousing and fleets of trucks (many poorly maintained, outdated, underpowered, and unsuited for long haul) but also teams of managers devoted to managing all these assets and processes. Much of this was simply not suited to the new demand of the post-reform economy.

But, some of it was naturally adaptable and formed the basis for some of the new logistics industry.

The US firm P&G, which manufactures fast-moving consumer goods, made an early move into China to capture market share and production capacity across a wide range of products including detergents, soaps, shampoos, and cosmetics. With a strong China HQ in Guangzhou, it also created multiple manufacturing points across China, for instance a detergent plant in Chengdu, Sichuan. It set about learning about distribution and logistics in China by partnering at the local level with Chinese firms that had formerly been part of the MOC "system." Having partnered with and shadowed those firms, it gradually created its own China-wide logistics network, locally adapted but more efficient than the legacy network it had learnt from.

This meltdown of the transportation and logistics infrastructure under central planning led not only to many entities simply going out of business but also to the emergence of new logistics entities based on that consolidation. Typical of this is China Logistics Group which was formed in 2021 with a registered capital equivalent to US$ 4.9 BN through the merger of a number of "materials" entities with origins in the by then dissolved MODT and in the railways. It has 120 railway lines, 4.9 MM m² of warehousing, and 3 MM trucks. We profile China Logistics Group later in Chapter 13.

The legacy that the first three decades of the PRC bequeathed to the post-reform China was overall negative and disabling. As central planning melted away, so China's logistics faced a long hard slog to upgrade itself so that it could deliver what was needed for the new vibrant economy. To illustrate the severe hangover left from the first decades of the PRC, we provide the following case study.

Case study: Dalian 1988 and the legacy of central planning

Before examining China's economic reforms which began in 1978, it is useful to remind ourselves of the impact the legacy of central planning has on China's logistics, even well into the reform period. How did an investor assess China's logistics in 1988, a decade after China's economic reforms began? A foreign manufacturer was about to invest over US$ 100 MM to build a float glass plant, with a capacity of 500 tons per day, in China's port city of Dalian, in the North-eastern Province of Liaoning. Float glass, which involves molten glass being poured over a bath of liquid tin, was a new process for producing flat architectural glass for high-rise buildings which was vastly superior to glass produced by the older vertically drawn method.

Dalian provided a good environment for foreign direct investment (FDI) in manufacturing. Early in the reforms, FDI had been guided to the Special Economic Zones (SEZs) in South China. But in 1984, China launched its program to encourage FDI in 14 Open Cities, including Dalian, each of which established an Economic & Technical Development Zone (ETDZ), in which foreign firms enjoyed the same incentives as in the SEZs. Dalian was very active in courting foreign investors. The float glass producer decided to set up in Dalian's ETDZ. It was permitted a 60% and controlling equity share in the JV that it formed with a local Dalian glass producer. Given China's shortage of foreign exchange, the plant had to commit to export 70% proportion of its production, to earn foreign exchange to service its US$-denominated debt and to permit the repatriation of profits. The deal got done. Float glass was ultimately produced efficiently in high volume and quality. But, before that as the project feasibility work was undertaken, logistics emerged as a major concern.

There were inbound logistics of raw materials. A primary source of quartz sand for the plant had been identified about 200 km inland. Naturally occurring soda ash had to be imported from the US (A local soda plant could not produce the high-density granular soda ash suitable for float glass). There was a good local source of dolomite rock. Outbound logistics involved exports by sea as well as distribution into the domestic China market.

Railways were seen by the investor as vital to the logistics but they fell short of what was needed. Contacts with the Ministry of Railways revealed the following. There was serious congestion due to the limited number of cars per train and the high-level usage of steam locomotives for freight. There was a shortage of railcars. There was the prospect of improvement as lines were double-tracked, and electrified, or changed to diesel. A rail line into the ETDZ was planned but would take some time to arrive. In the meantime, there would initially be a one-hour truck drive to the nearest railhead.

Trucks would be needed to truck sand 40 km from the sand mine to the nearest rail ramp, but with a truck weight limit of just 15 tons. The railways said that they would like to build a rail spur to the sand mine, but there were no funds to do so. Moreover, even from the rail ramp, they could not guarantee that the railcars, to ship sand to the plant, would be available or that they would be free of contamination that could affect the sand quality.

The roads and trucking were also difficult. The Dalian-Shenyang superhighway was only partly constructed. Most of the trucks in Dalian had 15 tons capacity. There were very few 25-ton dump trucks. When it came to container trucks in Dalian, there were more tractors than chassis. The chassis were mainly for 40 ft containers with only handful with a 20-ft chassis. There were also constraints imposed by bridge weight limits of 10–15 tons. Local truck firms expressed willingness to buy new trucks. But they cautioned that it would take at least one year to find the funds and to acquire them.

Dalian was planning a new port (8 km from the factory site) but it was scheduled to only start operation about five years later. At the old port, 40 km from the plant, things were far from ideal. While container vessels were given priority, this was leading to bulk carriers, such as those that would carry the soda ash, waiting for 10–20 days to get unloaded. Moreover, the poor-quality equipment used to unload bulk vessels led to "unacceptable losses." This meant that the ship carrying the soda ash would need to carry its own unloading gear. There was very little storage room for bulk cargo at the piers.

At that time, container ships calling at Dalian were small feeder vessels (200–500 TEUs) with direct routes only to Japan and Hong Kong, from where the glass would be transshipped. Open-topped 20-ft containers (suitable for the shipment of glass exports from the factory) were unavailable in Dalian. Bringing them in would cost double that of closed top containers, due to repositioning costs.[6]

Since 1988, Dalian, in common with the rest of China, has radically transformed its transportation infrastructure and logistics. The float plant was able to successfully address the complex issues discussed above. But that window in 1988 serves to illustrate the heavy burden placed on China by its legacy logistics.

The economic reforms from 1978: "The China Paradox"

In September 1976, Mao Zedong died and in October, the so-called "Gang of Four" was arrested, thus bringing an end to the Cultural Revolution which over the previous decade had seen China paralyzed by political turmoil. By 1978, Deng Xiaoping had gained full control and he ushered in a remarkable period of economic growth, an "economic miracle" that massively outranks other economic spurts such as West Germany's post-war "Wirtschaftswunder." This vibrant and fast-growing economic environment provided an excellent environment within which China's logistics have flourished.

Over the last five decades, the Chinese economy has grown by 82 times so that today it is second only to that of the US. China's per capita GDP has increased 57-fold, from US$ 229 in 1978 to about USD 13,000 today. How has that happened?

During the Mao years, 1949–1976, China did achieve GDP growth (around 6% per annum). However, due to the adoption of the Soviet heavy industrial model, which was ill-suited to agrarian China, the growth was at the expense of the people's living standards. After the Mao era came to a close, reform-minded China officials were quick to observe candidly that after three decades of "socialism," there was still the strict rationing of basic commodities. They criticized the Maoist model as one of "perpetual poverty."

After the failure of the PRC's economic system during the first three decades, the CCP faced a crisis of flagging legitimacy, relevance, and vision. In an unusual act of humility and honesty from a ruling Communist Party rooted in Stalin's ethos, the CCP determined that bold steps were needed to shore up its survival. The solution was the creation of a new hybrid model whereby capitalist-style management and economic levers and incentives were adopted in order to unleash economic growth, but all under the CCP which maintained its monopoly on power. In turn, China's citizens, in a Faustian pact, accepted the rule of the party-state, in return for a shot at wealth and happiness, which ultimately, for many hundreds of millions, was largely delivered.

This model can be described as the "China Paradox,"[7] whereby seemingly incompatible forces, an old-style communist party, on the one hand, and the capitalist-style liberation of economic forces, on the other, operated smoothly together. The Chinese have termed this new hybrid model as "socialism with Chinese characteristics."

The path forward was not always smooth. The dismantling of the centrally planned economy was slow, complex, and painful. Deng's preference for gradual experimentation, pilot projects, "crossing the river by feeling the stones," was in part designed to outflank those who remained opposed to the reforms. It also led to constant stop-starts and economic adjustments. Moreover, throughout the reform process, there have been times when the CCP's autocratic nature came close to destroying the reform program, notably during the Tiananmen crisis in 1989. Still, the delicate balance of forces that comprise the China Paradox has been remarkably sustained and successful.

The economic reforms have had three pillars – the reform of the state-owned sector, the rise of the private sector, and the introduction of FDI. As the reforms began, the state-owned enterprises (SOEs) were near collapse, propped up by government subsidies. Most of the smaller and weakest SOEs were then dissolved or sold off. The largest SOEs went through a process whereby they were corporatized (which included becoming responsible for their own profit-and-loss and with their own board governance) and then recapitalized through stock market listings. This is what happened to firms such as the logistics firm Sinotrans which we profile below and in Chapter 13.

As economic controls were relaxed, so private enterprises emerged. To this day, they do not receive the kind of financial support that SOEs get. But the fact remains that while the SOEs were going through open-heart surgery, the private sector propped up the economy and to this day outstrips the state sector in profitability, job creation, and innovation. Moreover, in China's logistics, it is the private firms that have led the charge, for instance achieving true innovation in the field of e-commerce.

The third pillar was FDI, whereby sector-by-sector the government provided market access for foreign manufacturers and service providers, in return for inbound capital flows, technology transfers, and the filling of major gaps in the economy, such as the automobile sector. This was heralded by the Chinese government as the "open-door" policy.

China's accession to the World Trade Organization (WTO) in 2001 was a milestone in the open-door policy in that it ushered in the freeing up to FDI in previously restricted areas of the economy and an overall relaxation of constraints on foreign players. That said, the WTO accession had less impact than the US and others had hoped for. While largely fulfilling its part of the WTO bargain, the Chinese government used other tools including its role in SOEs and in state procurement to ensure that the open door for some investors remained little more than just ajar.

Nonetheless, despite the barriers they face, many foreign investors to this day remain keen to participate in the China market given its scale and further growth potential.

These three pillars are in turn closely linked to another key factor behind China's rapid rise, namely China's international trade and investment. Initially, it was mainly cross-border trade as China became the "factory of the world," a trend enhanced by China's accession to WTO. More recently, through the Belt and Road Initiative (BRI) (discussed in Chapter 10), it has expanded beyond trade to include significant Chinese direct investment from Greece to sub-Saharan Africa. The three pillars coupled with international trade have created the conditions for a rapid and sustained growth in China's logistics.

There is much debate about Xi Jinping's period as CCP Secretary General and head of state, which began in 2012. It has featured a tightening of the autocracy and with that a reassertion of Party authority across society from universities to enterprises. Major economic policy decision-making has been shifted from the State (the Premier and the State Council) to the Party and Xi.

In the SOEs, including those in logistics, CCP involvement in corporate matters from strategic direction and acquisitions to compensation and bonuses is having a cooling effect on managerial boldness and competitiveness. When it comes to private firms, the government has clamped down on technology companies not only due to regulatory lapses or gaps but also because their massive wealth (much of it offshore) and the attitude of their leaders such as Alibaba's Jack Ma might present a threat to the power and authority of the Party.

What we can see clearly is that throughout the four decades of reforms, the Party has had two fundamental goals. First and foremost, the goal is the Party's long-term survival. This is based on the strongly pragmatic spirit that dates back to Deng: whatever supports that goal is useful and whatever conflicts with that goal is to be rejected. The key to the success of China's hybrid model has been that, so far, the economic reforms have created wealth and security for China's citizens which in turn has shored up and sustained the Party's legitimacy.

The second goal, which is more ideological and at times conflicts with the pragmatic approach discussed above, is to somehow "make socialism work." To achieve that, the focus is on creating a strong and dominant state sector. The state sector gives the Party a raison d'être and defines the nation as "socialist." Hence, resources are allocated to the state sector, at the expense of the private sector. While the private sector is often praised and encouraged for its vital role, the thinly disguised truth is that Chinese leaders remain suspicious of the independence and entrepreneurial spirit of the private sector. They stress the need to "guide" the private sector and are quick to rein it in when deemed prudent.

Some believe that the harsh treatment of China's e-commerce giant Alibaba marked a watershed toward an ever-stronger state sector at the expense of private firms. But notwithstanding the buffeting some private firms have faced, the party-state's commitment to logistics provides a political climate which is highly favorable to this sector, and that includes the private firms such as Alibaba's logistics arm, Cainiao. It is the private-sector logistics firms that are setting the pace in innovation, technology adoption, and service quality. This being the case, the party-state is likely to put aside its antipathy toward entrepreneurs and to pursue a policy of pragmatic support for all logistics firms across the board, regardless of their ownership.

This supportive role expresses itself through government planning. As we discuss in Chapter 4, China's five-year plan for logistics is extremely detailed and includes state intervention in building out the logistics infrastructure including logistics hubs and parks. Still, there is no return to the centrally planned economy. The party-state's involvement in and control over industry and commerce (both state-owned and private firms) is today undoubtably greater than in the first decades of the reforms. Nonetheless, to understand how China operates today, we need to emphasize the extent to which market forces and competition are still the predominant driving forces for China's enterprises, including the logistics firms we shall later profile.

Despite its stellar performance since the reforms began, China's economy faces a number of structural issues. It is easy to see why the government sees logistics as a key lever for improving matters. The growth of China's total factor productivity, which is a key measure of economic efficiency and technology advance, is slowing. China's logistics remains a large area of economic low efficiency and presents something that can easily be addressed, an obvious "low hanging fruit" when China's logistics performance is compared with that of other nations. Government support for the logistics sector as a whole seems assured.

The consumption side of the Chinese economy remains weak. Government investment stimulus is still vital to keeping things moving forward. Given that the social safety net in China is far from complete, Chinese citizens save much more than in other nations – for schooling, healthcare, and retirement. Largely driven by private firms, China's e-commerce, and with it the logistics that enable the physical delivery of goods, is a key tool for unlocking consumer spending and thus receives strong and positive government attention.

It should also be noted that the Chinese government has pushed forward with large-scale investment at the grassroots in technology parks aimed at nurturing start-up firms in areas such as the Internet of Things and Artificial Intelligence, much of which will directly benefit the digitalization of logistics.

China is concerned at its slowing growth, forecast by the IMF to be less than 4% per annum in the medium term. It faces the structural issues mentioned above, coupled with a weak real estate sector, local government debt overhang, an aging workforce and rising youth unemployment. On the international front, some parts of the BRI seem to be underperforming. But while some observers point to China's "stumbling economy"[8] and argue that China has peaked, "reached the pinnacle of its economic power," others are cautious about putting excessive weight on the issues that China's economy has recently encountered.[9] In the past, there have been many pessimistic views on China (notably in 2001, with *The Coming Collapse of China*, and in 2013 with the *Stumbling Giant*[10]). But China has proven to be agile at adapting and adjusting in order to mitigate these risks. While Xi's rule does look less pragmatic than that of earlier leaders, it is reasonable to assume that China's economic rise will continue and not subside. One experienced observer has commented on the "peak China" notion, stating that the view that China's best days are behind it is "ideologically freighted," concluding that "a hell of a lot of people are very excited to make money in China. It's objectively premature to use that phrase."[11]

China's current economic trajectory and the political goals that underpin it point strongly to logistics, both in the domestic market and internationally, enjoying not just sustained growth in volume and efficiency, but also to being the recipient of positive attention and support from the government.

Case study: how a state-owned firm frees itself from the legacy of central planning

To illustrate how the economic reforms played out at the corporate level in China's state-owned logistics firms, we turn to the transformation that took place in Sinotrans. From the early 1950s, under the centrally planned economy, Sinotrans (full name China Foreign Trade Transportation) had enjoyed a virtual monopoly over China's international freight forwarding, whereby is worked with China's industry-specific foreign trade companies to arrange the cross-border goods transportation, by sea and by land across the northern border with the Soviet Union. In the late 1990s that was already changing. Other Chinese firms were permitted to compete with Sinotrans on freight forwarding and the broader logistics. On top of that, China was moving close to accession to the WTO (it happened in December 2001) and foreign logistics firms were, step-by-step, going to be permitted to operate as wholly foreign-owned ventures rather than just as 50/50 JVs with Chinese firms. The then Premier Zhu Rongji issued the stern warning that old Chinese state firms, such as Sinotrans, needed to shape up or face an uncertain future. Analysis of Sinotrans, conducted by external consultants, substantiated these concerns, pointing to an ultimately terminal downward financial spiral for much of their business.

Sinotrans were fortunate in having a strong leadership team which was willing to take the painful medicine needed to ensure survival. Later on, in Chapter 13, we profile Sinotrans and discuss this team in more detail. But here we shall just focus on the role of the firm's Chairman Luo Kaifu as a catalyst for change. With his piercing eyes and strong empathy, he was able to engage at a personal level, to command attention and respect, and to build consensus around his goals. He exhibited the gritty toughness for which his native Hubei Province is famous. Born in 1940, he graduated in economics from China's Foreign Trade University in 1966, just before the Cultural Revolution broke out. Later, he was posted as a foreign trade diplomat to the Netherlands, the US, the Philippines, and Switzerland. His global experience left a major impact on Luo. When invited to his apartment in Beijing, one would be served grilled steak and potatoes. It was well known that if you wanted to get his ear you would take him out for a French meal at his favorite Justine's restaurant at the Jianguo Hotel in Beijing. But there was another strongly Chinese side to Chairman Luo. He is a well-known and accomplished calligrapher. His brushwork ranges from classical themes to Mao Zedong's poems. This connects with his fierce Chinese nationalism and passionate support for the Party.

So, around 2000, Sinotrans was confronted with an existential threat to its spluttering businesses that faced enormous competition from many quarters. Before the firm could be recapitalized by a stock market listing, it first had to be transformed into something that was sustainable and which merited stock market confidence. The issues were deep and tough to address. Chairman Luo pressed ahead on a number of fronts. But even in the reformist atmosphere of the time, there was no way to simply steamroller the way forward. Instead, he sought to persuade and win over those that stood in his way, often inviting key executives and advisors to his private hide-away office suite located on the top floor of the company's headquarters in Beijing.

Although, under the old centrally planned economy, Sinotrans had a subsidiary in each province, these were administratively highly autonomous and not suited to creating an integrated logistics approach. On the surface, it looked like Sinotrans had a strong operational network across the nation, better than any other player. But when one looked more closely, it was apparent that it could not function in a unified or coordinated manner to deliver the logistics services. Eastern China, comprising Jiangsu, Shanghai, and Zhejiang accounted for a large chunk of the firm's revenues and profits. But it was hard to get these provincial-level subsidiaries to work together. In the end, after going through many legal hoops and by knocking heads together, Sinotrans was able to forge a modern corporate governance system with regional entities in South China, East China, and Central China which reported into and accepted orders from head office.

Another painful issue was Sinotrans' workforce, which was not only too large but poorly qualified for the new logistics business. It was bloated with employees who were semi-retired but still on the books. Much of the workforce had not received an education beyond lower middle school. There was also a massive social burden from employee housing and related healthcare and educational infrastructure. Some Chinese state firms postponed cutting back the workforce until after the firm was listed on the stock exchange, only to find (as did PetroChina) that shortly later it had to take a large financial hit for the workforce reduction, which drove down the stock price. In Sinotrans, the CCP Party Secretary doubled as HR head. Mild-mannered and collaborative in nature, she nonetheless expressed concern against the social impact of job cuts in the firm prior to the stock listing, and the heavy financial cost of doing so. This is a predictable position from somebody who was in favor of the restructuring but not at the cost of a heavy loss of employment and by implication the risk "social instability." However, Chairman Luo, even as a devoted communist, knew what was at stake. He took to the whiteboard and put up his list of the factors that would make the stock market listing a success. The list included items such as a sound business strategy, a differentiated value proposition, a strong customer base, and a supportive government (which would still be the biggest owner after the IPO). But at the top of the list, he wrote the keywords "attractiveness to investors." He articulated calmly but forcefully that having a large and unreformed workforce, beyond what was needed, posed an unacceptable unresolved future financial burden and would make it impossible to attract investors, thus putting the entire Initial Public Offering (IPO) in jeopardy. If the firm were not attractive, there would be no listing and no future for the firm. And it should be added that, at that time, the pressure from Premier Zhu was such that there was no sure path to a bail-out by the government. Chairman Luo won that argument, and many more, on what should be done to turn the firm around. Of course, some businesses were left intact, such as the subscale container shipping line, which despite dire financial projections was permitted to survive the cuts. But overall, the process that Sinotrans went through was successful in building a new firm that could get listed on the Hong Kong stock exchange and grow. Much of this success was down to the company's extraordinary leadership which was willing to be bold and take risks in order to extricate it from the legacy of the centrally planned economy.

Notes

1 Sun Yat-sen, The International Development of China, 1922, cited in Richard Louis Edmonds, *The Legacy of Sun Yat-sen's Railway Plan, China Quarterly*, Sep 1987.
2 Ming-Ju Cheng, *The Influence of Communications Internal and External upon the Economic Future of China*, Routledge, 1930, pp. 63–64.
3 Led by banker and former Minister of Finance, T.V. Soong.
4 Kuo Tzu-ch'eng, Lecture 7: Transport Planning, in *Chinese Economic Planning, Translations from Chung-Hua Ching-chi*, edited N. Lardy, 1978, Taylor and Francis Group, pp. 37–48.
5 In 2003 I was the first non-Chinese to be elected as Executive Director of the Federation.
6 Paul G. Clifford, project notes, July 1988.
7 For a full exploration of the "China Paradox," see Paul G. Clifford, *The China Paradox. At the Front Line of Economic Transformation*, De Gruyter, Second edition, 2022.

8 Paul Krugman, *Why Is China's Economy Stumbling*, inon *New York Times*, Aug 13, 2023.

9 Nicholas Lardy, *How Serious Is China's Economic Slowdown?* Peterson Institute for International Economics, Aug 12, 2023, and Andrew Rothman, *The Coming Collapse of China?* in Sinology, Matthews International Capital Management, July 27, 2023.

10 Gordon G. Chang, *The Coming Collapse of China*, Random House, 2001, and Timothy Beardson, *Stumbling Giant. The Threats to China's Future*, Yale, 2013.

11 Ian Bremmer of Eurasia Group, quoted in Ephrat Livni, *Peak China*, in *New York Times*, Aug 20, 2023.

Chapter 3

Geography and transportation as the foundation

Geography is destiny

Understanding geography throws light on centers of population, natural resources, transportation, industry, and commerce and links to the outside world. It is the very foundation of defining how logistics facilitate the flow of goods through the economy.

Geography was kind to the US: in terms of rivers, the Great Lakes, large plains, and seaports on both coasts. Mexico is the very opposite: no navigable rivers, the population concentrated in semiarid plateaus, and, until modern times, only one major seaport, Veracruz. China falls somewhere between these two extremes.

In terms of topography, we can contrast China, which slopes up from the coastal plains of the eastern coast up to Mt Everest (Chomolungma) in the West with the US which is characterized by two coasts with lots of easily settled and highly fertile land in between. We should also point out that the US has a significant number of large and navigable rivers. Of the two great rivers in China, the Yellow River cannot be used for large ships while the Yangtze is navigable only for 2,700 km of its 6,300 km length. At many points, it passes through mountain ranges. Due to the locks on the Three Gorges Dam, the river is navigable up to Chongqing for vessels up to 5,000 DWT. Ocean-going ships up to 10,000 DWT can only reach the port of Wuhan. The Yangtze is also a huge barrier between North and South China. The first bridge over it, at Wuhan, was completed in 1957, with Soviet help, and the second one, at Nanjing was finished in 1968.[1] The Pearl River that enters the ocean near Hong Kong provides access just to Guangzhou (formerly known as Canton).

In order to understand China, there is a need to disaggregate it, take it apart, geographically, and that means in topography, climate, water supply, agriculture, culture, and diet, and with that also economic development, urbanization, and industrial capability. In turn, all that feeds into the challenges faced by China's logistics as it seeks to serve China's disparate regions and the nation as a whole.

DOI: 10.4324/9781003489115-5

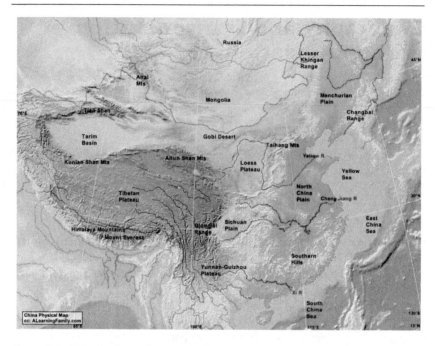

Figure 3.1 China's physical topography.

There are three regions that form quite discreet economies within which there is still a degree of self-sufficiency. Firstly, there is the North China Plain (Beijing-Tianjin-Hebei); secondly, the Lower Yangtze Delta (dominated by Shanghai); and thirdly, the Pearl River Delta (focused on Guangzhou, Hong Kong, and the new city of Shenzhen). Of course, there are other major development points, not least in Fujian (especially the city of Xiamen), Shandong Province (focused on the city of Qingdao), Xi'an (in Shaanxi Province), Chengdu (in Sichuan), and Chongqing. Beyond these tier-two cities, China's third-tier cities are also in rapid development. As we saw earlier, given the dysfunctional nature of central planning before the reforms, many of these regions developed a high degree of self-sufficiency and with that a duplication of manufacturing that was subscale and inefficient. Since the reforms, a key goal has been to create a more rational and efficient integration of the economy that requires logistics to link these regions and the cities within them.

In addition to those three main regions, there are also other parts of China that have their own clear identity and development path. In the West, Sichuan, based on the city of Chengdu, has transformed itself from a pleasant cultural center but an economic backwater focused on agriculture into a throbbing technology hub. Shaanxi's Xi'an has carved out a role for itself as a center of semiconductor production and high tech. China's Northeast (known under Japanese occupation as

Manchuria), which comprises three provinces (Liaoning, Jilin, and Heilongjiang), has cast off its history of smoke-stack industry. In particular, Liaoning's coastal city Dalian has emerged as an important center for IT and biotech.

We can illustrate the size and complexity of these key regions by looking at the Lower Yangtze Region. It comprises Shanghai Municipality and the Provinces of Jiangsu and Zhejiang which together account for 177 MM or 13% of China's population and, to highlight the region's high productivity, 19% of China's GDP.

Within this region, Jiangsu, with wide areas of wet-field cultivation was traditionally the richest region agriculturally which over the centuries supported a wealthy and intellectually prominent set of Mandarins (scholar-officials). Since the reforms, small workshops that were once part of now disbanded People's Communes (collective farms) became hybrid state-private factories (Township and Village Enterprises) on the path to becoming fully fledged private firms. Within Jiangsu, the railway and road corridor from Shanghai to Nanjing, passing through the cities of Suzhou, Wuxi, and Changzhou, has become intensely populated with new companies, Chinese and foreign-owned. For its part Shanghai, which had become China's commercial center under semicolonial rule in the 19th century, now took on the role of "dragon-head," leading the trade and commerce of the region through building the world's largest port, creating a financial services center that aspires to compete with Hong Kong, and linking the old Shanghai to the new Pudong area using numerous tunnels and bridges. Within Zhejiang Province, its capital Hangzhou, which entered the modern era not only with its beautiful West Lake but also with a significant industrial base, has energetically embraced high tech, with Alibaba being its most treasured asset. But within Zhejiang, there are other subthemes. The government in cities of Ningbo and Wenzhou become early pioneers in nurturing private companies, way before many other parts of the nation. Sitting in healthy remoteness from the nation's capital between the coast and mountain ranges, these cities traditionally had looked outwards and had been relatively free of interference from the hinterland. It is only quite recently that the railway has reached Wenzhou. We see a similar phenomenon with Xiamen and Shantou, down the coast south of Zhejiang in Fujian and Guangdong, respectively. Geography has strongly influenced economic outcomes.

Transportation as the enabler of logistics

China's domestic freight transportation mix

Over millennia China's roads were mostly rutted dirt tracks that were used by countless horse-, oxen-, mule-, and donkey-drawn carts to bring produce from the countryside to the towns and to take urban handicrafts, tools, and simple consumer products out to the rural areas. For shorter distances, farmers would

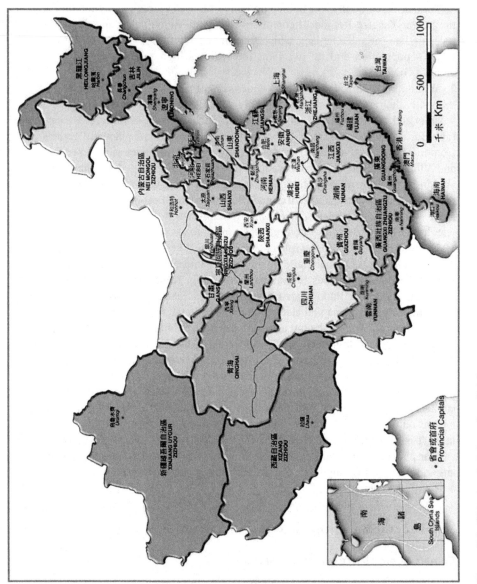

Figure 3.2 China's administrative divisions.

use wheelbarrows, a technology China invented. All this happened in the area around major markets within a range limited by this simple transportation.

Until the 20th century, China's only means of long-distance goods transportation was by its extensive network of inland waterways, plus the coastal shipping. At a local level, there was a myriad of canals and rivers that still crisscross the fertile deltas such as that of the Lower Yangtze. On a national level, the Grand Canal and other waterways were built to carry tribute grain to the capital for the imperial court and for the army.[2] Salt, which was a government monopoly, was also transported around the nation by water. Though Imperial China is often perceived as a stable, even stagnant rural economy, there was in fact significant commodity production of luxury goods such as porcelain, silk, lacquer, and tea which were transported on small boats and larger ships to the Mandarins and wealthy elites, not only in the capital but also in provincial centers and below. The transportation mix began to be transformed in the early 20th century as railways were built, primarily leading inland from coastal ports.

As discussed earlier, Sun Yat-sen and the Republic of China that he founded in 1912 had bold plans for upgrading China's transportation infrastructure but little came to fruition and this weakness was holding China back. In 1930, a Chinese economist stated that "undoubtably the greatest obstacle in the way of economic development in China today is the absence of a good transport system."[3] He was dismayed at China's poor railways network, linking it directly to China's poverty: "It is not an exaggeration to compare China's need of railways with a hungry man's need for food. Until an adequate network of railways is constructed, there will be no effective remedy for the scourge of famine in China."[4] He also described China's shipping situation as "deplorable," noting that 93% of China's foreign trade and 54% of China's coastal trade were carried by foreign ships.[5]

When the Chinese Communist Party (CCP) took power in 1949, there was an urgent need not only to restore the limited road and railway infrastructure that had been damaged by war but also to adjust the transportation mix to fit the nation's goal of rapid industrialization.

The transportation mix, that is the proportion occupied by various modes of transport, can be defined in three ways. If we use freight volume (tonnage) as the measure, then it necessarily places emphasis on heavy and often low-value items such as coal and construction materials, much of which is, within the domestic market, carried by rail. By using value as the measure, the data better highlights the high-value items, such as consumer electronics. A third measure is the actual economic turnover defined by weight-X-distance (ton/km) This latter metric is the key to the pricing of transportation services, though of course there are variations of pricing based on the complexity of handling any given product or commodity.

In the US, truck transportation is the dominant mode, with 68% and 67% in terms of weight and value, ten times that of rail (7% and 6%, respectively).

In terms of weight-X-distance, trucks are the preferred mode for distances up to 750 miles and also come close to the share of rail for much longer distances.[6] The major role played by trucking in the US is in part a consequence of the investment begun by President Eisenhower in 1956 in the nation's Interstate Highway System which today comprises over 48,000 miles. The US also has a further 19,000 miles of other freeways. This investment reflected the US's auto-centric economy, where what was good for GM was good for the nation. However, despite the small proportion of total transportation that US freight rail occupies, it is important to note its high efficiency and technical prowess that led it to become a model as China sought to upgrade its rail performance.

History initially left China with a rather different transportation mix. In 1949, China had little in the way of a road network but had the beginnings of a rail system albeit lacking certain key linkages. Also, and of critical importance, as China in the 1950s adopted Soviet-style central planning, it predictably opted to emphasize freight rail:

> In countries with large masses such as China and the Soviet Union, the volume of transport carried by the railroad is the largest. Consequently, the railroad transport plans of those countries occupy the most important position in their overall transport planning.[7]

In the years 1949–1958, the first decade of CCP rule, China's railway network grew from 22,000 to 31,000 km, while the roads expanded from 81,000 to 400,000 km. Waterways doubled in length but the navigable routes did not expand as fast. In that period, the volume of goods transported grew nearly ten-fold, not surprising given the low base as the starting point. By 1958, rail was carrying 60% of goods volume compared to roads at 27%. But when looked at from a turnover point of view (tons/km), which factors in the length of the journey of each load, the share carried by the railways was 78% compared to 19% by water routes and just 3% for roads.[8] China's statisticians from this period also point to large productivity and efficiency gains, whether with regard to turnaround times for freight wagons, distances traveled by each wagon and locomotives or the weight pulled by each locomotive. While we should not rely too heavily on those statistics that were provided around the time of Great Leap Forward when some data was falsified, we can see the extent of the rehabilitation and extension of China's transportation network, after decades of war. But that progress pales in comparison to the massive push achieved since the economic reforms began.

In the period 1978–2021, reflecting China's economic takeoff, China's freight transportation volume grew 17 times. At the same time, the economy was becoming more integrated with transportation over longer distances, as can be seen from the 22-fold growth of freight transportation in terms of turnover (ton/km).

During that period, China developed a road system comparable to the US interstate system. While rail freight grew, its proportion of the total mix declined dramatically, in volume terms, from 35% in 1978 to 9% in 2021. Even in turnover terms, which reflect distance carried, something which would seem to favor rail, rail's share of the mix declined from 53% to 15%. This shift is not only due to the superhighways that permit long-distance truck haulage. The economic surge has seen a huge increase in consumer products, such as fast-moving consumer goods and electrical appliances that shippers are reluctant to put at risk on the railways that were subject to delays and unreliability coupled with exposure to the vagaries of the weather. Between 1978 and 2021, the proportion of goods carried by the highways increased from 48% to 73% in volume terms (a 25X growth) and from 4% to 80% in turnover (a nearly 200X growth!). Transportation by waterways and pipelines also grew at the expense of railways.[9]

There is a strong contrast between the US and China in that China's domestic water transportation accounts for 14% of transportation compared to the US at 4% (and in the US, it is further declining due to low water levels on the Mississippi). China's pipelines (used for oil and gas) have grown rapidly in recent decades, but they still, at 2% of transportation, lag behind the US (18%).[10]

Chinese planners and commentators are concerned about the environmental impact of the growth in road freight. There is a policy to increase the rail's proportion of the mix, a focus on shifting from road transportation to rail and to waterways. Intermodal (from road to rail) is clearly an area where progress needs to be made. There is also a trend to create on-dock rail terminals so as to avoid using trucks for the first and last mile.[11]

Waterways and ports

China's main river artery, the Yangtze River, in the past was used by junks of all sizes, but the passage upstream to Chongqing through the Three Gorges required massive teams of workers to haul the vessels upstream. In the 1860s, after the Opium Wars and the Unequal Treaties, two British trading firms and one local firm began cargo steamship lines up to so-called Treaty Ports (where foreigners enjoyed extraterritorial rights) at Yichang, Zhenjiang, Nanjing, Wuhan, and elsewhere. By the 1920s, ocean-going ships of 10,000 DWT and above were operating up to Wuhan during the season when the water level was high.

After the People's Republic of China (PRC) was established, efforts were focused on restoring the waterways to the conditions that prevailed before the war with Japan and the civil war. This entailed not only extensive dredging but also the repairing and installation of navigation buoys and aids on land to guide vessels. Sailing junks were fitted with engines.

China's coastline is more than 14,000 km long. In the southern provinces of Guangdong and Fujian, there were countless inlets and ports that fostered a thriving coastal trade. Coastal navigation is still vulnerable to typhoons but the old threat of piracy has gone away.

China's progress on major seaports is impressive. In the 1970s, China had only one new purpose-built port, Xingang (New Port) in Tianjin in North China which became the main entrepot for transportation inland to nearby Beijing.

Located in the marshy Tianjin suburb of Tanggu, it had come under foreign occupation in the late 19th century and was where the Eight-Nation force of foreign troops landed on their way to put down the Boxer Rebellion. But it was not until 1952 that work began to put in modern wharfs and only in the late 1970s that it began to handle shipping containers. In the period 1978–1980, China's state shipping firm COSCO had its first container ships built. Today, Tianjin's port is the world's 8th largest port, with 217 berths and handling 20 MM TEUs annually. But it is overshadowed by other ports in China, such as Shanghai (47 MM TEU annually), Ningbo (33MM), Shenzhen (30 MM), Qingdao (26MM), and Guangzhou (25MM).

Traditionally, in most Chinese ports, ships were moored in deeper areas of a coastal river and goods were transported on and off the vessels using lighters or barges. That was the case in Shanghai's port. Even the deepwater port of Hong Kong relied on lighters before the container age. The advent of the shipping container transformed things. But China lacked the ports to handle them.

In the 1980s, the Chinese government facilitated the rapid growth of Shenzhen Special Economic Zone, in south China, close to Hong Kong. That included several new deepwater ports, such as Yantian, that competed with Hong Kong. In the 1990s, the Party turned its attention to fast-tracking the development of Shanghai which had been something of complacent laggard up to then. The new Shanghai city was built in half the time it took to build Shenzhen. A series of new

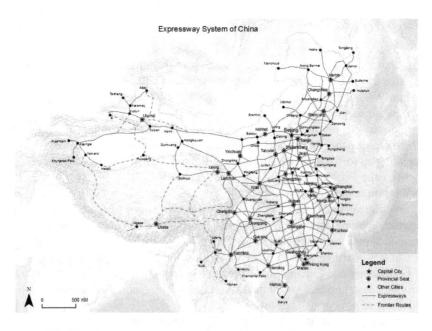

Figure 3.3 China's expressway (superhighway)network.

tunnels and bridges linked the old part of the city with a new zone called Pudong, on the other side of the Huangpu River. With this also came vast investment in Shanghai Port, really a series of ports, aimed at providing deepwater berths for the largest container ships. The new Yangshan Port was built on reclaimed land and connected to the mainland by a bridge over 32 km long. Over the last decade, Shanghai Port has been the largest port in the world.

In 1949, China's shipping sector was greatly hampered by the lack of a shipbuilding industry. There was the Jiangnan Shipyard (which dates back to 1865) and one in Dalian, which could build small coastal vessels. But today, China's shipbuilding industry is the largest in the world, with, as of 2022, 48% of global shipyard output compared to South Korea (25%) and Japan (15%). The capability and quality of China's shipbuilding are also now world class. Shipowners globally are happy to have their container ships and oil carriers built in China. China has mastered circular arc welding skills needed to build semi-submersible oil rigs. China's shipbuilders have recently launched their first cruise ship, in a highly technical segment of the market that hitherto had eluded China. China still relies on foreign firms for much of the machinery and electronics that go into the vessels. For instance, low-speed, two-stroke engines, and recently less polluting engines, for container ships, have been dominated by three firms, from Finland, Germany, and Japan. The Finnish firm, Wartsila has established a series of joint ventures in China with the state shipbuilders to produce marine engines and propellers. On the back of this learning process, it is to be anticipated that in due course, China will emerge as a major player in this area.

Roads, superhighways and trucking

China's achievements in road building since the reforms began in 1978 are breathtaking. By 2004, the total network reached 1.8 MM km, then 3.7 MM in 2008, and 5.28 MM by 2021. Of course, some of these are still unpaved. Most are still just the old-style national trunk roads (*Guodao*), which feature traffic lights and are often clogged with rural and suburban traffic. But the impressive superhighway network that China has built is a bold statement of intent. In the US, the Interstate system is often not fenced off and the risk of deer crossing is mitigated by years of cutting back of the trees and grass on the verges. In China, the superhighways are "closed off" (*fengbixing*), with strong fences along all of them, to make sure neither animals, tractors, nor pedestrians wander onto them.

In 1984, using World Bank financing, construction began on China's first expressway which was 400 km long, connecting the coastal city of Dalian with the Liaoning provincial capital of Shenyang. Far south in Hong Kong, entrepreneur Gordon Wu was pioneering a different approach. Through a joint venture with China, he built the 122-km Guangzhou-Shenzhen Superhighway. Its construction began in 1987, with completion a decade later, using fully commercial project finance which relied on road tolls to repay the debt.

In 1990, China's statistics showed that the nation only had 500 km of expressway. But by 2010, it reached 74,000 km, and by 2021, it was 169,000 km. The expressway network, which has long surpassed the US's Interstate system, is called the National Trunk Highway System. Its network configuration is summarized as 71118, or 7 radial expressways from Beijing, plus 11 going North-South and 18 East-West. China's longest expressway is 4,395 km, connecting Lianyungang on China's East coast with Khorgos in Xinjiang on the Kazakhstan border.

One Chinese commentator observed that "logistics is the foundation of the national economy, road freight is the basis of logistics, and truck drivers are the basis of road freight." He continues in a poetic vein that truckers are:

> like red blood cells, allowing the blood of China's economy to flow between China and neighboring countries, delivering oxygen to this large market and providing security for our lives, and they are closely related to the lives of each and every one of us.[12]

Trucks haul 70% of China's goods by tonnage and 30% by tons/km. But trucking is fragmented and highly inefficient. China's trucking industry does not resemble the US one which is dominated by large trucking specialists such as Werner, J.B. Hunt, and Schneider. There are some large trucking firms in China. But many of them are highly specialized such as Hengtong (largely shipping LNG), Beijing Changjiu (auto logistics), and Guangdong GenSho (auto parts). Deppon, which is listed on the Shanghai Stock Exchange with a market cap equivalent to over US$ 3 BN, provides a range of trucking services, including full-truckload, less-than-truckload, (often known as LTL) and express delivery. The Chinese e-commerce logistics giant JD Logistics recently gained a controlling interest in the firm, with its eyes on its last-mile delivery capability.

Many of the Chinese largest truck fleets are part of broader logistics operations. One of China's largest logistics players, COSCO Shipping Logistics, which we profile in Chapter 13, operates a significant fleet of trucks that are specialized in hauling containers, chemicals, refrigerated/chilled products, and "engineering" products (this latter category being the use of specialized vehicles for the land transportation of very large piece of equipment, for instance turbines for power stations). COSCO has been a pioneer in technology adoption, having used GPS tracking for its trucks for the last two decades. Sinotrans, the logistics platform of China Merchants, (also profiled in Chapter 13), runs their own fleet of trucks to link inland hubs with the coast and again with a high degree of product specialization. Large Chinese 3PLs such as COSCO, Sinotrans, and China Logistics Group are reluctant to outsource trucking to the fragmented and chaotic world of owner operators. They feel the need to have skin in the game and to own and operate these transportation assets in order to reassure their customers that the logistics will be reliable, resilient, and safe.

The condition of China's estimated 30 million truckers is not a pretty one. Based on a survey by a professor at China's Qinghua University, over 70% are self-employed and, in other words, are owner operators of the trucks. They come from an agricultural background, are mostly between 36 and 45 years old, and have two children. China's trucking workforce is aging and there is said to be a shortage of 10-MM drivers, more extreme than the hiring crisis in which the US trucking industry finds itself. The truckers borrow heavily to purchase their trucks and face pressure to repay, with the result that they do illegal overtime and cause accidents. The financial burden is increased by government regulations limiting the life of a truck to 10–15 years. They are "atomized and scattered" and live, eat, and even cook in their truck cab. Sometimes, they take their small children with them on the road. They suffer from severe mental stress. There are heartbreaking stories of drivers who, after being issued traffic fines, committed suicide by drinking poison. They fear stopping to rest due to the threat of goods being stolen and fuel being syphoned off by "oil guzzlers" (*you haozi*) and so risk their lives and those of others by driving through the night without rest. One trucker named Zhao was approached by a security guard who said "20 Yuan for a good's night sleep." He did not pay up and the next morning he found 700 liters of fuel had been stolen. The only mitigating factor is the feeling of solidarity between trucks that yields mutual help when needed.[13,14]

The government works hard to regulate the truckers, seeking to avoid overloading and excessive drivetime without rest. But the regulations bring with them what is called the "three types of chaos," the lack of standardization across the nation, the haphazard and inconsistent enforcement, and "unreasonable" and illegal fees levied on truckers.

All of China's superhighways are toll roads and for a long-distance driver, it mounts up. In the US, only 3% of its main highways are toll roads and tolls are quite modest compared to those in China. Chinese truckers are required by law to have a 20-minute rest after four hours of driving. But due to the absence of rest areas, 40% of Chinese truckers drive non-stop for more than 12 hours. The truck accident rate in China is 3.7 per km on all roads and 1.9 on superhighways. This compares to 0.1 accidents on all US roads.[15]

The Chinese government is mindful of the online chatter about the truckers being abused and forgotten. The Ministry of Transportation (MOT) and the government-organized trade unions have created a pilot program for "trucker homes" to be built along the superhighways, where truckers stop the truck without any risk, and then eat subsidized meals, sleep, shower, and get a change of clothes.

Railways and rail freight

China entered the modern age with a railway system that was the product of Imperialism, the results of the efforts of the Great Powers, during the 19th century to gain access to China, a process that the Chinese justifiably feared was a precursor to China being "carved up like a melon" (*guafen*), similar to what happened to Africa. The Great Powers ultimately stopped short of a full dismemberment of China, preferring instead to operate through Treaty Ports in which they enjoyed extraterritorial rights, outside the jurisdiction of the Chinese government. Behind these ports, the hinterland, while nominally controlled by the Chinese, became "spheres of influence" of the individual Great Powers. To permit the export of goods and raw materials out of China and imports into China, each Great Power built railway lines within its own sphere of influence, particularly after the turn of the 20th century. The British built a line from Shanghai up the Yangtze to Nanjing and another one from Kowloon, Hong Kong, to Guangzhou (Canton). In Shandong, the Germans built a line from their port of Qingdao up to Jinan. After World War One, Japan was awarded Germany's Shandong possessions. The Russians built a railway in Northeast China which after the Russo-Japanese War was folded into Japan's South Manchurian Railway. The French built a railway from Vietnam in their Indochina colony up to Kunming in China's Yunnan Province.

While these railways were well designed to support the economic goals of the Great Powers, they fell far short of providing China with a railway system that could integrate the national economy. What was to be built later, and in particular since 1949, was a complete network that provided North-South Routes in addition to the lines that began on the Eastern seaboard.

In the late Qing and the following Republic of China, a major issue for China's railways development was the high investment cost. Financing was provided by Russia, Japan, Britain, Germany, and France which all drove hard bargains in terms of operating control and resulting political influence. In 1930, it was estimated that China owed US$ 700 MM (a vast sum if converted to today's currency) on loans for their railway financing.[16]

As mentioned above, Sun Yat-sen promoted his "Railway Plan of China–1921" and urged China to emulate the US railway system.[17] Even though, due to invasion and civil war, little of this was achieved until after 1949, Sun's vision was highly influential. This can be seen today by taking the current network and laying it over the railroad map that he drafted.

In 1953, China established the Railroad Army Corp, similar to the US Army Corps of Engineers, to lead the nation's railway construction. With its 15 divisions and a training infrastructure of engineering colleges, it pushed railways into remote regions. Overall, in the early years of the PRC, there was significant progress in railway development. However, the surges of Mao's political radicalism during the Great Leap Forward (1958–1962) and the Cultural Revolution (1966–1976) saw a breakdown in the professional culture in the railways and a marked uptick in accidents.[18] After the economic reforms began, China sought to slim down the army and to move it out of civilian life. In 1984, the Corps' activities were transferred to the Ministry of Railways (MOR).

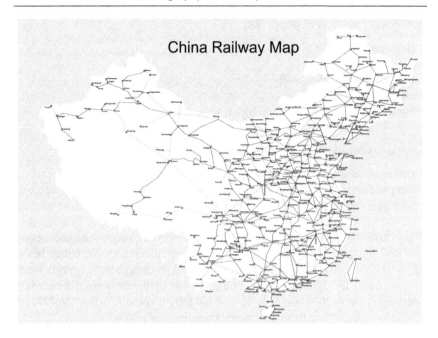

Figure 3.4 China's rail network.

In 2021, China had 151,000 km of railways, of which nearly 60% was double tracked and 74% was electrified, all of which benefits rail freight. The network is planned to expand to 175,000 km by 2025. In recent decades, the most stunning aspect of China's rail expansion has been passenger HSR which in 2021 had a total length track of 40,000 km of dedicated track and accounted for 27% of the network.[19] This in turn freed up rail capacity for freight on the remaining mixed passenger/freight lines.

China's rapid expansion of its rail network entailed the deployment of a wide range of skills. These were in civil engineering – building bridges, boring tunnels (using massive machines), laying rails, and installing overhead cables. It involved developing and installing complex electronic signaling systems. China developed and mass produced its own high-speed locomotives and rolling stock, doing so through copying others' technology and innovating on top of that. China's railway-building prowess is now being exported under China's Belt and Road Initiative to countries ranging from Indonesia to Kenya and Ethiopia.

China's rail construction has addressed the gaps left by the historical legacy that we mentioned above. Today, China has built five vertical North-South rail lines and three horizontal East-West rail lines. The distances covered by these lines are impressive.

North-South railway lines length (km)

Beijing-Shanghai 1,500
Beijing-Guangzhou 2,300
Beijing-Hong Kong 2,480
Henan-Guangxi 2,400
Shaanxi-Kunming 1,760

East-West railway lines length (km)

Beijing-Gansu 830
Jiangsu coast-Xinjiang 3,650
Shanghai-Yunnan 2,680[20]

China's railways have been slow to reflect the growth of China's consumer economy. Rail freight is mainly used for minerals (coal, metal ores, oil, coke), basic industrial products (such as steel), and agricultural products (such as grain). Coal alone accounts for 48% of freight volume carried by the railways. China's rail containerization in 2021 was only 15% of rail freight volume. In the US, 27% of railroad revenues come from intermodal containerized traffic.

Rail intermodal

China has been playing catch up in the development of its rail intermodal logistics, whereby containerized goods are transferred from trucks to rail. The World Bank has been mindful of just how China lags the rest of the world in this dimension:

> A more intense use of rail as part of the country's containerized freight delivery logistics system could be a game-changer for Chinese manufacturers and consumers alike, as we have seen in North America…That's because more and more manufacturing has moved to China's western provinces, which increases the distance of international and domestic shipments. At the same time, China's highways are becoming more congested, making it difficult to deliver goods and get value-for-money in trucking services.[21]

After decades of economic reforms, China's rail containerization (that is using shipping containers) was still embarrassingly tiny. Around 1% of containers left the ports by rail while 85% went by truck, with the remainder by waterways. This was a large and obvious area for improvement that had been staring China in the face, but which had not been adequately addressed. Twenty years ago, parts of the rail freight operations were hived off into a new firm called China Rail Container Transport which set about establishing intermodal terminals (for transfer road to rail and vice versa) across the nation.

But there was a more fundamental problem that needed to be fixed. China's MOR, as a Stalinist hold-out of central planners, was highly resistant to reform and change. China's highly effective Premier Zhu Rongji (he served from 1998 to 2003) tried in vain to reform the MOR which controlled the entire rail value chain – rail policy, operations, and rolling stock manufacturing. In 2008, China's roads, ports and shipping (the Ministry of Communications), air (the Civil Aviation Administration of China), and postal services (the State Postal Bureau) were merged into the new MOT. But it was not 2013 that the MOR was finally dissolved, with its regulatory powers being merged into the MOT and its operations reconstituted as the China Rail Corporation.

This long-drawn-out demise of the MOR as a legacy of Soviet-style central planning was one reason why China's rail intermodal logistics has been so slow to take off. Part of it had to do with the lack of investment in this new area. But much of the issue lays with the way the MOR obstructed reforms to permit pricing flexibility on a more commercial basis. As China began to spin off the intermodal business from the MOR, the hope was to interest major US rail freight players such as CSX in taking an equity stake in the assets to be listed on the stock market and thus become participants in this sector in China. However, MOR's unwillingness to consider flexible pricing for intermodal business was one issue that ended these negotiations between China and US players. But ultimately, China Rail Container did succeed in forming a JV which became listed on the stock market as China United Rail Container Co (CUIRC) (also known as CR International). A major and continuing feature of China's rail intermodal development has been Public-Private Partnerships, whereby heavy investment by the government is complemented by funding from the private sector. The Singapore ports firm PSA[22] (which has also invested in Antwerp) and Germany's Deutsche Bahn (DB Cargo) took minority stakes in CUIRC. DB's participation is closely linked to its broader cooperation with China on China-Europe rail links.

Today, CUIRC has 18 rail intermodal container terminals at strategic locations across China, including in Xinjiang, Sichuan, and Chongqing. At these terminals, it is deploying advanced loading equipment and providing warehousing and other logistics facilities.

A key aspect of efficiency in rail freight intermodal is the double-stacking of containers. In the US, double-stacking is now standard practice and permits one train to carry the same load as hundreds of trucks. However, double-stacking requires significant capital investment in increasing tunnel height and width, as well as adjusting bridge clearance. There is also the issue of a higher center of gravity from such tall loads. Greater axle loads have to be accommodated and rail lines have to be strengthened for the extra weight. Given the prohibitive costs of adopting double-stacking, it is not used in Europe or the UK. But both China and India are investing to make double-stacking possible. In China, progress on this has been slow. In 2018, China announced its first double-stacked freight train which could increase the load-carrying ability by 30%. However, it only traveled from the port of Ningbo to Shaoxing, still within the same province of Zhejiang.[23] There is also the prospect of double-stacking being used for China-Europe rail routes. But the challenges set out above make it hard to realize.[24]

High-speed rail freight

Until recently, China's rail freight traveled over the same rails as traditional, conventional passenger trains. The HSR lines, which represent 40,000 km of the total 130,000 km rail network, and which run at speeds of up to 350 km/hour, have been exclusively for passenger traffic. That is changing. The government's five-year plan for logistics spells out clearly the intent to create:

> Point-to-point high-speed high-speed rail express train services between qualified high-speed rail stations. ...Build a "one-stop" high-speed rail express service platform such as business acceptance, tracking enquiry and settlement handling, and promote the information sharing... with e-commerce and express logistics enterprises.[25]

In 2020, the first two high-speed freight trains, a converted passenger train with the seats removed, each carrying 40 tons of e-commerce goods, made the journey in opposite directions between Wuhan and Beijing. In the same year, China announced the production of a specially designed high-speed freight train with a 2.9-m wide-loading door. It travels at 350 km/hour, much faster than the until now fastest freight train in Italy which runs at 180 km/hour.[26] This new trend is closely related to the peaks of e-commerce caused by Single's Day which sees some 3 BN items being delivered. Road transport is too slow and traditional rail is slow and cumbersome. Air transport is too costly and polluting. HSR freight is useful in filling this niche.

Air cargo

Though it still remains a tiny part of domestic freight transportation, China airfreight is experiencing rapid growth due to two factors. Firstly, as China moves up the economic ladder, the proportion of high-value goods is growing. The second factor is the burgeoning China e-commerce sector and the fulfillment/delivery needs that create. In the period 2000–2021, China's domestic airfreight volume grew fourfold.

Twenty years ago, China's domestic air cargo industry was in its infancy. China Post had a couple of Y-(Yun)8s, Chinese derivatives of the Soviet-designed An (Antonov)-12. Those living in Beijing's Shunyi suburb close to the airport, could lie in bed and in the still night air of the North China plain hear at 2:30 AM every night the distant roar as that freight plane with four turboprop engines took off. As part of its Express Mail Service (known as EMS) it carried letters and packages down to Guangzhou. Other firms were to jump into China's domestic airfreight, especially in response to the explosive growth of e-commerce.

But domestic air cargo has not been an easy business. It was initially slow to take off. Smaller air cargo firms had to deal with tight regulation coupled with heavy competition from the large state-owned airlines that have easy access to investment capital and have vast belly cargo capacity (on passenger planes) on domestic routes. Some firms such as Donghai and Grandstar went bankrupt while others such as Shanghai Airlines' air cargo business were merged into other firms.

China Post Airlines' aging Y-8s are now supplemented by 22 narrow-bodied planes, Boeing 737 and 757 freighters and wide-bodied Boeing 777F freighters are currently being introduced. They have established an air cargo hub with an integrated logistics center at Nanjing Lukou Airport.

The fast movers in domestic airfreight are firms associated with e-commerce. SF Express in 2009 established its own airline which today has a fleet of B 767s and B 757s. It has airbases in Beijing and Shenzhen. Seeking to emulate the air cargo hubs of FedEx, UPS, and DHL in Memphis, Louisville, and Leipzig, respectively, SF is spending US$ 370 MM to establish a hub at Ezhou Huahu Airport in Hubei Province. JD Airlines, part of the e-commerce firm JD, is establishing an air cargo hub in Nantong, Jiangsu and says it will have 114 aircraft by 2025. YTO Express has an air cargo hub in Jiaxing, in Zhejiang very close to Shanghai, with 11 freighters including B 757s.

If we include airfreight between the Mainland and Hong Kong, Macau, and Taiwan, China's international airfreight has grown by five times in the last two decades. This sector has been dominated by the cargo subsidiaries of China's main airlines and by foreign players such as UPS, FedEx, and DHL, which have established their own hubs within China.

Development from the East Coast into the interior

As China's economic reforms began, development was focused on the Eastern seaboard and with that, the logistics were relatively straightforward. When, starting from the late 1970s, foreign investors flocked to China, they initially focused on places where the Chinese government provided the financial and tax incentives, namely in the Special Economic Zones, crucibles for economic experimentation in South China and then, starting in 1984, in a series of so-called Open Coastal Cities. These coastal locations also enjoyed convenient logistics with links to local ports for the import of raw materials and components and for the export of finished products. China, as the Factory-of-the-World, also naturally located its own export-oriented industry in the coastal plains of South China with easy access to container ports such as in Hong Kong, Shenzhen, or Xiamen. These factories were able to attract a seemingly unlimited supply of cheap labor from China's hinterland. Two decades ago, we conducted a survey to map the China logistics market and found that most of the 3PL activity were concentrated in the three regions discussed above: at that time, the urban and industrial concentrations of North China, the Lower Yangtze Valley, and South China accounted for 22%, 41%, and 37% of 3PL revenues, respectively.[27]

In the early days of China's opening up, in-bound logistics were relatively simple since the newly established foreign factories were located close to the ports. In the late 1980s, VW established a factory in Anting then in the rural suburbs of Shanghai. Initially, before local component sourcing became feasible, it imported completely knocked-down kits from Germany. China's largest container shipping line, COSCO, was able to win this important new client. VW decided to build warehousing at the Anting factory to permit a Just-in-Time (JIT) supply of components. COSCO's Chief Operating officer told VW that this was not necessary since COSCO would deliver containers from their ships on a regular schedule which permitted JIT. This assessment proved to be correct and the VW warehouse became redundant.[28] What this illustrates is that, in the first phase of China's economic reforms, since much of the foreign manufacturing was in coastal cities the in-bound land logistics were not complex – essentially just using a container truck to transport the container the short distance from the port to the factory. As multinational corporations moved in-land that was all to change.

Since then, we have seen a massive policy-driven shift in the economy. The Chinese government launched it "Go West" policy to encourage Chinese and foreign investors to open up the central and Western regions of China which had fallen behind as the coastal east boomed. Also, as wage levels in the coastal areas reached the level of those in the Baltic States, it became logical to seek lower cost labor in the interior. Foxconn, the Taiwan firm that assembles the Apple's iPhone, originally operated mainly in Shenzhen, just across the border from Hong Kong. Today its largest iPhone plant is in Zhengzhou, a large dusty inland city in Henan 950 km from the coast.

Foxconn was no doubt heavily leant on by the government to move to Zhengzhou. The same happens in other sectors. When automaker GM decided to take the plunge into China in the early 1990s, it selected (or was offered) Shanghai on the coast. Shanghai was embarking on a development rush and was keen to attract new auto investment in addition to VW, which had been there for nearly a decade. But when a few years later, Ford Motor decided that the time was ripe to invest in China, it was forced to accept Chongqing, an inland, (then) backward and populous city (population 32 MM), which looked like a worn-out inland version of Hong Kong with high-rise blocks perches on cliffs above the Yangtze. Chongqing was crying out for investment and the government made it happen.

During the war against Japan, remote Chongqing (Chungking) proved to be a safe haven for the government of the Republic of China. But today, being 1,685 km from the coast is an issue, a nightmare, not an advantage. Still, Ford seems to have had a fruitful relationship with Chang'an, the former arms manufacturer it teamed up with in Chongqing. Cummins (truck engine manufacturer) has also had a good experience there. But the logistics is a burden. A Korean producer of auto air-conditioning was lined up to supply the Ford factory there. The rational decision would have been to put their plant for the air-conditioning systems on the coast and simply have a warehouse in Chongqing where JIT inventory could be held. But Chongqing, keen to create jobs and bring in investment, drove a hard bargain and the Korean firm was compelled to build a full factory in Chongqing, while stopping short of producing the key component, their compressors, at that plant.

As the China head of the logistics arm of US firm Ryder System put it in 2007, "we will go the same way as other multi-national logistics companies have gone in Mainland China, from coastal cities to inland cities."[29] We profile Ryder in Chapter 14.

Case study: the corning example

To gain a vivid insight into how foreign firms tracked China's development Westwards into the interior and with that created the logistics to permit this, we can look at the record of the US firm Corning Incorporated that we mentioned earlier in Chapter 1. Corning's core competence is its mastery of materials science and processing which is applied to products such as specialty glass, complex ceramics, and photonics. It also epitomizes how smart firms constantly reinvent themselves in order to address market transitions, to respond to shifts in the external competitive environment. In the 1970s–1980s, it was known for its manufacturing of glass bulbs for TVs (the cathode ray tube or CRT). It also had a big business in consumer cooking ware. It was strong in miniature downlights (MDL).

But Corning was beginning a transformation into new directions. The consumer glassware business was spun off. The MDL business was abandoned due to Chinese competition. In 1970, it invented optical fiber and capitalized on that, not just producing the glass fiber and the cable but also moving into photonics (such as the erbium-doped fiber amplifiers or EDFAs needed to push the light along the fiber). As flat-screen TVs replaced CRTs, Corning transitioned into producing the glass substrates and finished products for LCDs used for TVs, computers, and tablets. It invented Gorilla Glass which today is used for the screen of virtually all mobile phones. It also pioneered the manufacturing of ceramic substrates which are the core technology for automotive catalytic converters.

Its involvement in China began in the 1980s when it deployed its CRT technology in that market and then extended its engagement to optical fiber and cabling. One of its boldest moves was in 2000 when it opened a plant in Shanghai to produce substrates for catalytic converters. Rather than locating the 5-MM unit per annum factory in South Korea, where there was already strong demand, Corning made the prescient move of putting it in China, where demand for cars would ultimately turn out to be much larger. To maintain full operating control and protect their Intellectual Property Rights (IPR), Corning chose a wholly-owned subsidiary rather than forming a joint venture with a local Chinese partner. The reform-minded Shanghai government was highly supportive of the project which was located in that city's Jinqiao Economic Zone.

Initially, the logistics around that project were not that complex. Shanghai Port was there to import raw materials and to export substrates to Korea and Japan where they were coated with precious metals by "catalyzers" and then "canned," to produce the final catalytic converter. Some of the substrates were shipped to catalyzers in the interior of China, but not far from Shanghai. They used a local 3PL recommended by the development zone.[30]

If, at that stage in their China presence, there was any complexity in the supply chain, it had to do with IPR protection. The eight types of mineral powders used to make the substrates were imported into China in especially secure containers. The highly proprietary dies for making the substrates were brought in by human couriers who personally carried them through customs.[31]

As China's automobile market reached an inflexion point and roared upwards, Corning's logistics became much more complex. Firstly, they were shipping to catalyzers, both foreign and Chinese, all-over China, including to the central regions and the West. The plot they owned in Jinqiao was ten times the size of the original factory. Ten years after the factory was established, it occupied the entire plot and a new site was needed. The decision was to locate 500 km inland in Hefei, Anhui Province where production began in 2019. The logistics had to handle this new dimension.[32]

This is a pattern across Corning's large China portfolio. Corning has invested US$ 9 BN in China, where they have 6,000 employees in 29 facilities, mainly factories. Their China operations include LCD, optical, catalytic converter substrates, life sciences (lab ware), and mobile (Gorilla Glass for mobile phones). One-third of its US$ 15 BN of global revenues come from China.

Corning did initially concentrate much of its business along or close to the coast in Shanghai, Shenzhen, Fuzhou, Haikou, and Beijing. But it has also taken bold steps to move into the interior with plants in central China (Wuhan and Hefei) and in the West (Chengdu and Chongqing). This move inland was in part driven by lower costs and land availability. But it also reflected the need to engage downstream with Chinese clients in those areas. It was tracking the waves of China's development surge.

Corning used its expertise in materials science to invent Gorilla Glass, an alkali-aluminosilicate which is strong and scratch resistance. It now dominates that global market for smartphone screens. Its production was the last part of its portfolio to face increasing logistics complexity in China as its footprint moved inland. To protect its intellectual property, Corning chose to produce Gorilla Glass in the US (Kentucky), Taiwan, and South Korea. The raw glass was then trucked to a port from where it was carried by container ship to Hong Kong. Occasionally, it was shipped by air to Hong Kong, with either Corning or the customer paying the extra, depending on which side caused the additional urgency. In Hong Kong, it was kept in a Corning warehouse, where the customers picked up the product and took title. This was convenient since the further processing of the Gorilla Glass took place just across the border in Shenzhen or Dongguan.

But soon the Gorilla Glass business was forced to follow the path of Corning's other product lines. Mobile phone production was moving inland (as with Foxconn mentioned above). In 2021, Corning announced that they were investing in a complete "hot-melt" Gorilla Glass factory in Chongqing, a city in the far West interior, where they already had an LCD plant. But Gorilla Glass is a very high value, relatively lightweight, and sought-after material. Even with the Chongqing production adding logistics complexity across China, Corning rarely uses distributors for this product and prefers to own and control the required warehousing, up to the point when title is transferred to the processor.[33]

Notes

1 Co-author Clifford first visited the Great Nanjing Bridge in early 1974. It was celebrated as a major achievement of the policy of Self Reliance, which was adopted after the Sino-Soviet Split.
2 T.R.Tregear, *An Economic Geography of China*, Butterworh, 1970.
3 T.R.Tregear, *An Economic Geography of China*, Butterworh, 1970, p. 34.
4 T.R.Tregear, *An Economic Geography of China*, Butterworh, 1970, p. 73.
5 T.R.Tregear, *An Economic Geography of China*, Butterworh, 1970, p. 98.
6 US Dept of Transportation, *Transportation Statistics Annual Report, 2022*, pp. 96–100.
7 Kuo Tsu-cheng, Transport Planning, in *Chinese Economic Planning, Translations form Chi-Hua Ching-Chi*, edited Nicolas Lardy, 1978, Taylor & Francis Group, p. 37.
8 The State Statistical Bureau, *Te34n Great Years. Statistics of the Economic and Cultural Achievements if the People's Republic of China*, Beijing, 1960, pp. 139–156.
9 State Statistical Bureau, *China Statistical Yearbook, 2022*, Beijing, 2023, p. 518.
10 International Council on Clean Transportation, *Towards Green Transportation and Sustainable Freight Systems, Comparison of Freight Strategies in the United States and China*, 2022.
11 International Council on Clean Transportation, *Towards Green Transportation and Sustainable Freight Systems, Comparison of Freight Strategies in the United States and China*, 2022.
12 Mao Ge, *Zhongguo wuliu de yinyou: kache siji qunti youhuan lu*, on Baidu, 14 May, 2022.
13 Shen Yuan, *Guonei jinyoude yifen kachesiji shendu baodao, buren cudu*, on *Wenhua zongheng*, Apr 10, 2021.
14 Mao Ge, *Zhongguo wuliu de yinyou: kache siji qunti youhuan lu*, on Baidu, 14 May, 2022.
15 Mao Ge, *Zhongguo wuliu de yinyou: kache siji qunti youhuan lu*, on Baidu, May 14, 2022.
16 Ming-Ju Cheng, *The Influence of Communications Internal and External upon the Economic Future of China*, Routledge, 1930, p. 71.

17 Sun Yat-sen, *The International Development of China,* 1922, cited in Richard Louis Edmonds, *The Legacy of Sun Yat-sen's Railway Plan,* on *China Quarterly,* Sep 1987.
18 Elizabeth Koll, *Railroads and the Transportation of China,* Harvard, 2019.
19 State Statistical Bureau, *China Statistical Yearbook, 2022,* Beijing, 2023, pp. 515, 528.
20 *China Travel Network,* https://www.travelchinaguide.com/china-trains/railway/network.htm.
21 Luis Blancas, quoted in *Containers on Rail: China Next Big Opportunity in Supply Chain Logistics,* World Bank, 2015. And in Luis Blancas, Gerald Ollivier and Richard Bullock, *Customer-driven Rail Intermodal Unlocking a New Sources of Value in China,* The World Bank, 2015.
22 PSA website, globalpsa.com.
23 Xinhua, *Double Stacked Container Train Put into Service in China Port,* on *China. org.cn,* Dec 18, 2018.
24 Raphael Zhang, Lou Gong-wei, *Double Stack Container for Increasing Capacity for Eurasian Transportation,* on *New Silkroad Discovery,* www.newsilkroaddiscovery. com, Nov 11, 2021.
25 State Council of PRC, *"Shisuwu" xiandai wuliu fazhan guihua* (14th Five year Plan, *Modern Logistics Development Plan*) issued Dec 15, 2022. Covers the period of China's 14th Five Year Plan, 2021–2025.
26 *China Takes Rail Logistics to a New Level. Freight Trains Run At 350 km/h,* in *Cargo Partner, 2021.*
27 *The State of Third-Party Logistics in China,* survey by Mercer Management Consulting, 2002.
28 Confidential interview by Paul G. Clifford with a shipping industry expert, London, Jan 5, 2024.
29 Christopher Woodward, cited in *Ryder expands Its China logistics infrastructure,* on *Payload Asia,* June 1, 2007.
30 Interview with a retired Senior Corning Executive, Nov 27, 2023.
31 Interview with a retired Senior Corning Executive, Nov 27, 2023.
32 Interview with a retired Senior Corning Executive, Nov 27, 2023.
33 Interview with a retired Senior Corning Executive, Nov 27, 2023.

Chapter 4

The hand of government guides China's logistics

Logistics role in forging national unity and economic integration

Throughout its history, China has encountered periods of disunity and national fragmentation. Anxiety about that still lurks in the minds of China's leaders. Modern logistics is seen as a powerful tool to integrate the economy and mitigate those risks.

In 1930, shortly after a period in which China disintegrated into a series of warlord fiefdoms, a Chinese economist stressed the role of transportation in fostering political unity:

> As soon as railways cover a country they create an economic dependence between its various parts......The economic interdependence of the parts of China will be a big step in the direction of political stability...Smooth and rapid communications is not only conducive to economic unity, but are also a condition of political unity.[1]

China's history can be seen as a series of cultural and economic flourishings when strong dynasties were able to provide the national unity, stability, and integration. China's first empire, the Qin Dynasty (221–206 BC) was short-lived due to its overreaching ambition and cruelty but was monumental in its impact. It is easy to see why Mao thought so highly of that dynasty's first emperor Qinshihuang. The Qin not only brought unity but also standardization of the currency, measures, of writing and of the axel length of wagons. This last reform held reduces the wear and tear on China's roads, especially in the soft Loess soil in Northwest China.

Other high points of unity followed. The Han Dynasty (206 BC to 220 AD) built upon the work begun by the Qin. Its armies expanded China's borders Westwards into what today is Xinjiang. The subsequent Sung, Tang, Yuan, Ming, and Qing dynasties were peaks of political unity. Throughout each dynasty, a core competence of the rulers was the capability to use central power to manage

DOI: 10.4324/9781003489115-6

China's hydraulic society, to build, and maintain the complex waterworks needed for China's intensive wet field cultivation of rice.

The Sui Dynasty (581–618), which was a precursor to the Tang, much like the Qin was to the Han, completed the linkage of a series of canals into the long Grand Canal between Hangzhou in central south China and up to the capital in Beijing. In its North-south route, it linked the Yangtze with the Yellow River. It was a major conduit for grain to be shifted from the central south to the capital (and to the military guarding the border) in the north. It obviated the need to transport grain around China's sea coast which was vulnerable to hurricanes and pirates.

Rather than looking at these peaks of dynastic power and glory, one can also see Chinese history through another lens. These peaks often ended with social breakdown, peasant rebellions, and invasion by nomadic peoples from the Steppes, resulting in periods of disunity, of chaos and a break-up of the national entity.

In the 1860s during the last decades of the Qing Dynasty, the Taiping Rebellion for a while established a separate regime based in Nanjing, while the Manchu emperors hung on in Beijing. After the 1911 revolution toppled the Qing, China broke up into a series of fiefdoms run by warlords. Even when in 1927 Chiang Kai-shek led his Northern Expedition to unite the nation, his rule during the Nanking Decade (up to the Japanese invasion of 1937) was marred by incomplete control over regional leaders which obstructed the central government and its policies.

It was only after the civil war (1945–1949) between the Republic of China (led by the Guomindang or KMT) and the Chinese Communist Party (CCP), that the CCP brought about national unity which extended ultimately to the remote areas of Tibet and Xinjiang. The CCP put in institutions designed to thwart any breakaway regions. Mirroring practices in imperial times, officials are regularly moved around to prevent over-close links being formed at the local level. China's formal military regions were shaped to ensure that they cut across provincial boundaries. Great efforts were put into fostering national unity through standardizing the spoken language. The new institutions, government processes, and job titles that the CCP borrowed from the Soviet Union were implanted across the nation down to the very lowest level, creating a massively homogenous, cohesive, and disciplined nation.

Recently, one observer did refer back to China's "failed empires and shattered hope" and argued that China will break up due to its "fractured" geography that "does not naturally hold together."[2] However the common wisdom today is to the contrary, namely that China is now in fact much less likely to break up than was the case during the nation's long history.

Over the centuries, the measure of a successful dynasty was its ability to centrally manage the waterworks that permitted intensive wet field cultivation, coupled with the capability to quickly act to nip peasant rebellions in the bud.

China's party-state today has infinitely more capacity to intervene across the nation when required. The surveillance system can accurately spot suspicious names and faces and link them to names and addresses. When floods wipe out the crops in one locality, a computerized system quickly ships grain to avoid starvation. Following the Severe Acute Respiratory Syndrome (SARS) pandemic (2002–2004), China instituted local disease-monitoring systems that kept the capital informed (albeit not perfectly in light of COVID-19), as opposed to being blindsided by local power. When the Wenchuan Earthquake occurred in 2008 in Sichuan, China as a whole swiftly moved to support the rescue and then the reconstruction efforts.[3]

Still, the lingering anxiety over China's history of disunity animates a never-ending desire for further integration of society and the economy. It is easy to see how, among China's leaders, the penny has dropped and there is now a real awareness of the prominent role logistics can play in this unifying process. Modern logistics is a force that can bring together parts of the nation hitherto largely excluded from development while at the same time driving economic efficiency and growth, bridging geographic barriers, increasing consumer and citizen satisfaction, and reducing carbon emissions. In early 2022, the CCP and China's State Council jointly issued a document that stressed the importance of logistics in "Accelerating the Construction of a National Unified Market."[4] The many dimensions of what can be achieved through upgrading the nation's logistics are closely aligned with the aspirations and policies of the CCP

The role of government

Wherever you look in the world, government plays a key role in creating the conditions for a thriving modern integrated logistics industry. It is often instrumental in building or helping to build the transportation channels, be they road, rail, air, or ports, which support the creation of a logistics network. Globally, the role of government also extends to the logistics parks that serve as warehousing hubs within that network. Government seeks to attract trade and investment to create local jobs and to drive supply chain efficiency. It plays a decisive role since it controls land zoning and planning permission and also has the power to offer tax and other incentives to potential investors in logistics parks. It also fosters logistics development through educational institutions.[5] Government on its own, or often working with private sector investors, clears the land, puts in the water, electricity, and fiber optics and often builds the warehousing. Sometimes, future warehouse tenants or owners may be locked in early. But often it is conducted on the basis of "if you build it, they will come." This puts a large burden on planners to figure out the major logistics routes and future demand.

In the international arena, national governments, bilaterally and multilaterally, play a central role in negotiating trade agreements, establishing the Law of the Sea, regulating and establishing telecommunications, payment systems, and much more.

National and local governments across the globe have established free trade zones that form logistics hubs. Typically, materials and components are imported into the zones duty free and then re-exported. This has happened in Rotterdam, Dubai, and in many locations in China. As we shall see later, China is trying to create a much larger zone using the entire Hainan Island (Hainan Free Port), trying to replicate the success of Dubai or Singapore (but without political autonomy being permitted).

Singapore is an excellent example of how government can take the lead in the economy as a whole and specifically in logistics. Singapore's life as a trading hub, as an entrepot, depends on it outperforming its competitors. Back in the 1960s it created the new Jurong Port and in the 1970s, the first container port in Southeast Asia. More recently, it has been working to use IT systems to make Singapore a digital logistics hub, what Tan Chin Hwee calls a "platform nation" providing an open digital platform to permit small- and medium-sized firms to participate in digital trade.[6] To facilitate the island's role as logistics center, Singapore has developed and fine-tuned a computerized customs clearance system. China has long sought to emulate Singapore's success story and logistics is one key aspect of that.

In the US, the Federal Government plays a key role in ensuring that the major transportation arteries, water, rail, and roads function efficiently. Waterways, notably the Mississippi and the Ohio, have for long been more efficient than railways and much more so than roads. 6%–7% of US domestic goods distribution is along the US 36,000 miles of waterways. However, that is declining precipitously due to falling water levels. The US Federal Government is active in providing funds to upgrade the nation's aging transportation network. In 2021, Biden's Infrastructure and Jobs Act allocated US$ 17 BN for the "Action Plan for America's Ports and Waterways."[7] The scope of the measures, designed to address the nation's "underfunded" infrastructure, included grants to help ports upgrade, assistance from the American Corps of Engineers to dredge deeper channels for larger vessels and for work on making the fragmented digital transportation infrastructure more integrated and interoperable.

When it comes to the supply chain itself, the recent federal measures in the US relate more to ensuring the nation is not over-reliant on semiconductors or pharmaceuticals made overseas than on directly facilitating the domestic logistics industry.[8] That is left to America's states and cities, coupled with their own investment corporations and agencies devoted to attracting inbound investment. Local trade associations and chambers of commerce also play a role. It is essentially a public-private partnership (PPP) approach.

The government-owned Port Authority of New York and New Jersey has developed a 350-acre logistics park in Linden just outside the port. In Memphis, Tennessee, the city-owned airport built a second runway and provided other benefits to entice FedEx to leave Little Rock (Arkansas) and build its global hub in Memphis.[9] In other places, it is business that takes the risk and foots the bill. The US railroad firm BNSF has branched out into building logistics parks that facilitate intermodal goods transfer. DP World built a pioneering logistics hub in Dubai.

In the UK, the story is one of private enterprise bearing most of the cost. But firms such as DP World, who are investing GBP 300 MM into its new port terminal and logistics hub called Thames Freeport, enjoy substantial local government incentives and other benefits. Thames Freeport advertises the fact that construction permits for new warehousing can be delivered by the government in 28 days.

In continental Europe, the local governments of Bremen, and Antwerp have energetically invested in logistics facilities close to their ports, as they battle with Hamburg Port to be the main point of entry in Northern Europe.

While governments globally play a key role in supporting logistics, through creating the fundamental infrastructure mainly in transportation and to lesser extent in establishing distribution hubs, the striking fact is that in China the role of government is broader and deeper than elsewhere in the world. The China party-state not only supports logistics in multiple ways and at all levels but is also highly interventionist in order to achieve the desired outcomes.

As mentioned earlier, there are strong and compelling reasons why the Chinese government is so supportive of the improvement in logistics in China. These relate not only to the obvious beneficial impact on economic efficiency and GDP improvement coupled with the green dividend but also the integration of poorer, less developed regions and populations into the modern economy and with that the fostering of a consumption led economy (as opposed to a government stimulus led one).

The role of government in China's logistics does fall well short of being all-encompassing. As we noted above, since the economic reforms began, China has developed a new hybrid system where market forces, enterprise autonomy, and competition are permitted and encouraged but all within certain boundaries (which are constantly changing) and under the strict supervision of the party-state. As China's new state logistics plan stresses: "Market leads, government guides" (*shichang zhidao zhengfu yindao*).[10] That guidance can be a light hand or a steel glove depending on how the party-state feels at any given time, depending on the extent to which it seeks to assert control over the economy.

The Chinese government's extraordinary level of support for the development of logistics manifests itself in a number of ways.

State planning. There has not been any return to the dysfunctional and discredited planning associated with the centrally planned economy that was unwound during the 1980s. China has what is largely a market economy. The government does interfere more than in true market economies but nonetheless relies heavily on market forces and levers (such as interest rates) to achieve its goals. However, what marks China off from other nations is the fine detail and extensive programs for direct intervention contained in its national development planning. As we discuss below, China's logistics are now the beneficiary of this government process.

Allocation of capital. A key element of government support is its direct influence on how China's state banks allocate capital to logistics firms. While China's private sectors, including logistics firms, as a key factor in economic growth, have largely been able to tap into bank loans,[11] it is also true that large state-owned logistics firms, as by definition the core of a "socialist" economy, can command the easiest access to such funding.

Another aspect of the government's role in the allocation of capital is its regulation and facilitation of stock market listings. A wide range of government approvals are required before a Chinese business can list. But given the high priority ascribed to logistics, the evidence is that not only large state-owned but also private logistics firms – large and also smaller emerging players – have access to those approvals.

Government investment. The Chinese government's investment goes far beyond the transportation infrastructure and includes directly funding the logistics parks and zones which, as we highlight below, are a key element in creating the logistics corridors set out in the national logistics plan. Most of this investment in logistics hubs comes from local government, usually at the city level.[12] Notwithstanding, the backdrop of critically serious issues with the real estate market and a resulting over-indebtedness at the local level, local government still energetically continues to invest in the infrastructure (parks, zones, and hubs) to attract industrial and logistics firms. Cities are competing against each other to attract capital, jobs, and tax revenues. This is being done through PPPs. A perfect example of this PPP approach, which we discuss later in Chapter 14, is the Supply Chain Smart Industrial Park being created in Xiaogan City, in Hubei in the middle of China, jointly by local government and companies that provide food, packaging, and logistics to McDonald's restaurants across China.[13] Later (in Chapter 10 on the Belt and Road), we also examine the powerful example of how the inland city of Xi'an (in Shaanxi Province) has invested heavily to carve out a key role for itself as a hub for China-Europe rail freight traffic.[14] Across the nation, China's central government is also pitching in through its investment in 20 national experimental logistics zones.

Forced consolidation. China's state logistics plan "encourages" logistics firms to "optimize and integrate resources through mergers and acquisitions and alliance cooperation."[15] The Chinese party-state has been unrelenting in driving consolidation across the state sector, including in logistics and transportation. State-owned logistics firms have also been active in their own Mergers & Acquisitions (M&A) activity, usually gobbling up much smaller entities that help build out their logistics network. But the government-forced mergers are quite different. They are not the result of strategic decisions by the firms themselves but are based on orders handed down to them by the party-state. Some of these mergers may make sense. Container shipping giant COSCO was told to merge with China Shipping an entity that lacked globally viable scale. The multiple subscale logistics entities left over from the meltdown of the former Ministry of Domestic Trade were merged with some railway-based firms to form China Logistics Group which offers the potential of a more integrated and competitive approach. But the rationale for other forced mergers looks less clear, for instance that of Sinotrans with China Merchants.

We should expect to see more of this kind of imposed consolidation that, overall, should be viewed as a positive contribution toward making China's state sector more competitive within China and globally.

Government support for logistics enterprises. The role of commercial entities under the rule of China's party-state remains ambiguous and constantly evolving. State-owned logistics firms have been permitted a degree of autonomy but still live under the shadow of the party-state. In some senses, that has helped them since they enjoy a favorable allocation of capital through bank loans and government subsidies compared to private firms. But on the downside, over the past decade, the party has clawed back much of its control over such firms. They find themselves in a much less free environment than was the case around the turn of the century.

Although private logistics firms have emerged very strongly and decisively, it is generally accepted have overall received less government support and have typically had to fend for themselves through reinvesting their own retained earnings or by tapping the equity markets. At the same time, they are subjected to increased oversight and "guidance" from the government. That said, the central and still growing importance of e-commerce to China's economy at home and internationally means that the government will broadly speaking act benevolently toward private logistics firm.

Nonetheless, there remains within China a constant tension between the drive for further reform and the old instinct for central control. This tension is well illustrated by words of caution over the need to rely on market forces, expressed by a leading Chinese expert on logistics;

> It must be pointed out that in the process of building a unified national market, it is appropriate to adopt a market-oriented approach to promote the construction of a modern logistics system, encourage various types of enterprises to operate independently, invest themselves, take responsibility for profits and losses, and develop themselves, including the introduction of foreign-funded logistics enterprises, and cannot be replaced or matched by governments at all levels.[16]

While the Chinese government leaves businesses (state and private) to deliver the logistics services that run over the infrastructure it has built, its influence over those enterprises may not be exclusively positive. It is clear to many observers, both foreign and Chinese, that the invasive nature of the Chinese party-state, whereby "guidance" may manifest itself in interference in rational business decision-making, may in some respects hold back or constrain China's logistics development. China's leadership seeks a balance between security and control on the one hand and growth and innovation on the other hand. The Party seems to be making the choice of stressing the control aspect even if reduces economic performance.

Progress toward a coordinated approach

In the past, a key factor holding back the development of China's logistics was the absence of unified planning. The situation was "scattered" and fragmented.[17] Policies relating to road and ports, aviation, and railways were all handled by separate government ministries or agencies. The situation was described using the Chinese saying "nine dragons controlling the water," (*jiulong zhishui*), that is "too many cooks in the kitchen," whereby responsibilities are unclear. Eventually, in 2008, ports, road, ports, and aviation were brought together as the Ministry of Transportation (MOT). But it was not until 2013 that the recalcitrant Ministry of Railways, which had stubbornly resisted reform on the grounds that any drastic change would lead to a seizing up of the overloaded rail network, was finally broken up and abolished, with its regulatory functions being folded into the MOT.

Two decades ago, under the excellent leadership of the reforming Premier Zhu Rongji, China's 10th Five-Year Plan (2001–2005) did include the goal of creating 30 national logistics centers or hubs and ten "large-scale" logistics enterprises. At the same time, China's key ministries involved in transportation came together to issue a document with "suggestions" that urged China's shippers to move from "enterprise [in-house] logistics" to "outsourced & specialized logistics." To address the issue of fragmentation in the logistics sector, it called for market consolidation. It also encouraged local government to do more to bring in foreign logistics firms.[18] Despite the useful focus on logistics in that period, these recommendations fell short of driving the change that was needed.

More recently, there has been significant progress. China's first logistics plan came in 2009 with the three-year *Logistics Adjustment and Revitalization Plan 2009–2011*, followed in 2014 by the *Medium and Long-Term Plan for the Development of the Logistics Industry, 2014–2020*. But, it was not until 2022 that China's logistic planning came of age when it earned the status of complete plan as a subset of the nation's overall five-year plan.

China finally has a five-year state plan for logistics

Logistics has been part of China's state planning for some time. But, only recently has it received the attention it deserves. In a groundbreaking move, on December 15, 2022, China's State Council issued the 14-page long China's *Modern Logistics Development Plan* (The Plan), as part of the nation's *14th Five-Year Plan for Economic and Social Development of the PRC* (2021–2025), marking the first time that modern logistics had its own five-year sub-plan. As one Chinese expert commentator aptly put it, "its forward-looking, comprehensive, guiding and professional nature represented a breakthrough."[19] It is hard to underestimate the significance of The Plan in setting the direction and in allocating resources.

As is customary in any context, the tough message that The Plan delivered on China's logistics was first prefaced with kind words of encouragement. It stated that over the previous five-year period, China's logistics had seen stable growth. The backbone infrastructure of logistics hubs had been improved, including for cold-chain products. Logistics, as a proportion of GDP, had fallen to 14.7%, a decline of 1.3% compared to 2015.[20]

There was also praise for the improvement of logistics in inland central and remote Western areas, for the increased volume carried by the railways including multimodal, and for the use of high technology in warehousing.

But it swiftly moved on to the challenges that China's logistics face, to the "stand-out problems" (*tupo wenti*) that needed to be fixed. The plan highlighted four areas.

First the question of how to "lower costs and increase efficiency." As it stood, there was not yet a "national unified market." The "allocation of logistics resources" was "unreasonable" and those resources not fully leveraged. The multimodal system (referring to containerized train intermodal) was "imperfect." Linkages between different modes were inadequate and transportation standardization was poor.[21]

Another issue to be addressed was "structural imbalances" whereby the basic logistics network infrastructure is "strong in the East [i.e. On the Eastern seaboard] and weak in the West, strong in the cities and weak in the countryside." It also found fault with the failure of logistics to adequately serve industry in certain areas of specialization such as cold-chain and air logistics.[22]

But, as we mentioned in our introduction, The Plan also made one massive criticism which was a striking admission, that China's logistics are "large but not strong. (da er bu qiang)." With extraordinary honesty and candor, China's planners lambasted the logistics industry saying;

The scale of the [our] logistics industry is large but its economies of scale and efficiency are not sufficient. This is particularly so with regard to undifferentiated and irregular competition in highway transport.... The level of logistics' organizational transformation, ... networking... is not high. At a national level our backbone logistics infrastructure is imperfect, and we lack modern logistics enterprises which possess the ability to compete globally, so that there is a still a gap [between us] and the world's countries that are strong in logistics.[23]

This strongly worded statement about China's logistics being "large but not strong" dovetails well into China's government's recent re-adjustment of economic policy through adopting the mantra of seeking a higher quality GDP, as opposed to GDP growth at any cost. It contrasts strongly with the initial decades of China's reforms when, under Deng Xiaoping's slogan of "development is a rigid principle," issues such as regional imbalance, wealth disparity, and pollution were largely ignored in order to achieve breakneck economic growth.

It sets the 2025 goal as "basically completing a modern logistics system that is responsive to supply and demand, that connects within China and with the outside world, that is safe and highly efficient, and is smart and green." It calls for China's logistics as a proportion of GDP to fall by about 2% by 2025, compared with the decline of 1.3% achieved in the previous five years.

The Plan envisages the "basic" completion of a logistics system that comprises "Channels + Hubs + Networks." In a sense, the networks form themselves through the commercial pressure to find the most rational flow for goods. But the government has a big say in the channels (based on the transportation infrastructure we discussed earlier) and particularly in the logistics hubs.

Globally, the hub-and-spoke model has now become the fundamental model for logistics. Regional distribution centers, with cross docking for trucks and automated warehousing and goods sorting, have sprung up in major global cities and in strategic locations between major conurbations. As in many other aspects of logistics, China is learning from this global experience and adopting the hub-and-spoke approach.

China has set the target of constructing about 120 "national logistics hubs," as the core, plus 100 "national backbone cold-chain logistics bases." Through this, the aim is to permit the operation of an integrated and smooth functioning "trunk and branch" (hub-and-spoke) warehousing system. Indicating that this will involve practical and direct investment by the government, the pledge is made to build 20 "national logistics hub experimental zones." The emphasis is on rebalancing the logistics to improve service in central China and in West of the nation. It also stresses the importance of bringing rail spur lines into these zones and parks and facilitating multimodal transportation, an area the plan repeatedly mentions as one major weakness of China's logistics. The "hubs construction project" also stresses the role of the hubs in driving logistics standardization, as well as the digitalization and green agendas.

It calls for logistics "channels" that rely on the transportation network to create linkages between the logistics hubs and the major conurbations and coastal ports. The logistics channel program for the domestic economy is summarized by four horizontals (East-West) and five verticals (North-South). When it comes to international logistics, there is the concept of "two alongs and the ten corridors," referring to international sea and land routes, something which is examined in more detail in Chapter 10.

The Plan puts emphasis on ways to lower logistics costs and drive efficiency. It also addresses a number of key areas which will have a major impact on the performance and direction of China's logistics. These include railways, international air cargo, cold-chain, technology, and closer linkages with manufacturing industry.

On the topic of costs and efficiency, it returns to the theme of the logistics being fragmented and "scattered" and calls for an optimization through larger truck fleets, shared warehousing, fewer empty back-hauls, and a reduction in the inventories (and with that lower working capital costs).[24]

It has details on the "standardization" of logistics, an area where the government has a direct say. It pledges to clamp down on unfair competition and monopolies and to achieve the simplification and rationalization of regulations which, in China, make life hell for truckers and logistics providers.

Correctly, it sees multimodal (also known as inter-modal) transportation as a path to efficiency improvement and cost reduction, both road-to-rail and road-to-water. In its "railway upgrading project," multimodal is at the top of the agenda and with it the growth of containerized rail traffic. Freight yards in major cities are to be converted into multimodal terminals. Linked to the multimodal theme, the plan calls for an expansion of the China-Europe rail freight lines. There is also discussion of how to build out the high-speed rail services for express goods items, something we touched on earlier.

The Plan sees shortcomings in China's international air cargo. This is spot on. As we pointed out in Chapter 3, China was slow to enter this business and has struggled to match the muscle and expertise of foreign competitors.

It spells out the transformative role technology will have on the nation's logistics and throughout makes repeated reference to the need for logistics to be green and ecologically sound. We explore those themes in more detail in later chapters.

The Plan is undoubtably a heftier and more detailed plan than what is typical in Western economies. The pledges of government intervention and funding go far beyond what we see for instance in the US. While this should not be construed as a reversion to the Soviet-style centrally planned economy, it does exhibit China's approach to economic management which still gives the party-state a major role in shaping and manipulating the economy while at the same time relying mainly on market forces to drive the final outcome. That delicate balance is articulated in the Plan's "basic principles," of "market-led and government-guided." Of course, the Chinese planners may easily say this but are also capable of doing something else, such as using a heavy controlling hand that stifles innovation and creativity. There remains within China a constant tension between the drive for further reform and the old instinct for central control and "security."

More self-reliance. Domestic-international dual circulation

In the wake of uncertainties sparked by the increasingly hostile posture of the US and also the impact of COVID-19, in 2020, China launched an economic readjustment based on the concept of domestic-international dual circulation (*guonei guoji shuang xunhuan*) which, as Xi put it, "takes the domestic market as the mainstay while letting internal and external markets boost each other." It represents a shift of emphasis toward stimulating domestic consumption, as an alternative to state investment-led growth. It is also a safety mechanism, a hedge against an increasingly difficult global economy for China, fraught with geopolitical tensions. However, it should be added that although it does call for "self-reliance" that does not resemble that self-defeating notion of self-reliance under Mao which was forced on China after the Sino-Soviet Split in the early 1960s. Under this new concept of dual circulation, China still intends to engage with the world, while making sure the domestic economy gets more attention. This has important ramifications for China's logistics. On the domestic front, there will be accelerated development in the less wealthy interior regions of China and with that a burst of logistics support for that push. On the international front, the growth in logistics will depend on global trade patterns and China's imports and exports, the growth of which has slowed recently. But as we see from China's new five-year plan for logistics, outlined above, the government is clearly wedded to growing Chinese firms' share of cross-border logistics, including in air cargo.

The transition to a consumption-led economy

The development of China's logistics is seen by the government as supporting its goal of moving from the current economic model that has relied heavily on government stimulus investment toward a model where consumer spending plays a bigger role in driving economic growth. China's citizens continue to save much more than those of other countries, in large due to the absence of a complete social safety net and the need to put money aside for healthcare, children's education, and retirement. China's five-year plan for logistics focuses on logistics' role in "expanding demand and upgrading consumption, optimizing and improving the commercial and express logistics network." The plan also highlights the weakness of logistics' reach into the rural areas, calling for "basic direct delivery" of express logistics into the villages so as to "support the expansion of the supply of high-quality consumer goods."[25] This emphasis on logistics supporting the "people's livelihood" (*minsheng*) is unmistakably closely linked to the goal of releasing consumer demand as part of government's goal of rebalancing the economy and weaning it off the government investment-led approach.

Government takes the lead – the Greater Bay Area (GBA) and the Hainan Free Port

These two highly significant government-led initiatives in South China vividly illustrate the key role the Chinese government takes in driving economic development and with it the growth of logistics.

The Guangdong-Hong Kong – Macau Greater Bay Area (GBA). Since the beginning of China's reforms in the late 1970s, South China's Pearl River Delta, from Hong Kong up to Guangzhou, has been the crucible of China's industrial and commercial transformation and innovation. Supporting this extraordinary performance has been strong logistics founded on a highly efficient transportation infrastructure whether the highways and bridges built by entrepreneurs and financed by tolls or the multiple border crossings opened up between Hong Kong and Shenzhen. That high degree of economic and logistical integration is now being further enhanced by the bold Guangdong-Hong Kong-Macau GBA (*Yue Xiang Ao Dawanqu*).

In 1997, Hong Kong ceased to be run by Britain and was handed back to China, becoming a Special Administrative Region of China which was to have a "high degree" of autonomy for 50 years. Though that degree of independence from the rest of the PRC, whether politically or economically, has not matched the expectations of many, it still remains a separate entity with its own currency, taxation system, financial markets, trade and tariffs, and legal system.

But as we reach the halfway point of the "fifty years without change," there are abundant signs that China is slowly but steadily forcing the pace of further integration of Hong Kong into the Mainland through the GBA, which encompasses Hong Kong, Macau and nine cities in Guangdong (including Guangzhou and Shenzhen) which together currently account for US$ 1.8 Trillion or 10% of China's GDP. The GBA has three of the world's largest container ports and five international airports. With the GBA, the existing excellent linkages, especially between Hong Kong and Shenzhen, will be further simplified and automated to permit the free flow of goods within the area. In the marshy areas, besides the Shenzhen River which marks the border between Hong Kong and Shenzhen, a massive new high-tech zone is being constructed, bringing the two cities closer together. It is not clear if and when the border between Hong Kong and Shenzhen will ultimately be dissolved. It may be difficult to do until 2047 when the 50 years is up. In the meantime, this region continues to enjoy highly efficient logistics which help it maintain its status as an engine house of China's economic growth. Most critically, this flow of goods around this key economic area will in turn drive its further social and political integration.

The Hainan Free Trade Port. Hainan is a tropical island in the far south of China, just across the water from Vietnam. Its area (32,000 km²) is slightly more than that of Taiwan. But, its population is only 10 MM, less than half that of Taiwan. Formerly part of Guangdong Province, in 1988, it became its own province and also China's fifth Special Economic Zone (SEZ) with special incentives to foreign investors. While other SEZs such Shenzhen flourished and grew rapidly, the story with Hainan was less glorious. Tourism took off strongly in Hainan. But broader attempts to industrialize were not that productive. Hainan's location, far from the major markets of China, was a hindrance.

Recently, the Chinese government has set forth a bold program to revitalize the development of Hainan. A process, started in 2018, culminated in 2021 with China's State Council establishing the Taiwan Free Trade Port (HFTP) (*Hainan ziyou maoyi gang*). In some ways, it resembles Singapore or Dubai, but obviously without separate nation-state status. The HFTP enjoys zero tariffs for certain products. Products imported and processed in Hainan with 30% added value in Hainan can travel duty free into the rest of China. Corporate tax and personal income tax are both capped at 15%.[26]

Due to its tropical climate and sandy beaches, Hainan is already a major tourist destination, largely for Chinese citizens. The HFTP status brings the added attraction of large-scale duty-free shopping. A massive duty-free complex has been built in Hainan's main city Haikou. This will spawn a greater flow of goods between Hainan and the rest of China. Since 2020, there have been air cargo flights into Hainan's three main airports, from Hong Kong and Amsterdam bringing in cosmetics, perfumes, and jewelry. But, the ambitions of HFTP go far beyond duty-free products for tourists. Hainan Yangpu Port located in the Northwest of the island, close to the Yangpu Economic Development Zone (with an area of 30 km^2) and linked to Hainan's capital Haikou by superhighway, has begun direct container shipping lines to SE Asia and Australia. Hainan is also seeking to ramp up its exports to China and the rest of the world of tropical fruits and tropical products such as natural rubber and palm oil. Hainan University is playing a key role in supporting R&D in tropical agriculture.[27]

A gamechanger in making Hainan a logistics hub is the commitment made in 2021 by Alibaba's logistics subsidiary Cainiao (profiled later in Chapter 13) through a comprehensive PPP with Hainan's government. Under this program, Cainiao is building 150,000 m^2 of "smart and bonded" warehousing, to house luxury goods, pharma, and cold-chain products to help make Hainan "a duty-free haven." Cainiao is building a digital platform to help merchants bring products through customs and to the stores. They are upgrading Hainan's transportation capability through providing air cargo terminal operations with flights to Singapore, South Korea, and Japan and with sea routes to Hong Kong which link Hainan into the GBA[28] which we discussed above.

Given the checkered history of Hainan's recent development, there may be some skepticism about this latest effort. Hainan is not blessed with a strategic location whether in terms of global transportation or proximity to major markets. There is no certainty that Hainan can become more than just a tourist center with enhanced duty-free shopping. It is unclear whether Cainiao signing up for major investment to help Hainan along the path to becoming a significant logistics hub is motivated by sound strategic vision or by patriotic duty/pleasing the party-state. Most likely, it is a mixture of those motivations. Regardless, there is no denying the new bolder vision and scope of what has been mapped out for Hainan.

Flaws in the regulatory environment

China's regulatory environment for logistics and transportation is at times overly restrictive and furthermore is highly inconsistent in it regional and local practical application. These elements present an obstacle to the goals of raising the level of the logistics industry.

There are, by some estimates, 18–30 MM truckers in China, ten times the number in the USA. Like truckers everywhere, they complain bitterly about the abuse and control they are subjected to. But some of this anguish is well-placed. China's superhighways are subject to very heavy road tolls, which for a trucker going from Shanghai to Xinjiang can amount to a great deal of money. Then at the local level, illegal tolls are often levied to augment local finances. Out-of-province truckers are particularly vulnerable. China's MOT will tell you with true candor that it has little power to halt this kind of banditry, especially in the more remote areas.

Road tolls are measured by distance not weight, a fact which encourages overweight trucks which cause accidents and wears out the roadways and bridges.[29] The widespread spot checks on weight that we see on Chinese roads are not enough to rectify these problems.

Resentment among truckers does boil over in China, just as it does with taxi drivers. China's trade unions are controlled by the party-state and there is no freedom to strike or even to protest. But that does not stop truckers periodically flexing their muscles through strikes or blockades to protest official bullying and interference. However, there is nothing to suggest that this issue amounts to anything like the labor disputes in the US at ports or at UPS.

As we move on to discussion of the issues and opportunities faced by China's logistics firms, it is useful to keep in the rear-view mirror the critical symbiotic relationship between these enterprises and China's government at the central and local level. That relationship, which we regard as by and large a positive one, is one that these enterprises, state and private, large and small, Chinese or foreign, have to constantly take into account.

Notes

1 Ming-Ju Cheng, *The Influence of Communications Internal and External upon the Economic Future of China*, Routledge, 1930, p. 169.
2 Peter Zehman, *Accidental Super Power. The Next Generation of American Pre-eminence and the Coming Global Disorder*, Hachette, 2014, pp. 291–223.
3 Co-author Clifford, while with Cisco Systems in China, saw the Wenchuan Earthquake efforts close up. He was involved in establishing remote healthcare networks as part of the recovery efforts.
4 Wu Youxi, *xiandai wuliu shi jiakuai jianshen quanguo tongyi dashichang de zhongyao zhicheng (Modern Logistics Is an Important Support for Accelerating the Construction of a National Market)*, on zhanglian, Apr 24, 2022.
5 Yossi Sheffi, *Logistics Clusters: Delivery Value and Driving Growth*, MIT Press, 2014.

6 Tan Chin Hwee and Sangeet Paul Choudary, *Singapore Must Think Like a Platform to Thrive as a Digital Hub*, on *Smartkarma Content*, Feb 20, 2018.

7 *The Biden-Harris Plan for America's Ports and Waterways*, issued by *The White House*, Nov 9, 2021.

8 *Executive Order on America's Supply Chains*, issued by *The White House*, Feb 24, 2021.

9 Yossi Sheffi, *Logistics Clusters: Delivery Value and Driving Growth*, MIT Press, 2014.

10 State Council of PRC, *"Shisuwu" xiandai wuliu fazhan guihua (14th Five year Plan, Modern Logistics Development Plan)*, issued Dec 15, 2022.

11 See comments by Meg Rithmire in her presentation on Critical Issues Confronting China, at Fairbank Center for China Studies, Harvard, Feb 14, 2024.

12 Xiangming Chen, *Reconnecting Eurasia: A New Logistics State, The China–Europe Freight Train, and the Resurging Ancient City of Xi'an*, on *Eurasian Geography and Economics*, Apr 2021.

13 *CFLD Introduces McDonald's Smart Supply Chain to Central China's Hubei*, on *Global Times*, Dec 23, 2020.

14 Xiangming Chen, *Reconnecting Eurasia: A New Logistics State, The China–Europe Freight Train, and the Resurging Ancient City of Xi'an*, on *Eurasian Geography and Economics*, Apr 2021.

15 State Council of PRC, *"Shisuwu" xiandai wuliu fazhan guihua (14th Five year Plan, Modern Logistics Development Plan)*, issued Dec 15, 2022.

16 Wu Youxi, *xiandai wuliu shi jiakuai jianshe quanguo tongyi dashichang de zhongyaozhicheng (Modern Logistics Is an Important Support for Accelerating the Construction of a Unified National Market)* on *Baidu*, Apr 24, 2022.

17 Wu Youxi, *Jiaqiang tongchouguihua, tuidong goujian xiandai wuliu tixi (Strenthen Overall Planning and Promote the Construction of a Modern Logistics System*, on *21 shiji jingjibao*, Dec 17, 2022.

18 MOR/MOC/CAAC/Moftec, *Suggestions to Speed up China Logistics Development*, Mar 2001.

19 MOR/MOC/CAAC/Moftec, *Suggestions to Speed up China Logistics Development*, Mar 2001.

20 State Council of PRC, *"Shisuwu" xiandai wuliu fazhan guihua (14th Five year Plan, Modern Logistics Development Plan)*, issued Dec 15, 2022.

21 State Council of PRC, *"Shisuwu" xiandai wuliu fazhan guihua (14th Five year Plan, Modern Logistics Development Plan)*, issued Dec 15, 2022.

22 State Council of PRC, *"Shisuwu" xiandai wuliu fazhan guihua (14th Five year Plan, Modern Logistics Development Plan)*, issued Dec 15, 2022.

23 State Council of PRC, *"Shisuwu" xiandai wuliu fazhan guihua (14th Five year Plan, Modern Logistics Development Plan)*, issued Dec 15, 2022.

24 State Council of PRC, *"Shisuwu" xiandai wuliu fazhan guihua (14th Five year Plan, Modern Logistics Development Plan)*, issued Dec 15, 2022.

25 State Council of PRC, *"Shisuwu" xiandai wuliu fazhan guihua (14th Five year Plan, Modern Logistics Development Plan)*, issued Dec 15, 2022.

26 Xinhua, *Five Years on, China Speeds Its Way to Build Hainan Free Trade Port*, on *China Daily*, Apr 13, 2023.

27 Based on contacts with Dr. Feng Da Hsuan and Dr. Carter Tseng on the International Advisory Board of Hainan University.

28 Rachelle Harry, *Cainiao Partners with Hainan Government to Help It Become a "Smart Supply Chain Zone,"* on *Aircargo News*, Jun 18, 2021.

29 Dave Wickenham, *A Glimpse into Driving Long-Haul in China*, on *South China Morning Post*, Jan 13, 2020.

Challenges and goals; from backward to world class

Chapter 5

Strategic issues and opportunities

From backward to world class

As we pointed out in the introduction, China's relative backwardness in its adoption of modern integrated logistics does itself have a bright side, in that improvement and progress from such a low base can be both rapid and of great economic significance. China's leaders have rather belatedly realized the enormous opportunity that the transformation of this sector presents. Some Chinese logistics providers have moved beyond the catch-up phase and are now setting the pace in global e-commerce. Later, we shall provide detailed case studies and profiles portraying how specific companies, Chinese and foreign, have set about meeting China's logistics needs domestically and in the international supply chain. But here we first introduce not only the fundamental weaknesses that have held back China's logistics but also the factors that provide grounds for optimism with regard to China's progress in this hitherto neglected area.

Unmet needs in China's logistics around the year 2000

To set the scene, it is useful to get a snapshot of how China's logistics were performing about two decades ago. At that time, we interviewed shippers in China, both foreign and Chinese about the basic logistics services that were available. This is a sample of their feedback:

"Providers can't deliver what they promised, overall weak control over the operations."
"Critical issues with trucking – transit time, damage and loss, availability."
"Lack of information visibility."
"National coverage not integrated to provide consistent service level."[1]

These unmet needs not only demonstrated the poor condition of China's logistics but also presented a significant business opportunity for firms that could fill this gap.

DOI: 10.4324/9781003489115-8

The strategic challenges

Reluctance to outsource to 3PLs

China's shippers (the manufacturers) have been slow and reluctant to outsource their logistics to 3PLs. Two decades ago, a survey of China's 3PLs stated that about 70% of multinational shippers outsource logistics services but only 15% of Chinese shippers did so.[2] Despite efforts to rectify this, it still remains a serious problem. In 2023, a leading Chinese logistics expert put it bluntly;

> There are still some [manufacturing] enterprises… that retain or develop internal logistics, investing their own funds in the construction of warehousing, docks, container yards, vehicles and other facilities, objectively resulting in the occupation of valuable land in the urban areas, and in the insufficient internal use of or idle resources. Also due to this diversified investment and operations, there is a [negative] effect on the competitiveness of these firms' core businesses.[3]

He adds that the Chinese government's goal is to

> Encourage the development of third-party logistics, encourage traditional commercial manufacturing enterprises to outsource logistics, to break the concept of small production and of local protectionism. … This is a major strategic issue.[4]

The main reason has been that most shippers had their own existing in-house transportation and warehousing capabilities. After central planning melted away, China's manufacturers were forced to create their own truck fleets to ensure reliable service. They also have had insufficient confidence in the ability of emerging 3PLs and transportation firms to provide the level of service required.

Another reason why China's shippers have been slow to outsource to 3PLs is that they do not have adequate knowledge of their logistics costs. Across the board, from old state-owned firms to emerging private firms, the Management Information Systems that provide such data have been rudimentary at best. The in-house fleets of trucks were often regarded as a cost center which did not receive sufficient scrutiny. This situation was most serious when it came to warehousing. There was little or no data on how long inventory was held or on the working capital costs of doing so.[5] Without any clear picture of their logistics costs, Chinese firms have been slow to move from relying on in-house capability to using 3PLs. And when they do move to 3PLs, without that data, it is hard for the 3PL to demonstrate efficiency gains and to set the price accordingly. Still, Chinese manufacturers have made great strides in the last two decades and are fast adopting more rigorous financial management and reporting. The best among them are also benchmarking their performance in these areas against international competitors.

Today China's outsourcing to 3PLs still lags behind the rest of the world. Smaller Chinese manufacturers are the ones most likely to outsource. As we profile in Chapter 13, many of the largest industrial players, such as home appliance producer Qingdao Haier, built their own in-house logistics capability. Other large manufacturers have chosen what is really a halfway house whereby they take an equity position in a logistics firm. This may be termed a form of "collaboration" rather than straight out outsourcing to a 3PL.[6]

Market fragmentation

China has already produced a strong stable of large logistics firms ranging from the state-owned giants, which have been revitalized through restructuring and recapitalization, to e-commerce firms and their related logistics operations. But, as China's state planners reiterate, China's logistics industry remains fragmented and "scattered." There is a clarion call for efforts to "integrate fragmented transport, warehousing and distribution" through the sharing of resources and facilities. The heart of the issue is that many of China's logistics providers are small, without economies of scale, and are unable to meet the needs of the market. The Chinese government calls for "the nurturing of a raft of modern logistics firms with international competitiveness."[7]

The five-year national logistics plan calls for China's logistics firms to "integrate resources" through mergers and acquisitions and through alliances to create firms that have "international competitiveness." Private logistics firms are urged to become "refined, bigger and stronger."[8]

Intense competition and poor profitability

China's subscale trucking and logistics providers are poorly differentiated and compete mainly on price, reducing profitability and service levels. The poor profitability in turn makes it harder for them to invest in more efficient and technology-enabled transportation, warehousing, and in the IT systems that integrate it all. The consensus in China is that "the main problem remains the low profit rate of logistics enterprises."[9] Official statistics show that between 2010 and 2019, the operating profit margin of China's top 50 logistics firms declined from 11.3% to 6.1%.[10] Below, we discuss asset intensity and the investment this entails as one of the factors causing this declining poor profitability.

The poor profitability in turn hampers the firms' ability to pay decent salaries and undermines their "attractiveness" to "outstanding social talents." It also restricts these firms' ability to invest for growth. Logistics firms are also subject to "unreasonable" road tolls and land-use payments, all of which reduce their profitability.[11]

But the heart of the matter is;

> the business model of some domestic warehousing and vehicle transportation companies is mainly low-price competition. Low prices are accompanied by inferior services, or they make profits through illegal methods such as [truck] overloading and [illegal] overtime.[12]

The government is seeking to improve the industry's profitability through forcing the pace of mergers and consolidation. In so doing, it also explicitly seeks to "effectively guide the withdrawal of excess capacity." The goal is to create a strong core of "specialized, refined, special and new modern logistics enterprises."[13]

Even Sinotrans, which has scale and muscle, turns in a net profit margin of 3.7% which does not stack up against its global peer the Swiss firm Kuehne + Nagel which enjoys a margin of 6.5%.[14]

The debate over asset intensity

Globally, there are some players, notably the "integrators" such as UPS, who integrate ownership of transportation and warehouse assets into their business. Nonetheless, the trend in logistics has broadly speaking been toward "asset-light" 3PLs, that is those that chose not to own most of the transportation or warehouse assets and, wherever possible or prudent, to outsource those elements. This "lean" approach in turn reduces capital expenditure, financing needs, and balance sheet pressure. It provides business flexibility.

We say they do this only when *prudent* since customers sometimes insist that their 3PLs have some "skin in the game" to ensure high-quality delivery of services. 3PLs, while seeking to free themselves from the heavy capital requirements of such assets which can burden their balance sheet, may also find it useful to have some limited participation in these assets since it provides industry knowledge and control, for instance in being close to and fully understanding the trucking business.

When it comes to China, the argument for a 3PL owning or leasing its own transportation or warehousing assets becomes much stronger. The fragmented and chaotic market has made it vitally important to have more control over matters at the operating level. Without that, the shippers may not feel confident that their goods will arrive at their destinations safely and on time.

That said, some major global players, who are active in China, stick to an asset-light approach. Swiss firm Kuehne + Nagel (K&N), states that globally it continues to "operate an asset-light business model."[15] K&N is strong in air logistics especially in China since itsr acquisition of Apex in 2021. But K&N has chosen not to own its own fleet of aircraft but instead to book space or lease aircraft with others. As an example of this, K&N has entered into a long-term dedicated charter agreement with Atlas Air for two B 747-8 freighters that will bear K&N livery. This contrasts with the asset-intensive approach of UPS and China's SF.[16]

Of concern and related to the decline in profitability of the largest firms mentioned above is a new trend toward an asset-heavy approach. This is a repeat of a pattern which was seen before.

Around the turn of the century, a number of state-owned logistics firms, notably Sinotrans, went through a restructuring whereby they initially chose a relatively asset-light approach. When it came to the assets they did own, such as warehousing and truck yards, most had been built before the reforms began and were fully depreciated, so had no impact on profitability or the balance sheet. But as these firms listed on the stock exchange, they did use these funds to increase their fixed assets, to build out their own transportation fleets and storage facilities. This asset-heavy build-out has gathered pace as, for instance, they establish costly cold-chain hubs.

But when around 2016, China's e-commerce and express delivery took off, these traditional 3PLs, which were used to providing services to old-style manufacturers, found themselves ill-equipped to satisfy the high frequency and timeliness required by the new digital consumer economy.

The e-commerce and express delivery firms that emerged after 2016 either built their own logistics capabilities or relied on new types of 3PL. Using the funds from stock market listings and other fund-raising, this sector moved toward what is essentially an asset-heavy model. Firms such as JD, SF, Cainiao, ZTO (Zhongtong), YTO (Yuantong), STO (Shentong), Yunda, and Pinduoduo began investing heavily in distribution centers, truck yards, and IT systems.[17]

How was it that, in 2021, JD Logistics, while growing fast in terms of revenues and with a customer base of 600 MM, was still loss-making? One reason for this is the sustained investment in expanding its footprint across China. In the years 2018–2021, JD Logistics invested RMB 2 trillion. By 2021, it has had 1,300 warehouses, 41 "intelligent logistic zones," 400,000 employees, and a total storage area of 23 MM m^2.[18]

The Chinese government is investing heavily in the transportation and logistics infrastructure. But in the final analysis, it is up to Chinese firms to step up to the plate and create the services needed, and with that invest in more fixed assets. But even if, as is likely, this shift toward an asset-heavy model is required, there is another factor that needs to be addressed – setting prices that reflect the value provided and making sure there is a reasonable return on the investment.

One Chinese logistics expert states that China's logistics firms are "underpricing their services."[19] He argues that even though e-commerce firms have easy access to equity markets, which he calls a "blood transfusion," this is not sustainable. Furthermore, traditional 3PLs are reluctant to get into this new market segment due to its "money-burning" model.

Given the capital intensity coupled with the low profit margin, most firms lack sufficient internally generated funds and can only maintain a "level of simple reproduction." This situation is most acute in road transportation. His conclusion is that:

> The fundamental problem restricting the development of logistics enterprises is that the service pricing...does not correctly reflect the value of logistics services.... Without facing this problem, even if logistics enters the intelligent and green stage, the dispute between light and heavy asset models will reappear, and it will be difficult for supply chains to develop healthily.[20]

It is apparent that the legacy of logistics being poorly understood and undervalued lingers on. Just as it has been hard to get shippers to outsource to 3PLs, it is hard to persuade them that the state-of-the-art services are worth the price premium they deserve.

Standards and regulation

China is still working to create clear and implementable standards for basic logistics, around issues such as palletization and packaging, around specialized areas such as drugs, cold chain, and hazardous chemicals. Even more demanding is creating the standards and regulations with respect to technology adoption in logistics ranging from logistics internet platforms to warehouse automation and transportation monitoring. Given the strict and narrow definition of the business a Chinese company can engage in (as defined on a company's business license), traditional logistics firms have experienced regulatory obstacles to gaining access to e-commerce.

Over the last 40 years, China has built a relatively complete system of laws, regulations, and industry standards. But the thorniest issue has been and remains the even implementation of these measures at the local level. Local authorities may be reluctant to enforce important regulations on their local firms. Meanwhile, "irregular" (illegal) road tolls and other charges are widely levied on logistics providers, especially those with out-of-province license plates. The central government has little power to halt these practices which cause havoc to China's logistics and undermine their profitability and efficiency. To its credit, the government, facing pressure and even protests from truckers, is seeking ways to simplify matters through reducing the red tape and unnecessary restrictions.

Sources of funds and capital allocation

The general pattern in China is that capital allocation has favored State-owned Enterprise (SOEs) more than private firms. China's state banks have been more ready lend to SOEs, not just because private enterprise firms were perceived to have a higher credit risk, but also because the party-state deep-down has a preference for the state sector which helps define the nation's "socialism." This principle of course also applies to logistics firms.

As China's largest SOE logistics firms were taken apart and restructured to give them a new lease on life, and were afforded countless lifelines, they were also required to be "responsible for their own profit and loss" (*zifu yingkui*). The government's helping hand came in approvals for SOE logistics firms to list on the stock exchange, thus providing a valuable and continuing source of funds that could be plowed into investment in upgrading and expanding its services and capabilities across China. Lending from state banks was also assured.

Chinese private logistics firms initially found a lack of access to sources capital to be a major handicap. They were perceived as a high credit risk and also suffered from the party-state's disdain for private business. They were forced to rely on retained earnings or organically generated funds that could be deployed for capital investment. However, given the government's priority given to e-commerce, private logistics firms have over the last decade found it more straightforward to tap into bank loans or to obtain the government approvals required for stock market IPOs. The explosion of energy from China's private sector social media and e-commerce giants, such as Alibaba and JD.com, paved the way for the private logistics firms related to them to gain access to large quantities of funds from the equity markets, which have been invested in building-out their services and the technology and infrastructure which support it. As an example, in 2021, JD Logistics raised US$ 3.2 BN through an IPO on the Hong Kong stock market. The same year, its parent, JD.com, raised US$ 12 BN through listings in New York and Hong Kong.

Talent and training

In the late 1990s, China's nascent modern integrated logistics firms faced a series gap in terms of skills and experience.

Veteran foreign logistics experts who labored in China in those early days to support their MNC clients entering the market will recount how they worked tirelessly to train local staff, only to find that Chinese firms quickly moved in to poach them. But that was never going to fill the gap and China embarked energetically on a program of logistics education based on Western theory and practice.

When the state-owned Sinotrans started its transformation into a modern 3PL, less than 25% of its employees had received an education beyond upper middle school. Of those with higher education, few were versed in modern logistics, which even in the West was a relatively new discipline. Sinotrans took the bold step of sending key members of its 3PL business to study at the UK's Cranfield University which specializes in supply chain studies. But soon the West came to China.

Today, there are numerous Chinese universities that offer supply chain and logistics at a first-degree and postgraduate level, with specializations in operations, marine transport, warehousing, and railways. Foreign universities offer logistics and transportation degrees in China through joint ventures with Chinese universities such as Georgia Tech with Tianjin University (in Shenzhen), Liverpool University with Xi'an Jiaotong (in Suzhou), Nottingham University (in Ningbo), and McGill with Zhejiang University (in Hangzhou). Foreign training firms such as Unichrone offer certificates in logistics through online courses and also at physical locations across China.

But a shortage of "talent" (*rencai*), of qualified professionals, remains a continuing challenge for China's logistics. As we pointed out earlier, the poor profitability of China's logistics firms restricts their ability to compete for top talent against firms in high tech, financial services, and management consulting. In its five-year plan for logistics, the government puts emphasis on further upgrading the educational system to support the logistics industry through research and higher degrees to vocational training. Enterprises are urged to work closely with these institutions to design courses and rotate employees into training. There is a call to "increase the introduction of overseas high end-end talents."[21]

Weakness of Chinese 3PLs in foreign markets

While foreign 3PLs have had a strong position in the cross-border logistics business in China, in the intra-China (domestic) market, they have struggled to compete against Chinese firms, for reasons such as government regulation and cut-throat price competition. The flip side of this is that, when it comes to the international market, Chinese 3PLs have also found it heavy going. Chinese firms are adept at customs clearance at the China border. They have created a logistics presence globally through their container vessels and through owning and operating ports such as in Piraeus in Greece. However, they find it hard to offer an integrated and seamless logistics service globally. In 1996, COSCO established a 3PL subsidiary in the US (in Secaucus, NJ). Today, it has offices across the US and its own truck fleet and warehousing. However, it still lacks the scale and reputation to compete against local 3PLs in the US.

Rather than struggling to grow their overseas operations organically, an obvious alternative is to make acquisitions. A good example of this is the merger in 2021 of the Chinese firm SF Express, often regarded as "China's FedEx," with HK-based Kerry Logistics. SF spent US$ 2.2 BN to acquire 51.5% of Kerry. The combined firm became the second largest Chinese logistics company (after Sinotrans which has revenues of US$ 11 BN) and gives SF greatly enhanced reach across Asia where Kerry is strong. SF made it clear that they had found it hard to break into overseas markets due to the strong existing relationships between shippers and 3PLs, stating;

> Frankly, we don't have a global footprint at this moment; we are in only about 20% of the countries that DHL and FedEx are in. In 10 years, I believe we will have at least comparable capability to the big three [DHL, FedEx and UPS].[22]

Sinotrans claims to have coverage in 38 countries and regions with 78 operating points globally. A decade ago, it had partnered in a JV with a US firm that provides logistics to Best Buy. Best Buy had launched a big push into China through its acquisition of Chinese consumer electronics retailer Jiangsu Five Star Appliance. Sinotrans helped the foreign 3PL deliver the required services in China, while Sinotrans gained reach into the US for Chinese manufacturers. Sinotrans was able to;

> learn some new operating models and technologies. Processes and IT can be operated according to US standards, and the US can train marketers to carry out marketing activities in the US market.

This JV did not last long, since things did not work out well for Best Buy. Best Buy first tried to market itself using a Chinese version of its US name. When that failed, it reverted to the old Chinese brand. None of that worked and in 2014, after only eight years, Best Buy pulled out of China due to poor profitability. Although the linkup that Sinotrans had with that foreign 3PL was mutually beneficial, it did not give Sinotrans the ownership and control of the foreign operations that were needed to be a convincing player. As a former executive of Sinotrans puts it;

> For Chinese companies active in the international logistics market, how to get out of the Chinese market, how get rid of the status quo of only [being strong in] port handover service capabilities, and gradually move towards global supply chain management, especially to enter the logistics market of developed countries in Europe and America. This is a long-term subject.[23]

To achieve a world-class international service, Sinotrans has become active in overseas M&A. In 2020, Sinotrans spent Euros 386 MM to acquire the Netherlands-based logistics firm KLG (Kuijken Logistics Group) which has 17 branches across three countries in Europe, 140,000 m² of warehousing and 1,300 employees. Sinotrans pledged to maintain the firm's identity and deal carefully with cultural integration. Post-acquisition, KLG's IT platform became Sinotrans' platform for Europe.[24] Through this transaction, Sinotrans also acquired KLG warehousing and operations in China (Shanghai, Qingdao, Xiamen, and Shenzhen) thus further plugging into foreign expertise and talent.

Bifurcated market

20 years ago, foreign MNCs selling to and investing in China would almost exclusively work with trusted foreign 3PLs who followed them into China. They were happy to pay a premium for such services. Meanwhile, China's manufacturers worked mainly with Chinese 3PLs, since they had strong existing relationships with them and, above all, because the costs of their services were much

lower than those of foreign 3PLs. One striking exception was the ability of the US firm Ryder to work with Chinese firms (More on that in Chapter 14).

This bifurcated market still exists to some extent but has been heavily eroded by two factors. Firstly, as we saw with Corning earlier, foreign manufacturers followed China's economic development from the Eastern seaboard inland into central and Western China. Foreign 3PLs were effective in the regions close to the ports but have to this day struggled to build out their services into the interior. Foreign MNCs increasingly have been forced to rely on Chinese logistics players. They also built their own in-house logistics knowledge in China, as was the case with early entrants such as the US firm P&G.

The second factor is that major Chinese logistics players, both re-invigorated SOEs and newly emerged private firms, increasingly can provide the efficiency and reliability needed by foreign firms in China. Two decades ago, the goal of winning a long-term logistics contract from foreign MNCs was the "holy grail" of Chinese 3PLs. At that time, the "contract logistics" arms of Chinese providers were nipping at the heels of their foreign competitors. The Danish firm Maersk Logistics provided logistics to the French tire manufacturer Michelin which in 1995 had established a large production facility in Shenyang, in Northeast China's Liaoning Province. The logistics were relatively complex given Shenyang's inland location. But Sinotrans studied Maersk's approach that included special ways to stack the tires during transportation. They were able to displace Maersk and win a contract. "We learnt how to do it and they took over those skills," said a former Maersk employee.[25] Today, the very top Chinese logistics firms are well equipped to meet the needs of MNCs in the intra-China market and have achieved the goal of breaking into that segment which requires high-quality service and offers better pricing than Chinese shippers would accept.

It should also be added that the MNCs in China were anxious to cut costs in China, since they faced growing competition from local producers. Notwithstanding their close long-term relationship with foreign 3PLs, these foreign shippers were becoming tired of the high service fees charged by the foreign 3PLs and were highly receptive to Chinese providers that increasingly could offer a level of service that was acceptable.[26]

Weakness in China's foreign trade

Contrary to expectations, after Covid-19 passed, China's exports remained weak and, in some months, declined precipitously. This was largely due to weak global demand triggered by sluggish economic growth. China's exports to Europe were especially affected. China's imports were also hit, since China imports many components for assembly into finished products that are then re-exported.[27]

On top of this, geopolitical tensions between the US and China have prompted some foreign firms that source from China to "de-risk" their supply chain and diversify their sourcing to countries such as Vietnam and Indonesia. So far, this is a slow and limited trend, not yet a wave. This cooling of enthusiasm for China is also occurring with foreign direct investment. Still, even though there has been some capital flight from China, many foreign investors remain in China for the long term since China is not just a supplier but also a market with further growth potential.

This poor foreign trade performance has a direct impact on the logistics that facilitate the flow of goods in and out of China. In that sense, its greatest impact is on foreign 3PLs active in China, who have a strong position in the cross-border business. In turn, it is less significant for Chinese players that are strongest in the intra-China market. Furthermore, China's rapid growth in e-commerce and related logistics within China goes some way to compensate for the concerns over foreign trade.

If this litany of challenges that China's logistics face seems long compared to the opportunities set out below, it should be added that many of the issues are being actively and systematically addressed and, as progress is made, they in themselves present opportunities. As the Chinese are fond of saying, one can "turn a bad thing into a good thing" (*ba huaishi biancheng haoshi*).

Case study: Tsingtao Brewery

This brewery, based in Qingdao, Shandong Province, is to this day China's best known beer brand within China and globally. Founded in 1903 by Germans after Qingdao became a German colony, it went through many transformations, under Japanese occupation, then with nationalization under the Chinese Communist Party (CCP), and finally privatization and listing on the Hong Kong Stock market in the 1990s. In 2001, it not only had a strong quality reputation, brand, and market share in China but also something that many Chinese breweries lacked – large-scale production.

However, being a stock-market–listed company, there was increased scrutiny of its financial performance. Tsingtao's domestic outbound logistics costs were an estimated 10%–12% of the total product cost. If that percentage could be brought down by just one or two percentage points, there would be significant cost savings and a positive impact on the bottom line. Transportation and inventory accounted for about half and one-third, respectively, of the total logistics costs. Tsingtao traditionally had handled its own logistics in-house. A major Chinese 3PL came forward with a plan to improve the nationwide outbound distribution performance which addressed the following logistics costs and bottlenecks:

- Greater overall administrative efficiency, in the simplification of external processes and the reduction of data errors.
- The reduction of transportation costs through the optimization of the distribution network, service consolidation and with that lower freight rates.

- Inventory reduction through addressing damage, shrinkage (theft), all of which reduced the cost of insurance and the capital cost of financing the inventory.
- Outsourcing the logistics to a 3PL. Tsingtao owned many transportation and storage assets. With a 3PL, those assets could be reduced. The 3PL would also permit a more tailored or adaptable logistics service and the more efficient management of transportation providers.
- Digitalization of the logistics processes to permit better staff productivity and enhanced service levels.

This is a powerful example of the way in which a modern Chinese 3PL, even two decades ago, went about winning business through proposing a comprehensive solution, based first on a diagnosis to identify the areas for improvement, then followed by measures to implement these cost reductions. This kind of value-based approach not only brings demonstrable fact-based improvement but also permits the Chinese 3PL to differentiate itself from the countless other players whose appeal is based principally on price, not outcome or service quality. This is part of the pattern of the upgrading of China's logistics whereby global best practices are introduced and internalized.

The opportunities

Anybody who knows China well will be suitably skeptical and scornful of gushing statements about the opportunities in China. It is not only the case that foreign 3PLs have labored, largely in vain, to gain a strong presence in the intra-China logistics market. Chinese 3PLs also face serious headwinds and obstacles to profitability as we mentioned above. But there are positive trends and bright spots that indicate strongly that, if the business model is well-designed, focused, and realistic, and if the offering is differentiated and appreciated by shippers, then there are indeed significant opportunities in logistics, be it for Chinese or foreign providers.

Market growth, quality, and increased sophistication

If it were just that China's logistics are growing at 15% per year and are likely to continue to do so for some time, the news would not be so positive for those running businesses or investing in this sector in China. We would be simply getting further into the mire of cutthroat competition, weak pricing, and heavy investment without a suitable return. Fortunately, the rapid growth is happening alongside a widespread adoption of global management skills and smart technology, which is propelling the market to increased sophistication, in terms of quality of service, be it in terms of efficiency, reliability, and environmental sustainability or in terms of value-added-services throughout the supply chain.

All this in turn helps encourage shippers to outsource to 3PLs and also opens up a path toward improved value-based pricing and enhanced profitability which then in turn permits the investment that can drive the further upgrading of this sector. It is a virtuous circle.

Higher value goods

Before China's economic reforms began, the nation's market for consumer products was extremely basic and underdeveloped. Logistics was mostly around low-value raw materials such as coal, iron ore, and coke and basic products such as steel and grain. Since the reforms, China's logistics have needed to respond to a number of massive changes. Firstly, China moved from basic manufacturing to more added-value items. Since the reforms began, China has established a comprehensive auto industry, which requires great agility and coordination in linking the parts suppliers to the Original Equipment Manufacturers (OEMs), and making sure the after-sales service network is fully stocked. Now with the high-tech electronics industry, the complexity and the value-added have grown exponentially. The myriad of components and supplies that go into manufacturing semiconductors, that go into assembling the mobile phones, requires an extremely sophisticated logistics network linking the ecosystem of suppliers to the product assembler. Given their high value, Apple's iPhones, which are assembled in China, are shipped out to the world in Boeing 777 C cargo aircraft – likewise with semiconductors.

Secondly, China's consumer market has created a strong demand for logistics. This ranges from lower value fast-moving consumer goods to higher value consumer durables such as TVs, washing machines, and refrigerators. The explosive growth of e-commerce has further enhanced the critical importance of logistics, putting a premium on high-quality, technology-driven service which in turn makes it an attractive business, especially if the provider has scale and strong sources of funding for investment.

Enterprise transformation

We discussed earlier the difficult historical legacy left to the Chinese economy including its logistics. Around the turn of the century, China's Premier Zhu Rongji turned up the heat on the reform of China's SOEs, insisting that they transform themselves in preparation for the post-World Trade Organization (WTO) accession competition from foreign firms. Sinotrans, which we profile in Chapter 13, went through a painful but necessary process of restructuring and strategic re-focusing prior to a stock market listing which permitted it to re-capitalize the firm for future investment and growth. Today, with revenues of US$ 11 BN, Sinotrans is China's largest homegrown 3PL and a good example of a new breed of SOE "national champions" in this sector. While Sinotrans became a modern

3PL on the back of its earlier role as a freight forwarder, the Chinese largest shipping firm COSCO Shipping came to it from a different direction, using its muscle in container shipping to build a highly successful land-based 3PL in China. Notwithstanding the fragmentation and poor performance in much of China's logistics market, these revitalized SOEs are today perfectly capable of providing world-class services.

As China embarked on its reforms, it relied heavily on newly emerged private firms to underpin the economy. In providing innovation, profitability, and job creation, they continue to outpace the SOEs. From a raft of a myriad sub-scale and weak private logistics firms, some strikingly successful entities have emerged such as J.D Logistics, SF Express, and Cainiao, which we profile later. Their emergence has largely been on the back of China's e-commerce.

The presence of these reformed SOEs and newly emerged private logistics provide strong grounds for optimism with regard to China's upgrading of this sector to global standards.

Government intervention and support

There are serious concerns about the party-state's heightened control over the economy and the interference in enterprises which saps their autonomy, vitality, and entrepreneurial spirit. Nonetheless, as discussed above, the Chinese party-state has fully taken on board the strategic importance of the logistics industry and is highly supportive of it in a number of ways. Logistics are now fully integrated into the five-year planning process and are accorded high priority. The government is active in not only building the transportation infrastructure over which the logistics can run but also in investing heavily in logistics parks, including those with specialization such as cold chain. Bank funding is channeled into this sector. The government also encourages China's logistics firms to list on stock exchanges.

The government is rightly concerned about the continuing fragmented nature of the logistics sector. It seeks consolidation and urges firms to merge. When it comes to smaller private firms, it has little power to get this done. But when it comes to SOEs, it has absolute power to force mergers on these firms. As discussed above, this has happened with the formation of China Logistics Group, China Merchants' acquisition of Sinotrans, and the merger of COSCO with a smaller shipping firm.

E-commerce fuels the growth

One of the largest factors driving the development of world-class logistics in China is the flourishing of e-commerce that has made China the largest retail market in the world. Its annual e-commerce volume has reached about US$ 15 trillion, way ahead of the next largest e-commerce nations, the US

(US$ 600 MM) and the UK (US$ 135 MM).[28] In 2020, there were 2.29 trillion e-commerce transactions in China. China's online retail sales are growing faster than anywhere in the world. Depending on your source, they account for over 35%–40% of the China retail market compared to around 11%–15% in the US.[29] In global terms, China has three of the top five e-commerce firms in terms of online sales volume: Alibaba (US$ 780 BN, ahead of Amazon at US$ 691 BN), with Pinduoduo and JD.com (US$ 445 and US$ 363 BN) ahead of eBay (US$ 78 BN).[30]

Alibaba, JD.com, and Pinduoduo (which focuses on group buying) together account for about 80% of the China e-commerce market. Alibaba remains dominant with about 50%. Others include Vipshop, which is focused on luxury goods, and Suning, which is big in consumer electronics and started out as a bricks-and-mortar business.

The social media giant TenCent which runs WeChat and others such as Walmart has invested in JD.com as a way to combat the muscular Alibaba and its Taobao e-commerce platform. But recently, Tencent has shown signs of getting more directly involved in e-commerce.

As a measure of the scale of China's e-commerce, we can look with astonishment at China's Singles Day (November 11 or Double 11) which is twice as large as the US Black Friday and Cyber Monday combined. On November 11, 2021, China's dominant e-commerce players Alibaba and JD.com did US$ 85 BN and 55 BN of business, respectively, compared to US$ 23 BN and 31 BN in 2018.

In the West, e-commerce is typically separated from social media and online payment platforms. China is leapfrogging the rest of the world through combining many of these online functions. Alibaba, China's largest e-commerce firm has its Alipay payment function, while Tencent, which is allied with JD.com on e-commerce, China's #2 e-commerce player, has WeChat Pay. 68% of China's e-commerce payments are through these payment platforms, versus only 6% using credit card.

A fundamental aspect of e-commerce is that at the end of the day, there has to be the physical delivery of the goods, something referred to as "fulfillment" (meaning getting it to your doorstep rather than achieving one's life goals!). In the US, Amazon for a long time relied on others for its logistics, principally UPS, FedEx, and the United States Postal Service. But in recent years, it has been active in building its own in-house logistics and transportation capability. In China, the big e-commerce players were quicker in seeing the benefits of having their own logistics network.

In 2013, Alibaba launched its own logistics arm called Cainiao Smart Logistics Network which today has grown into one of China's largest logistics firms. Alibaba's founder Jack Ma has been a passionate advocate of this subsidiary. In 2018, he pledged to spend US$ 15 BN on building Cainiao, stating "this network is not only national, but global, [We want to] connect every courier, connect every warehouse, every hub, every city and every house." He set the goal of achieving "single-day delivery across China and 72-hour delivery to the rest of the world." Ma fully understood the opportunity for China in this area. He noted that, in developed countries, logistics constituted 7%–8% of GDP and by lowering logistics costs, China could reduce logistics' proportion of China's GDP from 15% to under 5%.[31] He made the critical connection between his technology-driven Alibaba and Cainiao, saying:

> If we can use data to solve the problem of low transport efficiency and high logistics costs, we can create huge profit margins for the manufacturing industry and [the] logistics sector. I think this is what Cainiao and our logistics industry should do for the country.[32]

JD.com has its own in-house logistics firm which it claims is the largest logistics firm in China, with a focus on fast-moving consumer goods, apparel, home appliances, and fresh produce. It is active in pioneering automated drone delivery. Pinduoduo has built its own logistics platform to support manufacturers in route planning, automated warehousing, and parcel sorting.

In this way, China's e-commerce and its visionaries such as Jack Ma are playing a central role in shaping China's logistics development which offers the prospect of leapfrogging the rest of the world. We profile these Chinese e-commerce logistics innovators later in Chapter 13.

Cross-border e-commerce takes off

Chinese users of e-commerce are increasingly seeking international luxury goods from Europe and North America. Chinese firms such as Cainiao and JDL provide efficient logistics to bring these products into China. Earlier we discussed how Hainan Island is becoming a duty-free shopping hub for Chinese consumers for such items that are shipped in from overseas by air. Still, overall, the Chinese domestic e-commerce market is relatively separate from the global market due to consumer behavior and tastes and broader cultural factors.

But cross-border logistics flowing in the opposite direction, that is e-commerce retailing that ships Chinese products such as garments and shoes to online shoppers in Europe and North America is booming. At the heart of this major trend are two Chinese e-retailers, Shein and Temu, which we profile in Chapter 13.

Notes

1 Paul G. Clifford, project notes, 2000.
2 The state of third-party logistics in China, a survey by Mercer Management Consulting, 2002, sponsored by The China Federation of Logistics & Purchasing.
3 Wu Youxi, *xiandai wuliu shi jiakuai jianshe quanguo tongyi dashichang de zhongyaozhicheng (Modern Logistics Is an Important Support for Accelerating the Construction of a Unified National Market)*, on *Baidu*, Apr 24, 2022.

4 Wu Youxi, *xiandai wuliu shi jiakuai jianshe quanguo tongyi dashichang de zhongyaozhicheng (Modern Logistics Is an Important Support for Accelerating the Construction of a Unified National Market)*, on *Baidu*, Apr 24, 2022.
5 The state of third-party logistics in China, a survey by Mercer Management Consulting, 2002, sponsored by The China Federation of Logistics & Purchasing.
6 Confidential interview with a Chinese academic logistics expert, Feb 2024.
7 State Council of PRC, *"Shisuwu" xiandai wuliu fazhan guihua (14th Five year Plan, Modern Logistics Development Plan)*, issued Dec 15, 2022.
8 State Council of PRC, *"Shisuwu" xiandai wuliu fazhan guihua (14th Five year Plan, Modern Logistics Development Plan)*, issued Dec 15, 2022.
9 State Council of PRC, *"Shisuwu" xiandai wuliu fazhan guihua (14th Five year Plan, Modern Logistics Development Plan)*, issued Dec 15, 2022.
10 *Quanguo zhongdian qiye wuliu tongji diaocha baogao (Investigation Report on National Key Enterprise Logistics)*, issue by China's NDRC, State Statistical Bureau and China Federation of Logistics & Purchasing, cited by Wu Youxi, *wuliu hangye qingzhong zichan jingying moshi zhi zheng beihou (Behind the Battle over the Light and Heavy Asset Asset Model in the Logistics Industry)*, on *Caijing*, June 13, 2022.
11 *The Dilemma and Prospects of China's Logistics Development*, on website of Shanghai Sunlit Logistics Co., Jan 6, 2021.
12 *The Dilemma and Prospects of China's Logistics Development*, on website of Shanghai Sunlit Logistics Co., Jan 6, 2021.
13 State Council of PRC, *"Shisuwu" xiandai wuliu fazhan guihua (14th Five Year Plan, Modern Logistics Development Plan)*, issued Dec 15, 2022.
14 Sinotrans Ltd, *2022 Annual Report*, Sinotrans Ltd., 2022.
15 *2019 Annual Report*, Kuehne + Nagel, 2020.
16 Kuehne + Nagel website Feb 17, 2022.
17 One definition of 'asset light' is when fixed assets account for less than 40% of the assets on the balance sheet.
18 Wu Youxi, *wuliu hangye qingzhong zichan jingying moshi zhi zheng beihou (Behind the Battle over the Light and Heavy Asset Asset Model in the Logistics Industry)*, on *Caijing*, June 13, 2022.
19 Wu Youxi, *wuliu hangye qingzhong zichan jingying moshi zhi zheng beihou (Behind the Battle over the Light and Heavy Asset Asset Model in the Logistics Industry)*, on *Caijing*, June 13, 2022.
20 Wu Youxi, *wuliu hangye qingzhong zichan jingying moshi zhi zheng beihou (Behind the Battle over the Light and Heavy Asset Asset Model in the Logistics Industry)*, on *Caijing*, June 13, 2022.
21 State Council of PRC, *"Shisuwu" xiandai wuliu fazhan guihua (14th Five year Plan, Modern Logistics Development Plan)*, issued Dec 15, 2022.
22 Eric Kulisch, *SF Express Merger with Kerry Logistics Creates Logistics Powerhouse. Analysts Say Deal Gives China's 'Fedex' International Reach, Import/Export Services*, on *Freight Waves*, Feb 12, 2021.
23 *The Dilemma and Prospects of China's Logistics Development* on website of Shanghai Sunlit Logistics Co., Jan 6, 2021.
24 *Sinotrans Acquires Seven European Companies for 2 Billion Yuan*, on *www.seetao.com*, Dec 11, 2020.
25 Interview with former Maersk executive, Aug 30, 2023.
26 Interview with former Maersk executive, Aug 30, 2023.
27 *Fears for China Economic Growth after Exports Plunge in May*, interview with Clifford Coonan, on *DW News*, June 2023.

28 Graham Charlton, *E-commerce in China: Stats and Trends*, on *E-commerce Guide*, Aug 5, 2020.
29 Katharina Buchholz, *This Chart Shows E-commerce Is Growing Faster in China*, on *World Economic Forum*, Jan 26, 2021.
30 *Leading E-commerce Retailers Worldwide in 2022 and 2027*, on *Statistica*, Nov 25, 2022.
31 Alizila Staff, *Jack Ma Bets Big on Logistics*, on *Alizila* (Alibaba site), May 31, 2018, and Emma lee, *Jack Ma Goes All-in on Smart Logistics Infrastructure Network*, on *TechNode*, June 4, 2018.
32 Alizila Staff, *Jack Ma Bets Big on Logistics*, on *Alizila* (Alibaba site), May 31, 2018.

Chapter 6

Specialized niche markets and capabilities

In developed economies, it is taken for granted that there is a high degree of specialization in logistics services. 3PLs have a clear focus on the specific needs of different segments of their market, whether it is with regard to cold-chain or auto logistics. They commonly choose to differentiate themselves by focusing their capabilities on certain areas of specialization. In contrast, China is a latecomer to logistics specialization and these capability gaps are urgently being addressed both by the Chinese government and by companies that see market opportunity in addressing unmet needs. The government-sponsored China Federation of Logistics and Purchasing has over a dozen subcommittees focused on logistics specialization in cold chain, auto, pharma, medical equipment, white goods, electronic goods, express logistics, dangerous chemicals, steel, energy, agricultural products, wines and spirits, and more.

Cold-chain logistics

In the past, it was common for Chinese truckers to save fuel by switching off refrigeration while not being watched, thus compromising the products. It was also common for products to be shifted onto a non-refrigerated truck for part of the journey and then back onto a refrigerated truck when it got close to the destination. The Chinese government has made determined efforts to turn around the situation. The improvement of cold-chain logistics, which is essential for food and pharmaceutical distribution, figures prominently in China's five-year plan for logistics. The focus in part has to do with food safety. Cold chain is also critical for the quality of many pharmaceuticals, even though that segment of the market is nowhere as large as for perishable food. But in the wake of COVID-19, there is a greater awareness of how important the cold chain is for pharma. The push for a fully functioning cold chain is also driven by the government's desire to achieve economic growth through increased consumer consumption. There is also close scrutiny of how to balance the reduction of food wastage against the need to make the cold chain energy efficient, given its significant contribution to greenhouse gas emissions.

DOI: 10.4324/9781003489115-9

"四横四纵" 国家冷链物流骨干通道网络布局示意图

Figure 6.1 China's planned network of cold chain logistics backbone corridors.

The Chinese government has set a target of 100 "national backbone cold-chain bases" or hubs across China by 2025. Multiple smaller cold-chain storage facilities in agricultural areas will then feed into these hubs. Cold-chain corridors will link the major urban centers and agricultural regions (see the map above). There is an emphasis on upgrading rail cold chain and also rail water intermodal cold chain. Attention is also paid to the standardization of cold-chain trucks. The Plan also spells out the importance, in cold chain, of product traceability and of temperature and humidity monitoring, which can be achieved by new technology. Beyond just the cold-chain specialization, additional sophistication is being adopted, specific to meat, seafood, dairy, frozen food, and pharmaceuticals.

In 2020, China's cold-chain logistics market was US$ 60 BN and the refrigerated storage area was 180 MM cubic meters.[1] But this is behind the rest of the world on a per capita basis. From its low base, China's cold-chain logistics is growing very fast and between 2023 and 2026 is forecast to nearly double.[2]

On the corporate side, China's cold chain is being built by the pioneering efforts of firms such as the innovative private Chinese logistics provider SF (Shunfeng). As an indication of how hungry SF is to absorb state-of-the-art skills from foreign firms, SF has formed a joint venture, in which it has a controlling interest, with US firm Havi Group which runs McDonald's logistics in China. Havi in turn is also heavily focused on the cold chain, as the key to food safety in that fast food chain. (SF and Havi are profiled in Chapters 13 and 14.)

China has recently launched cold storage freight train services from China to Laos and to Vietnam. They export Chinese fruit and vegetables and import tropical fruits from Vietnam and Laos.

A key element of achieving a sound and resilient cold chain is refrigeration technology, whether on refrigerated shipping containers (reefers), rail wagons, or trucks or in warehousing. This is an area where China has leaned heavily on imported foreign technology. Preeminent in this has been the US firm refrigeration and air-conditioning firm Carrier which today in China has 5,000 employees, multiple factories, and two R&D centers. Carrier's Transicold subsidiary has managed to dominate the Chinese market for refrigeration used in logistics. Within China, it has developed new refrigeration products for heavy-duty trucks used for hauling food and pharmaceuticals. This new Transicold technology also addresses the need for energy savings and the reduction of carbon emissions, as urged by the government in the five-year plan.

Auto logistics

As China entered the economic reform in the early 1980s, a key gap in the nation's industrial capability was the automotive industry. 30 years of the centrally planned economy found China with only two truck factories of any scale and miniscule passenger car production. This is not remarkable. Given the poor road system and government policy, most long-distance goods shipments were by rail. When it came to passenger cars, there was no consumer demand, with bicycles being the preferred way around town. What small demand there was for passenger cars came from China's government and Party officials, and this was satisfied by the uninspiring Shanghai sedan and the Red Flag limousine.

Initially, China sought to fill the gap in two ways. One way was through the import of finished cars. In 1985, China imported more than 350,000 vehicles, mainly fleets of Toyotas for use as taxis. Earlier, a small number of Polish cars had been imported as well. The other way was to put China on the path toward large-scale modernized auto production using foreign direct investment. The pioneers in this were Volkswagen (VW) (Shanghai 1984), American Motors/Jeep (Beijing 1984), and Peugeot (Guangzhou 1984). Given the absence of qualified parts suppliers in China, these plants initially simply imported completely knocked-down kits for assembly. These kits arrived in containers at Chinese ports and were then trucked a relatively short distance to the factories. The logistics on the China side were simple, with the complexity concentrated overseas where the containers were loaded.

This model based on kits was a short-term solution, while local parts supply was being established. China was very short of foreign exchange and tightly rationed its use by these plants to import the kits, thus greatly limiting their progress toward large-scale production and profitability. China also imposed ever-tighter requirements on local content (i.e., the proportion of the car's value that came from local components and materials). Shanghai Municipality went even further, setting up a committee to put pressure on VW to have its component suppliers base themselves not just in China but in Shanghai or nearby. Other foreign firms decided to wait until the eco-system of auto component suppliers was well established. Notable in this respect was General Motors (GM) which held fire, waiting until 1997 to establish their plant in Shanghai. Japanese firms that had enjoyed significant import orders from China were also slower in establishing auto assembly plants in China.

The Western auto manufacturing model that China introduced was a far cry from the early days of GM and Ford when production was heavily vertically integrated, meaning that they owned and ran most of the upstream production of components that went into the later assembly process. Under the new decentralized model of today, the car maker or original equipment manufacturer (OEM) still does more than just the final assembly along the production line. What they do includes welding and painting and handling some of the other car manufacturing tasks be it the engine block or pressing of body panels. But more generally speaking, most of the production is handled by Tier 1 suppliers (those who supply and deal directly with the OEM) and by Tier 2 suppliers, who provide components for the Tier 1 players. Logistics providers handle the flow and storage of auto components between all these three parties, which can be grouped as inbound logistics. They also handle the shipment and storage of finished vehicles (outbound) as well as the complex after-market supply of replacement parts for the service network.

So, auto component producers followed their OEM customers into China. This partial list provides just a glimpse at the enormous investment made to create this galaxy of suppliers.

Selective auto component suppliers invested in China

Eaton (steering, hydraulics, air conditioning, axle assemblies)
BorgWarner, Aisin Seiki (power train)
Bosch (electrical systems and lighting, wipers)
Visteon, Delphi (electrical systems and cockpit design)
Valeo (generators, wipers)
BASF, PPG (auto coatings)
AC Delco (starters and generators)
Faurecia, Adient, Lear (seats)
SKF, Timken, TNT, NSK (bearings)

Michelin (tires)
Corning (catalytic converter substrates)
Hella (lighting)
Hanon Systems (air conditioning)

Source: Primary research for the book

The factories of these firms and countless others across China all need logistics services linking them to their own suppliers and downstream to the OEMs themselves.

The arrival of electric vehicles (EVs) means some reduction in the number of components and with that slightly less logistics complexity. Suppliers are busy adapting and transforming themselves for the new environment, for example, BorgWarner which in 2023 opened a new plant in Tianjin that will supply e-motors for EVs. The other phenomenon is the degree to which OEMs are partnering to have a stake in the battery production facilities. OEMs such as Mercedes, Ford, and Tesla are partnering globally with China's largest battery producer CATL. VW is investing over US$ 200 MM in its own battery plant located at the Anhui site of its third and latest EV plant in China.

In the late 1990s, as China's auto industry finally reached an upward inflection point, China's logistics firms correctly perceived the urgent need for inbound logistics services that could take cost and risk out of what was becoming a very stretched supply chain. A key element of this process was creating Just-In-Time supply which reduced the inventory and the working capital carrying cost for the OEM. As elsewhere in the world, this often entailed the supplier or the 3PL providing off-site warehousing close to the OEM. To optimize this, advanced technology has been deployed for Warehouse Management Systems and for Transport Management Tracking.

At the turn of the century, China's liner shipping firm COSCO (now called COSCO Shipping) made the strategic decision to build out its ground transportation capabilities into a fully-fledged ground transportation 3PL. COSCO Logistics, which was formally established in 2003, made auto logistics a high priority, deeming it to be "very attractive" based not only on the market potential (sales of private cars were growing at 80% per annum) and high return but also on the fact that the business (especially inbound) was technically sophisticated and demanding, which played to COSCO's scale and strengths. There was a strong addressable market in terms of auto OEMs with high-volume production. The top 10 OEMs in China accounted for 1.6 million of the total 2 MM unit annual output at that time. COSCO projected that their auto logistics revenues would grow sixfold in two years. The scope for their auto logistics covered inbound, outbound, and spare parts (the after-market). On the inbound logistics side, they had established a regional distribution center (RDC) center in Shanghai from which they were doing trucked "milk runs" to Beijing Jeep (in Beijing) and to Dongfeng-Nissan (in Wuhan) with a sequencing center in each location, providing a value-added service (VAS) whereby COSCO matched the parts to different stages and assemblies along the production line. Other VASs offered included the sorting and the subassembly of components.

On outbound logistics, back then COSCO already had a fleet of 400 CBU (Completely Built Unit) transporters serving customers such as Changan (in Chongqing), Hyundai (in Beijing), Brilliance (in Shenyang), and Nissan (in Wuhan and Guangzhou) using three RDCs.

China's export auto logistics are ramping up on the back of China's strong position in EVs. A decade ago, COSCO was operating two Ro-Ro (Roll-on, Roll-off) auto-carrying ships each with a 5,000-vehicle capacity. Today COSCO Logistics are riding the wave of exports from China, which were over 3 MM vehicles in 2022 and are expected to rise to 5 MM in a short while. COSCO is working closely with Chinese EV producer BYD to ship vehicles on container ships from Shenzhen's Yantian Port to Europe and by rail freight from Chongqing to the Middle East. COSCO has formed a JV with Chang'an Auto for vehicle exports. Jointly with SAIC Anji Logistics and Shanghai Port, it has ordered three large Ro-Ro vessels.

Foreign logistics firms specializing in auto logistics are deeply entrenched in the China market. The French firm CEVA in 2002 formed a logistics JV in China, through a partnership with SAIC Anji, which has in recent years been expanding beyond its auto logistics origins. German auto specialist 3PLs Hellmann, DB Schenker, and BLG have all focused heavily on shipping components to China and finished vehicles to Europe, using the 11,000 km, 23-day rail freight land bridge. D.B. Schenker's trains begin in Leipzig and end in Shenyang, the location of BMW's main production facility in China. In 2022, BMW sold 392,000 vehicles in China making it its largest market in the world.

The French auto logistics specialist Gefco is adapting to the switch to EVs. As they explain,

> EVs need fewer moving parts than ICE [internal combustion engine] powertrains, which means less transportation of spare parts in the future... Moreover, transportation assets and schemes will need to be adjusted to comply with regulation on battery transport.[3]

This is a reference to complying with tight safety regulations for battery transportation. Gefco has specialized in shipping EV batteries to Europe by rail freight and in 2019 signed a five-year agreement with China's CATL battery producer.

Dangerous goods logistics

China's regulations on the transportation and storage of dangerous goods (explosives, flammable, toxic, corrosive, and other hazardous chemicals and materials) are stricter than in the US and Europe. There are carefully set levels of hazmat certification of logistics providers and rules for packaging information.

This unfortunately has not prevented disasters such as the 2015 explosions of ammonium nitrate at a port area in Tianjin which left 173 dead. In 2019, six ministries together issued new regulations covering the 3 MM tons of dangerous goods transported in China each day, and the 12,300 dangerous goods road transportation firms with 373,000 vehicles. 70% of hazardous goods are carried by road. Part of the problem remains that of multiple agencies sharing responsibility coupled with, at times, poor local compliance or supervision. But the other big factor is the fragmented nature of trucking in this specialized area as in others.

However, some large players have emerged in dangerous goods logistics. NORINCO is one of China's largest manufacturers of small arms (weapons). Its in-house logistics subsidiary had a unique government license to transport AK 47s and other such weapons to China's ports. However, around the year 2000, NORINCO had the vision to see that they could leverage their privileged position in dangerous goods transportation and decided to take their in-house capability and transform it into a 3PL providing specialized logistics for external customers in chemicals and other dangerous goods. To do so, it formed a joint venture with the US hazardous goods logistics specialist firm IMC. Other Chinese firms such as DFH (Dongfanghong) have carved out a niche for themselves in hazmat logistics, most recently in handling the transportation by sea and by air of lithium-ion batteries from China to export markets. Other firms such as the Japanese firm NRS have formed partnerships in Chinese ports for bulk storage tank farms for fuel and chemicals.

Specialized to serve a social purpose: promoting people's livelihood

The social purpose of logistics in improving the "People's Livelihood" (*Minsheng*) is spelt out strongly by the Chinese government. It is seen as a key tool to "better meet the needs of urban and rural residents… to expand domestic demand and consumption."[4] Much of Chinese economic growth has over the last four decades been propelled by government policy-led infrastructure development and stimulus spending. Improved logistics for the general population offers the prospect of moving toward a more consumption-led economic model.

The Chinese government quite correctly focuses heavily on seeking to bridge the urban and rural gap. This gap manifests itself not just in terms of wealth and opportunity but also in the linkages between rural residents and businesses into the broader economy. This imbalance in turn relates directly to the weakness in China's logistics. As China's national logistics plan bluntly states, the basic logistics infrastructure is "strong in the East [in the coastal regions] and weak in the West. The cities are strong and the countryside is weak."[5] There is an emphasis on upgrading logistics in the most remote and mountainous areas. The goal is to improve the express logistics in rural areas, using county-level distribution centers and village-level e-commerce "service stations." To facilitate farmers' access to national markets, rural chilled warehousing is being installed for agricultural products. In addition to this, efforts are being made to improve China's "emergency logistics" which are deployed in response to natural disasters such as earthquakes, floods, typhoons, and pandemics.

Notes

1 Ouyang Shijia, *Quality Cold Chain Logistics Top Priority*, on *China Daily*, Dec 14, 2021.
2 Benjamin Ritter and Kevin Karl, *Expanding Global Cold Chain: Effective Adaptation, or Dangerous Contribution to Climate Change*, on *Phys.org*, Jan 30, 2023.
3 Steve Garnsey, *Automotive to Play a Key Role in Gefco's China Strategy*, on *Automotive Logistics*, June 3, 2019.
4 State Council of PRC, *14th Five-Year Plan Modern Logistics Development Plan*, Dec 15, 2022.
5 State Council of PRC, *14th Five-Year Plan Modern Logistics Development Plan*, Dec 15, 2022.

Chapter 7

The digital revolution and technology advances are transformative

This chapter focuses on how the digital revolution – the internet, fiber optics and broadband, mobile telephony, the Internet of Things (IoT), cloud computing, blockchain, artificial intelligence (AI), and data analytics – is inevitably and inexorably transforming China's logistics. Though China's technology adoption has been hesitant and patchy, it is now accelerating due in part to the need to automate as a means to address rising labor costs and skills shortages, brought on by aging population and a falling birth rate. Beyond the digital revolution, we also examine how some more traditional technologies in logistics are being revamped to meet contemporary needs.

High tech has been transforming global logistics for some time. From the 1980s to the 1990s, there was Electronic Data Interchange (EDI). But, EDI was "expensive and limited in reach," and proprietary systems were only available to large firms while smaller companies were "locked out of the game."[1]

The arrival of the internet in the early 1990s "leveled the playing field,"[2] in effect having a democratization effect with regard to technology adoption. It opened the door to the wholesale digitalization of trade and commerce, transforming supplier-customer relationships and the logistics industry that made them function. In turn, high-speed fiber optics and broadband that the data passes over and routers that know where to send the data played their role. A further revolutionary step came with mobile telephony, first mainly voice (with First Generation or 1G in the 1980s) but now (in its fifth generation – 5G – and soon to reach 6G) capable of remotely and reliably transmitting in real-time large volumes of data and images. This in turn has opened up the IoT, which is deployed so heavily in logistics, and with it, AI-driven analytics.

But, as the pace of technology accelerated dramatically over the last two decades, how has the global logistics industry responded to this unrelenting drumbeat? The Danish firm Maersk, the world's second-largest container shipping firm which is actively diversifying into ground logistics, puts it bluntly; "logistics is behind the curve when it comes to technology."[3] This can be accounted for by a number of factors. Manufacturers deployed technology for their core business but neglected it when it came to logistics. The supply chain

DOI: 10.4324/9781003489115-10

is heavily fragmented with providers operating in silos, with poor technological connectivity between them. Many shippers and logistics providers were reluctant or slow to update their legacy IT systems. Technology adoption was also hampered by a focus "on extracting value from a heavily cost-focused model. We sacrificed visibility and flexibility in favor of reliability and cost and, until now, this hasn't needed to change."[4]

While global logistics lag other sectors in technology adoption and upgrading, China is still further behind, albeit catching or even overtaking in some areas. As a leading Chinese logistics expert candidly explained:

> For leaders to emerge and for the industry to meet its customers' needs, it will need to employ new technologies, such as advanced analytics and machine learning. Few traditional logistics companies in China, however, have sufficiently invested in analytics capabilities. Even fewer have studied how smart logistics might fit into their strategies.[5]

China's government fosters technology adoption

China's national five-year plan for logistics focuses heavily on the transformative role of technology. It acknowledges the part already played by "mobile internet, big data, cloud computing and the Internet of Things." It calls for the further "empowerment of logistics digital technology" and its "intelligent transformation" through AI. It calls for "smart" approaches using automation, through robotics in warehousing (for handling and sorting), logistics hubs and ports and through unmanned transportation. Since the largest Chinese 3PLs are already far along the path of adopting new technologies, The Plan has a strong emphasis on the need to design IT systems and platforms for small- and medium-sized enterprises.[6]

The Chinese government has launched its own "open, public and shared"[7] National Transportation and Logistics Public Information Platform (LOGINK) which "aggregates data from various sources — including domestic and foreign ports, foreign logistics networks, hundreds of thousands of users in China, and other public databases — to provide the most comprehensive picture available of the world's logistics activities" which some argue could provide China firms with "unmatched" advantage in global markets.[8]

The US government has been quick to take notice, describing the platform as follows:

> LOGINK provides users with a one stop shop for logistics data management, shipment tracking, and information exchange needs between enterprises as well as from business to government. China's government is encouraging global ports, freight carriers and forwarders… to adopt LOGINK by providing it free of charge…China is promoting logistics data standards that would

support the platform's widespread use. A second generation of LOGINK... would offer a cloud-based suite of enterprise software applications, such as advanced data analytics and business partner relationship management tools.[9]

This may sound extremely useful, especially since it is open to all. But the platform no doubt plays a dual role, facilitating not only more efficient logistics but at the same time providing China's party-state with enhanced surveillance capability. Given the latter element, the US has predictably highlighted the risks of the platform:

> Widespread adoption of LOGINK could create economic and strategic risks for the United States and other countries... LOGINK could undercut U.S. firms that provide more innovative products at higher costs without state support. LOGINK's visibility into global shipping and supply chains could also enable the Chinese government to identify U.S. supply chain vulnerabilities and to track shipments of U.S. military cargo on commercial freight. Though LOGINK claims users can share only the data they want, the security of the platform is unclear. The Chinese Communist Party (CCP) could potentially gain access to and control massive amounts of sensitive business and foreign government data through LOGINK.[10]

We should note the words "could" and "potentially" in the above risk analysis that is typical of recent new Cold War rhetoric. But even if the risks of using this platform are perfectly accurate and not overstated, the anxiety seems based on a false understanding of how China's economy functions. Notwithstanding the Chinese government's undoubted access to private data on national security grounds, the fact remains that market forces predominate in the economy. Chinese firms, shippers, and 3PLs alike, as they compete and serve their customers, are strongly incentivized to use their own confidential IT systems. It stands to reason that the LOGINK platform can give a leg up to small Chinese firms. But it is also perfectly obvious that it cannot substitute or supplant the proprietary IT platforms used by Chinese firms. Given the US's dominance in logistics and related technology, the notion that the Chinese government platform somehow puts US firms at a disadvantage is curious and bizarre, to say the least.

Deploying the new IT systems and tools

25 years ago, container shipping lines had their own proprietary computer systems to help them plan their routes and the utilization of the onboard space for containers. But in recent decades, we have seen logistics providers utilizing IT systems that seamlessly span the entire supply chain. These systems may be developed in-house, acquired through mergers, purchased, or leased through cloud computing (through Logistics Platforms as a Service or LPaaS).

Today, there is no doubting the critical importance of assets such as trucks, ships, and warehousing. But the IT systems sit at the core of modern logistics firms, integrating the entire flow of goods and representing a key factor for competitive success.

Logistics firms are able to create an integrated end-to-end supply chain using an array of computers and related gear and specialized software all linked through the Internet (the World Wide Web or WWW). The firm's employees plug into these systems through fiber cable or 5G mobile telephony using an array of devices, ranging from old-style desktops, to laptops, tablets, and mobile phones. These devices are now linked seamlessly through "collaboration" software, transmitting, real-time or instantly, data, voice, images, and video.

In the past, data storage was typically done in an in-house data center. But, over the last two decades with the vast ramp-up of data volume and the analytics that go with it, there has been a remarkable shift toward cloud computing whereby data storage is done by specialized firms with their own data centers or server farms. Some of this is "private cloud" where the IT storage is outsourced to a facility dedicated to one customer. But more often, it is the Public Cloud, where a data center is shared by a number of customers, whose data is, of course, carefully segregated and firewalled. More generally and with logistics, the concerns over security and data loss in cloud computing have melted away as "cloud" has become the dominant trend.

Within the supply chain and logistics more narrowly, data security is of paramount importance. A feature of modern logistics is the extent to which the IT systems have to be configured not only to drive internal operations but also to interact seamlessly with its surrounding ecosystem, that is those outside the firm that need to be kept in the loop. The customer requirement for visibility and flexibility across the supply chain makes it essential to proactively "push" messages providing alerts on time of delivery and any delays. The IT systems integrate multiple parties upstream and downstream, the shippers/customers, the providers of transportation of transportation and warehousing, the recipients of the goods, and the customs officials at the border. But to achieve this, the IT systems are designed to permit these outside parties to gain access, but only to certain areas and with varying levels of security.

This awesome computing power available today is utilized to design logistics approaches customized to individual customers across the range of attributes we discussed earlier. Specialized software is used to design and optimize the "milk runs," the order in which goods are picked up and dropped off. The IT systems also permit automated and speedy customs clearance at ports. They facilitate the space-booking by freight forwarders (the travel agents of goods transportation) whether on ships, trains, or aircraft. Trucks, which in the past often returned with a backhaul, now have a better chance of identifying a load for the return leg, thus transforming the efficiency and economics of trucking. In logistics, as elsewhere in society, the digital revolution is facilitating the more rational utilization of capacity. GPS permits the tracking of goods and the vehicles carrying them, down to a few yards. GPS, as with passenger cars, in the realm of logistics facilitates real-time adjustments to delivery routes based on congestion and weather. Truckers are assisted in avoiding congestion and guided to routes where they turn right rather than left, thus speeding things up. IT systems have become transformative in goods logistics just as they have been for ride-hailing firms such as Uber, Lyft, Didi Chuxing (China), and Grab (Singapore).

Across the supply chain, IT systems are used to track the goods. Barcodes are now ubiquitous and logistics staff scan the products in and out at each step of the process. While in the past the scanning devices stored a batch of data that would later be dumped into a computer back at the office, now this data is transmitted in real time back into the firm's network.

Radio frequency identification (RFID) tags, which can transmit and receive, are now also widely used to track inventory. Each tag has an Electronic Product Code, with a generic part and one which relates to the individual product items. Automatic trackers monitor and record inventory as it loaded onto or unloaded from a shipping container. But, when it comes to warehousing, most still use barcodes rather than RFID tags. Warehouses have become expressions of how technology is transforming old processes. Robots and other automated systems often now deposit and retrieve items in warehousing.

China is a front runner in *The Internet of Things (IoT)*, which at the end of 2020 accounted for around US$ 376 BN of annual activity globally, ranging from specially designed semiconductors to sensors and related mobile communications gear. China is using IoT to transform existing cities and new urban development, creating so-called smart cities across a range of dimensions including public safety (surveillance), healthcare, e-government, mass transit, and, last and not least, logistics, transportation, and warehousing.

In logistics, IoT uses sensors and the mobile internet to send data back from trucks, ships, trains, and warehousing back to the logistics provider. Trucks increasingly have onboard computers that collect data that is transmitted via telematics. This has implications for operational efficiency, safety, and regulatory compliance. Truckers in the US are forbidden to use cell phones and the computer is used to communicate with home base. New trucks also have collision avoidance systems. The computer also collects data on the vehicle speed and the time spent by the driver at the wheel or resting. IoT now plays a vital role in the chilled chain. Sensors in the truck, container, or warehouse transmit real-time data on the temperature the goods are at, providing not only a perfect record, for health, safety, and liability reasons, of how they have been transported but also permitting swift action to rectify a failing refrigeration system.

Blockchain technology also has the potential to play a transformative role in logistics, in improving both trust, efficiency, and speed. It electronically permits a series of distributed ledgers which are linked securely through encryption. This offers the opportunity to increase visibility throughout the supply chain while maintaining a high level of security. But this technology is not yet proven beyond proof-of-concept.

Using blockchain, and the encryption it brings, cyberattacks and manipulation can be combatted. Through a robust digital contract combined with Electronic Proof-of-Delivery (ePOD), it is possible to reduce disputes and facilitate payment. At the same time, blockchain can enhance track and trace across the supply chain.

This data has to be stored. Some large logistics firms have their own data centers. But these represent a large investment, often needing multiple locations and redundancy to ensure resilience, coupled with high operating costs in terms of electricity for cooling. As we mentioned, there has been a major shift toward outsourcing data storage, using cloud computing whereby one's data is kept in an outside vendor's data center. But it should be stressed that China does not permit foreign ownership of data centers. Moreover, foreign logistics have to comply with complex Chinese requirements for local data storage.

In 2017, China announced its goal to be "a world leader" in *Artificial Intelligence (AI)* by 2030[11] and is deploying its state planning weight and investment to achieve that. While the US led in developing the theory of AI, China is fast implementing the technology. The gap between China and US on AI is fast being closed. One can point to an upsurge in China's academic publications and patents on AI. But quantity in this does not directly imply results. The Chinese government has plowed funds into high-tech parks for IA start-ups and many of these are now reaching commercial scale and achieving stock market listings. This is one aspect of Xi Jinping's industrial policy that seems to have worked well.

Many correctly point to the fact that China has focused on the use of AI to achieve strict surveillance of its citizens, while the US had focused more on marketing and sales applications. But China is also bringing AI knowledge to bear in many other areas, whether in medical research, in industrial automation and robotics, or in analyzing and predicting demand and performance within the supply chain and in logistics. Alibaba is pushing hard into AI and, given its roots in e-commerce, is applying it to issues relating to the supply chain.

The data collected through IoT and through countless communications between humans represents a potential treasure trove which can be used to guide future action and fuel continuous improvement. When it comes to logistics, AI and *machine learning* are used to spot, decipher, and learn from patterns, or algorithms, within what were formerly unwieldy data dumps. These analytics are used to optimize logistics and improve customer service, to adjust operations real time while they are under way and to improve the design of future service offerings, and to provide better tracking and visibility for shipper and recipients (through generative AI). It can help forecast demand patterns, optimize inventory levels, reduce transportation costs, and provide better security and risk management. All this feeds into enhanced financial reporting and strategic planning.[12] AI, when applied smartly to the right data, is beginning to contribute globally and in China in logistics to matching operational performance with customer needs.

There is strong evidence of the benefits that IoT and the resulting AI analytics could have on improving China's transportation fleet asset management. One estimate is that 15% of the fuel and maintenance cost for trucking in China could be saved through AI-driven optimization of routes.[13]

In the past, across industry and commerce, IT systems were often an afterthought and poorly represented in senior management. Today, IT has become a core corporate function, central to both internal operations and for the interaction with customers and beyond. IT is represented at the top by the Chief Technology Officer and the Chief Information Officer.

IT platforms for logistics

Foreign logistics firms operating in China come equipped with their own IT systems. Many of these are proprietary. 3PLs such as Expeditors, Kuehne & Nagel, and DB Schenker and the so-called "integrators" (UPS, FedEx, and DHL) who dominate in express goods have developed their own in-house IT systems platforms, their core asset which differentiates them and makes it difficult to replicate their services and compete against them. As strategy consultants put it, these platforms provide massive "strategic control." UPS employs a small army of software engineers to build, update, and maintain its IT systems. These platforms look inward, controlling and integrating the service offering, the delivery coupled with finance, human resources, and regulatory compliance. They also look outwards making the firm a hub that provides carefully structured tiers of access to achieve friction-free links whereby monitoring and tracking are communicated with customers, suppliers, and outsourced providers.

In the US, some firms, such as Flexport, started out as developers of software for logistics and have moved on to become providers of entire logistics platforms whereby they serve as a virtual 3PL, asset-light – without their own transportation or warehousing. In 2018, Chinese express courier logistics firm SF Express invested US$ 100 MM in Flexport, with the goal of bringing their technology to China.[14]

A key element of these IT platforms is *Transportation Management Systems (TMS)*. While in the US the largest 3PLs have the resources to develop their own proprietary systems, smaller providers opt to purchase or lease road freight TMS software from firms such as Oracle, MercuryGate, and Blue Yonder. When it comes to air and ocean freight the largest is CargoWise. A benefit of leasing the software (through Software as a Service [SaaS]) is that it is constantly updated and refined. Such off-the-shelf IT solutions are customizable, in terms of the type of logistics, the specialization required. These TMS streamline a wide range of services from shipping and route management, to warehousing, tracking, and accounting.

Sinotrans, with annual revenues of US$ 16 BN (in 2022) is an excellent example of how China's largest 3PLs have moved fast to develop their own in-house proprietary logistics technology capabilities. In 2022, it registered 22 new patents and 15 software copyrights. Its technology subsidiary, Sinotrans Innovation Technology Co, has launched Sinotrans' own SDCC Transport Management System which controls a wide range of functions ranging from using AI algorithms for transport scheduling with a capacity of handling 100,000 trucks, to electronic billing and settlements. It is migrating each of its specialized services, including outbound auto logistics, onto SDCC. Sinotrans has also digitalized its shipping space-booking through Sinotransbooking.com, a platform that covers eight of China's largest sea ports.

Sinotrans, under the banner of "internet + logistics," has also built a public logistics e-commerce platform, called y2t.com (in Chinese *yunyitong*), focusing on the B2B (Business-to-Business) market, providing services from inland truck haulage and rail to cross-border shipping, air cargo, and rail links to Europe and S E Asia, plus related customs clearance. It claims to already link tens of thousands of manufacturers and smaller logistics firms. The network states that it is focused on "the construction of a high-value logistics big-data system" which will use AI not only to enhance the service offering but also to identify additional customer needs. It should be added that Sinotrans'2022 revenues from e-commerce were only US$ 1.7 BN or around 10% of its total business. And most of this was cross-border e-commerce. The business directly attributed to y2t.com, albeit growing at over 100% per annum but from a low base, was less than US$ 200 MM and with a miniscule profit.[15] In this field, it is a minnow compared to Alibaba and its logistics subsidiary Cainiao. But the entry of this state-owned firm into this business is a clear indicator of where the future growth is expected to come from.

China's smaller 3PLs already can already rely on array of China-developed TMS, provided by firms as vTradeEx (*weizhi*), e6 (*yiliu keji*), Litin, Flux, Kinnsoft, and Yida. Although most of these are new start-ups, Yida was established back in 1984 and in addition to developing software also operates cold-chain logistics and has invested in business parks.

Smart warehousing and robotics

In China, warehousing accounts for about 40% of total logistics costs and requires a large high trained workforce. Its traditional warehouses are highly inefficient. The huge growth of e-commerce is continuing to expand China's warehousing needs. It is fertile ground for technology and automation. China already has many thousands of so-called "smart warehouses."[16] Warehousing and regional distribution centers consume a great deal of land and automation can permit greater use-intensity. In addition, according to Chinese e-commerce logistics firm JD.com, automation can reduce labor costs by 70%.

In these smart warehouses, complex computer systems dispatch goods to designated locations and also retrieve them likewise, when the time comes for them to be further shipped. This is accomplished by a series of specialized robots: sorting robots (that reduce and remove human error from this critical step in the process), the palletizing robots (that put the goods on pallets for easy handling), autonomous mobile robots (AMRs) (mini electric vehicles that buzz around getting the goods to the right spot), picking robots (that reach into an open carton to pick one of or more pieces which are often assembled to create a single shipment to a store or a customer), and robot forklifts that put things away and retrieve them (that put the goods up on a high shelf and then remove them when the time comes).

This kind of automation has been around for some years and is not entirely new. But AI is being deployed to further optimize where the goods are placed in the warehouse and right up to the ceiling. In so doing, it can permit the warehouse to be shared by multiple firms, much like cloud computing on a server. Thus, rental space needed can be reduced. AI can also be used to match the palletization as it leaves with the layout of the warehouse where it arrives. All of this implies greater logistics efficiency and cost reduction.

Warehousing technology remains an area where China is still playing catch-up. China imports a wide range of items, ranging from software for automation controls and the sensors used on robots. But as an indication of the rapid progress China is making, Cainiao, the logistics arm of Alibaba, recently launched its complete "Enterprise Smart Warehouse Solution."[17] For planning purposes, it provides digital two- and three-dimensional space visualization. It used AI, cloud computing, and automation, supported by Autonomous Mobile Robots (AMRs and automated guided vehicles [AGVs]). This drive to streamline processes and improve efficiency, which Cainiao claims has achieved a 99% accuracy rate in parcel sorting, is highly significant when one considers that on China's Double 11 (or Singles Day) which falls on Nov 11 each year and is the largest e-commerce day, Alibaba achieves around US$ 38 BN of Gross Merchandize Value (the usual measure of e-commerce volume). On Hainan Island which is now designated a Free Port, Alibaba's logistics arm, Cainiao, is developing a smart supply chain pilot zone that will have 150,000 m² of digitalized bonded warehousing. Cainiao is also deploying its complete warehouse "solution" internationally, for instance in Thailand and the rest of Southeast Asia.

Sinotrans' Tianjin subsidiary, which focuses on cross-border business including customs clearance, has worked with Tianjin Little Bee (*Mifeng*) to install state-of-the-art RFID technology in its warehousing, using not only handheld devices but also automated RFID readers on doors and on forklifts.

Foreign players are also active in this field. Danish logistics provider Maersk is investing US$ 174 MM in what is described as its first "green and smart flagship logistics center" in China. Located in the Shanghai Free Trade Zone, it will have 150,000 m² of warehouse space, including a 24-m high warehouse with an automated storage and retrieval system.[18]

Trucking and related technology

Trucking Management. Globally within logistics, trucking management has traditionally been a major headache. Not only is the sector fragmented and inefficient with a preponderance of owner-operators, but it also does not respond easily to regulation, resulting in serious issues of safety and reliability.

In the US, the issue of how to ensure trucks have a backhaul (that is having a load when they return) remains a thorny one. 15%–20% don't have a backhaul and of the remainder 36% are not full loads. In the US, digital freight brokers have emerged. They do not own trucks themselves but play the role of automatically matching shippers and their loads to truckers who have empty legs, a sort of online dating for trucks. This capacity is achieved using software which harnesses the power of AI algorithms.[19] Freight brokers use "load boards" put up on the web, which facilitate the pooling of truck resources and reduces empty backhaul. They are online but the shippers still post manually and the truckers then check the boards to see what is needed. 3PLs often offer much the same services as freight brokers but handle a much broader range of supply chain functions.

In China, where the trucking is much more fragmented, the backhaul problem is even greater and harder to resolve. China's truckers are already belabored by cut-throat competition and rising costs for labor and fuel, coupled with the heavy burden of tolls, many of them "irregular" (that is illegal). Empty backhauls further eat into any profitability there may be. Online discussion on this issue in China produces discussion of solutions such as "penalties" for those with no backhaul and the broader utilization on IT system's such as load boards alongside logistics.[20]

China is now fast introducing the concept of digital freight brokers, known in China as "network freight companies" (the network being the digital element). The leading Chinese digital freight broker is probably the Full Truck Alliance which claimed that in 2020 20% of Chinese heavy- or medium-duty trucks used their digital platform. As a caveat, that may be for only one load in a year. The old patterns persist. Its growth is assisted by tax refunds from local governments which rightly see the benefits that the platform brings.[21] Full Truck Alliance sings the praises of their platform which increases truck utilization and truckers' income by 50% and 30%–40%, respectively, while reducing transaction costs by 6%–8%.[22] Another fast-growing Chinese digital freight broker is the Rockcheck (Rongchen) Group, Tianjin's largest private steel producer. It uses its "intelligent dispatching" function to match trucks with loads and in the four years after the platform was launched in 2018 racked up 172,000 trucking users with cumulative shipments of 82 MM tons.[23]

To deal with what hitherto has been a regulatory gray area, in 2022, the Chinese government issued regulations on Road Freight Transport on Online Platforms. Since then, the government has intervened to protect "drivers rights" and has criticized these platforms for predatory pricing and arbitrary increases in membership fees.[24]

At the end of 2022, these platforms in China accounted for about 100 BN or 14% of the total China highway freight market of US$ 735 BN. There were over 2,500 of these "network freight enterprises." 94 MM waybills were uploaded onto the platforms that year, an increase of 36% year-on-year.

While these platforms clearly play a vital role, fuller resolution of the back-haul issue in China is only likely to come firstly from a consolidation of the trucking sector and the emergence of more larger scale line-haul trucking firms and secondly from further government initiatives to bring owner-operators into groupings that share a common software platform.

When it comes to broader technology platforms for trucking, Chinese firms are also stepping up to the plate. Beijing-based G7 Network, founded and led by China logistics' pioneer Zhai Xuehun, offers a complete platform for truck fleet management, from order processing to route planning and asset tracking using GPS. It used IoT sensors to monitor in real-time driver fatigue through cameras, to warn the driver if there is insufficient space between it and the next truck, and to monitor weight to prevent theft.

Founded in 2010, G7 Network has been financed by the Chinese government and by private equity firms. Based on a recent fund-raising cycle, the company is valued at US$ 2.2 BN. It uses a SaaS business model.[25] G7 Network has also formed a joint venture called Inceptio to develop autonomous trucks, with funding from e-commerce firms Meituan Dianping (focused on meal delivery) and JD.com.

In line with global developments, the Chinese government has already introduced commercial vehicle Event Data Recorders (EDRs), which are the "black boxes" that store data on truck speed, ABS functioning, and seat belt use. It has yet to make Electronic Logging Devices universal on China's trucks.

Heavy-duty trucks: filling the gap. As China entered its economic reforms in 1978, after three decades of Soviet-style planning and rapid industrialization, it found itself still poorly equipped in many respects. One striking failure was to develop the capability to produce heavy-duty long-haul trucks.

In 1935, the Republic of China established China Heavy Duty Truck (CHDT) in Jinan, Shandong but that came to nothing due to the war with Japan. In 1956, with help from the then Czechoslovakia, CHDT began to produce a version of an 8-ton Skoda truck. Unfortunately, the annual capacity of the Chinese factory never rose above around 100 vehicles. The only volume truck production was carried out by two truck factories, the First Auto Works (FAW) (established with Soviet help in 1953 in Changchun, Jilin Province) and the Second Auto Works (established in 1969 in Shiyan, Hubei Province) with both factories annually producing around 100,000 trucks. The FAW's Jiefang (or Liberation) truck was of Soviet design and the SAW's Dongfeng truck was very similar. They were medium-sized trucks with a tonnage of 2.5–5 tons and with gasoline not diesel engines. Given their military origins, they performed well in rough conditions. In the modern age, they proved sufficient to haul containers to locations relatively close to the seaports. But they did not have the capacity or power for long-distance routes and heavy loads. This was a major gap.

As China embarked on creating an arterial system of superhighways, there was a vital need for trucks that could serve long-haul routes. CHDT, later listed on the Hong Kong stock exchange as Sinotruk, took the lead in importing technology from Stehr of Germany and then from Volvo of Sweden. But unlike China's passenger vehicle market which by the early 1990s showed commercial volumes which warranted foreign direct investment, the China market for heavy-duty trucks remained largely served by exports to China. US firm Paccar (Kenworth and Peterbilt trucks) focused on exporting mining and oilfield trucks to China. After its early unsuccessful involvement with CHDT, Volvo Trucks reverted to focusing on exports to China, in 2020 shipping 4,300 vehicles into that market. The remainder of China's demand for heavy-duty truck has been met largely by local production by firms such as FAW, Dongfeng (former SAW), Sinotruk and a breakaway success with Foton, a subsidiary of Beijing Auto that boldly entered this market segment with new designs, and a new facility in Huairou, just outside Beijing.

But in recent years, China's demand for high-quality, heavy-duty trucks, reflecting, with a time lag, the completion of China's superhighway network and the increasing integration of the economy as a whole have finally reached an inflection point thus creating attractive economies of scale for local production by foreign firms. Between 2016 and 2020, annual sales of heavy trucks grew from 728,000 to 1,617,000 vehicles.[26] Foreign players are now finally making the leap from exports to local production (or assembly) in China. Volvo Trucks has acquired a Chinese heavy-duty truck company in Taiyuan (Shanxi Province) where it will initially annually assemble 15,000 units of its FH, FM, and FMX heavy trucks. Daimler Truck has also recently taken a bold step forward. Back in 2012, Daimler had formed a 50/50 joint venture with Beijing's Foton. Daimler provided technical for Foton's Auman line of heavy trucks that were folded into the JV.[27] But it was not until late 2020 that Daimler felt the China market had achieved sufficient maturity and with an adequate ecosystem of qualified local suppliers to mitigate the potential reputational risks associated with local production. They announced assembly in Beijing of its iconic heavy truck, the Mercedes-Benz Actros with a load capacity of 18–26 tons and the fuel-efficient turbo-charged OM471 engine. The design production capacity of the new plant will be 60,000 units. In 2022 the first China Actros was produced. Daimler describes China as the "largest heavy-duty truck market in the world" which they will continue to serve by exports as well as through the local assembly.

Autonomous trucks. Globally, AVs (autonomous vehicles) or AGVs (autonomous guided vehicles) are already transforming the logistics industry. China was one of the first to deploy AVs to move containers at ports. Shanghai's Yangshan Port, the largest in the world, launched its first automated terminal with AGVs in 2017. Qingdao, Tianjin, and other Chinese ports also now have automated terminals with AGVs.

AVs are also deployed widely in state-of-the-art warehousing, to move the palleted goods around and then up into the computer-designated spots in vertical warehouses. Deploying AVs on public highways is more complex and is taking some time to be realized. Some trucks already are largely automated but still have a human sitting in the cab alongside the computer. One vision being developed in the US is to start with a few key routes. They may be point-to-point but that will be between hubs where goods are transferred to traditional human-operated trucks for shorter distance local haulage.[28]

In China, government investment is flowing into automated truck development. In the US, this trend is constrained by regulations which deter experimentation due to legitimate safety concerns. In China, there is the ability to experiment more boldly, through it should be added that public opinion is a serious factor in China and therefore the government is often inclined to make conservative baby steps to avoid the risk of public blowback. Foreign firms are using China as a test bed for this technology.

China's long-haul intercity trucking requires around 8 MM trucks and two to three drivers per truck. It is claimed that driverless trucks could reduce trucking costs by 50%. Baidu (China's Google) has partnered with Beijing truck manufacturer Foton to produce a prototype self-driving truck,[29] one which would permit the driver to rest for long periods. US firm Plus is partnering with Changchun-based truck makers FAW to develop driverless trucks, using its PlusDrive Driver Assist System.

TuSimple, a US-based start-up specializing in autonomous transportation, has provided the software to enable the Chinese firm Foton's driverless, heavy trucks. But as an indication of how logistics and related technology can get caught up in geopolitics, in 2022, it was told by the Committee on Foreign Investment in the United States (CFIUS) to stop transferring technology to China due to national security concerns, since the driverless truck technology has military applications. After an investigation by CFIUS and a settlement[30] (without admission of guilt), TuSimple's Chinese founder decided to scale back its US operations and focus on working within China.

A Chinese firm, the Shanghai-based Inceptio Technology, which as mentioned above is a joint venture formed by G7 Network, lays claim to bringing into operation in China the "industry's Ist autonomous truck for line-haul logistics." It has partnered with Chinese truck makers Dongfeng (in Wuhan) and Sinotruk Huanghe (in Jinan) to deploy its proprietary Level 3 (L3) driverless truck technology (Truck Navigation Autopilot). They have conducted a study which claims that, when fitted with this technology, the trucks are 98% less to likely to have an accident than a conventional truck. Now approved for mass production and having clocked up 50 MM km without an accident, these L3 trucks use onboard radar (imported from Bosch), cameras, and computer platform (rated at "up to 245 TOPS" which refers to Trillions of Operation Per Second," a typical measure of an AI capable computer)[31] to achieve L3's "conditional automation," which requires human presence and override. Inceptio has formed strategic alliances with STO Express and ZTO Express which recently placed orders for 500 and 200 of these trucks respectively.[32] In 2022, after some years of piloting, Sinotrans made its L4 autonomous long-distance trunk line freight trucks fully operational, with accumulated distance of 300,000 km.

While these are all major steps forward, there is a long way to go. Some firms claim to already be at L4 (fully autonomous but still with man in the cab). But the reality is that in China, L4 is still largely experimental. Most of China's autonomous trucks are still L2 or L3, a technology advance that makes it possible to lower costs by moving from two drivers per truck to one.

L5, full automation – driverless and without a man in the cap – still remains just experimental or even aspirational: not about to be realized in a full operational sense. In late 2023, Dongfeng Sharing, part of the Dongfeng Motor, announced that it had received a license to operate a 13-km test track for L5 autonomous truck driving in Lanzhou, Gansu Province. It includes an array of intelligent roadside devices for telecommunications and radar guidance.[33]

Case study: the Jiuquan-Mingshui Autonomous Highway (green digital highway)

A perfect illustration of the way the Chinese government is intervening to drive innovation in China's logistics is the Jiuquan-Mingshui Highway, also, due to its use of green hydrogen, referred to as the Green Digital Highway. This is a demonstration or pilot project which entails a 438-km dedicated (that is only used by driverless trucks) route that is being constructed in the Hexi Corridor of Gansu Province. The corridor's strategic significance goes back to ancient times when it was a key link in the Silk Road. It is a narrow 1000 km strip of land that connects Xinjiang (in the West) with the rest of China.

The Chinese government is investing RMB 10 BN in this project which it hails as the "world's first driverless, and fully intelligent smart highway."[34] It is designed to carry 13,000 trucks/day and annually 80 MM tons of freight. The goal is to tackle two key issues – the inefficiency of Chinese trucking and its negative environmental impact, which together is described as a "double carbon" reduction – both heightened performance and the adoption of renewables. It is pointed out that China's total fleet of 40 MM trucks represents only 11% of Chinese vehicles but accounts for 65% of vehicle carbon emissions. Heavy-duty trucks in China account for 84% of these emissions.[35]

Gansu province is well suited to capturing solar and wind energy which is to be used to create green hydrogen for the autonomous trucks running on this new highway. Hydrogen refueling stations are to be constructed along its length.

Since this new pilot project is a dedicated highway just for autonomous trucks, it represents a vital opportunity to test and refine L4 autonomous trucks (driverless but with man in the cab) so that is reliable, safe, and suitable for broad adoption.

There is another key innovative element to the Jiuqiun-Mingshui Autonomous Highway. This is the role of government in creating the smart and intelligent infrastructure which includes a private 5G network, roadside optical fiber cable, cameras, and high-precision GPS.

There will also be a real-time traffic reporting system. As one expert explains:

> The biggest enemy to autonomy is edge/corner cases (the engineering term for event outside normal operating parameters) such as a pop-up accidents, emergency vehicles and construction sites. The system can notify autonomous vehicles to be prepared.[36]

This infrastructure is highly significant since, once it is in place, the software needed to operate the driverless truck can be simplified[37] and implemented more smoothly. The role that government has played in this project is in itself a pioneering innovation with great promise.

Drones

Drones are already widely deployed for photography by real estate agents, film makers, ardent amateurs, and of course for reconnaissance and bombing by the world's militaries. China dominates not only the world's cheap yet smart drones that fly off the shelves of Walmart but also complex drone-based commercial platforms. China's leader in this field is Guangzhou-based Ehang Intelligent Technology which uses "cloud computing and Autonomous Aerial Vehicles" (AAV) (unmanned drones) to transport goods or people, as well are conduct aerial photography and surveillance. In 2019, it signed a strategic agreement in China with Sinotrans-DHL, the express package joint venture, to deliver packages over the last mile. Initially, the goods were to travel 8 km to and from that firm's Dongguan service center, located close to Shenzhen in Guangdong. As it celebrated this milestone, Ehang stated that use of the AAV would reduce the delivery time from 40 to 8 minutes and cut the delivery cost by 80%.[38] The expectations were that, in China, this would achieve more acceptance and success compared to DHL negative experience in 2013 in Germany when it experimented with drones (Paketkopter) using a German-made drone but did not proceed with that project. EHang is also working with Chinese retailer Yonghui Superstores to use drones for food delivery.

Rail technology

China entered the post-Mao economic reforms not only with a rail network that needed to be radically upgraded but also with freight locomotive technology that was inadequate for the economic lift-off.

We talked earlier about how in many respects China's geographic scale and with it the logistical challenges resembled that of the US. It made perfect sense for China to turn to the US for technical assistance on its locomotives. The US freight rail system is world class, with highly efficient lines passing from the ports on the West Coast (Los Angeles-Long Beach, Oakland, and Seattle) where the goods from China arrive, across the continent to the major markets in the Mid-West and on the East Coast. These freight trains operated by firms such as Union Pacific and BNSF are often over 1 km in length and can reach up to 5 km long, made possible by "distributed power," that is with multiple locomotives spaced through the train.

In the mid-1980s, US firms GE and GM's EMD (Electromotive Division) sold hundreds of diesel-electric locomotives to China. In 1984, GE's 3,000 HP C39-7 diesel-electric locos began their journey from the plant in Erie, PA plant to Newport News where they were loaded onto ships to China.

By 2005, the China market's demand for freight locos remained hot. But the Chinese government was insistent on some localization. Both GE and EMD signed multi-hundred million dollar agreements with China whereby both agreed to build or assemble locomotives jointly with China. GE's contract called for 300 6,250 HP diesel electric locomotives to be built with China's Ministry of Rail's (MOR) factory in Qishuyuan, in Jiangsu, while EMD built 334 6,300 HP locos jointly with a MOR factory in Dalian, Liaoning Province. These US locomotive designs were compliant with US EPA emissions regulation. In 2007, the Canadian firm Bombardier signed a US$ 1.4 BN contract to produce 500 of its Europe-designed 9.6 MW electric freight locomotives jointly with the MOR's Dalian plant.

China's rail freight development was held back by the conservatism and caution of its railway officials and experts who were reluctant to adopt US-style MU (or multiunit) cabling that permitted the brakes and the throttle on various locomotives to be controlled from a single location on the train, thus achieving greater hauling power. Once that reluctance was overcome, Chinese rail freight was able to fully emulate the US model.

The supply of technology extended beyond the locos themselves to the complex braking and control systems that made these long freight trains viable. In 2009, the US firm WABTEC (which recently bought the GE loco business) formed a joint venture in China to produce pneumatic-control valves and other braking equipment for use on freight rail cars.

Today, based on further development of technology from foreign partners (and no doubt through some IPR "rub off"), China now has developed its own range of locomotives. GE thought it had a chance to supply a large proportion of the 6,500 electric locomotives needed. That was not to be. Just as an indication of what China has achieved, in 2023 China announced the arrival of its Zhuzhou, (Hunan Province)-built six-section electric locomotive with 28.8 MW power, to be used to haul 10,000 tons of coal.[39]

The build-out of China's high-speed passenger rail network, which uses new lines, has freed up some capacity which can be used for rail freight. But with the explosive growth of e-commerce especially on "Singles Day" or Double 11 (November 11th) when, in 2020, about 3 BN packages were on the move, there is a need for high-speed rail for express freight. In 2020, there were two significant events which heralded the arrival of China's high-speed freight. On November 1 of that year, two express freight trains set off, one from Wuhan to Beijing (300 km) and the other in the reverse direction. They were repurposed high-speed passenger trains, with the seats removed, and each carrying 40 tons of e-commerce freight at up to 300 km/hour. A month later one of China's main producers of railway rolling stock put on display a totally new high-speed freight train. It had 8 wagons and 2.9 m wide loading doors. It can travel at up to 350 km/hour.[40]

China's goal is to reduce harmful emissions by creating an air-rail cargo intermodal approach which moves e-commerce products off of aircraft on onto express freight trains. This would reduce carbon emissions by over 2 MM tons annually and 57%, compared to if the goods were just carried by the domestic air network.[41]

Automation at the ports

As we will discuss in Chapter 10, China has globally deployed the skills in ports construction and management it had developed domestically. A key element of this is China's fast adoption of technology that automates ports, improving efficiency and reduces carbon emissions. Ports were initially fairly slow to upgrade their technology in part due to sunk costs in the older gear, coupled with pressure to maintain jobs. But now the race is on to automate. China, as in the rest of the world, is widely deploying a range of new technologies in part to achieve the goal of "sustainability," that is to reduce emissions. Firstly, there are automated rubber-tired gantry cranes powered by electricity rather than diesel and with one person remotely overseeing five cranes. Ship-to-shore (STS) cranes are also automated. Down below there are driverless automated terminal tractors (ATs or AGVs) which move the containers around. Beyond this, 5G mobile telephony is being deployed to link all these steps in the process, while AI is being used to monitor and optimize performance and efficiency. In the US, the Port of Virginia has invested US$ 140 MM in computer-automated cranes. In the UK, container ports such as Felixstowe (owned by the Hong Kong firm Hutchison), Immingham, and Teesport are introducing the same new technology.

In 2021, China's Xingang Port in Tianjin announced it was building its first "emission-free terminal," through using solar and wind power, through automating the cranes using only electric power, and by utilizing AI monitoring, with the result that energy consumption can be reduced by 17%. Shanghai's Yangshan Port has also gone through this technical transformation and is now the world's largest automated port.

China's near monopoly in the global market for STS cranes used at container ports has attracted significant controversy. Shanghai Zhenhua supplies 70%–80% of the world's STC cranes in over 100 countries. Chinese cranes account for around 200 or 80% of the national total in the US. This has prompted the US to issue a presidential executive order to combat this perceived China cybersecurity threat. Though the software installed on these highly automated cranes comes from the Swiss firm ABB, it could be monitored by the Chinese and is also updated by Zhenhua remotely using IoT, thus creating a potential national security risk. There are also unsubstantiated suggestions that the Chinese could use these cranes to track the origins/destinations and contents of containers. The US government has instructed ports with Chinese cranes to undertake a set of cyber security initiatives, something that makes good sense. It has also said it will provide US$ 20 BN in financial aid to a subsidiary of Mitsui (from Japan) to build new cranes in the US. This move is driven not only by security concerns but also by a desire to bring manufacturing jobs back to the US. However, as it stands, given that this new US-based STC crane manufacturing would be carried out by Mitsui,[42] there may be new jobs but the technology and the software will be Japanese, albeit deemed to be less risky than acquiring it from China. Moreover, there are also signs that US ports are not inclined to reduce their dependence on Chinese cranes. The Port of Seattle and Tacoma said that, having already complied and done its national security due diligence, it does not plan to replace the Chinese cranes.[43] This issue perfectly reflects the geopolitical headwinds that logistics and related technology face. However, in this case, it remains to be seen what the full impact will be and whether this initiative is for real or instead represents a loud noise, but little action, aimed at assuaging domestic concerns in the US.

When it comes to new ports that China is managing overseas, the goal is to be automated from the outset, permitting them to leapfrog other older ports which remain heavily invested in earlier technology and processes. SIPG's, the Shanghai ports group, has invested in, constructed and operates part of Haifa port. Israel's first new port for 60 years, it is a "smart port," bringing "automation, efficiency, energy saving and top service quality."[44]

Notes

1 David Bovet and Joseph Martha, *Value Nets. Breaking the Supply Chain to Unlock Hidden Profits*, Wiley, 2002. This book was translated into Chinese and published in China in 2001, under the title Jiazhiwang. P. 198.

2 David Bovet and Joseph Martha, *Value Nets. Breaking the Supply Chain to Unlock Hidden Profits*, Wiley, 2002. This book was translated into Chinese and published in China in 2001, under the title Jiazhiwang. P. 198.

3 *Logistics' Digital Revolution. The Transformation of Data and Technology in Supply Chain Logistics*,A-P Moller-Maersk, Aug 2020.
4 *Logistics' Digital Revolution. The Transformation of Data and Technology in Supply Chain Logistics*, A.P. Moller-Maersk, Aug 2020.
5 Detlev Mohr, *Fast and Furious. Riding the Next Growth Wave of Logistics in India and China*, McKinsey & Company, Sep 2019.
6 The State Council, *14th Five Year Plan Modern Logistics Development Plan*, issued Dec 15, 2022.
7 Gu Jingyan, *National Transport and Logistics Information platform in China*, at UNESCAP conference, Bangkok, Dec 2015.
8 Avery Ruxer Franklin, *China's Logistics Data Management Platform Could Give It Unmatched Power in Global Market, Experts Argue*, Rice University, Apr 25, 2023.
9 The US-China Economic and Security review Commission, *LOGINK: Risks from China's Promotion of a Global Logistics Management Platform*, Sep 20, 2022.
10 The US-China Economic and Security review Commission, *LOGINK: Risks from China's Promotion of a Global Logistics Management Platform*, Sep 20, 2022.
11 *China Announces Goal of Leadership in Artificial Intelligence by 2030*, on *CBS News*, July 21, 2017.
12 Silvai La face, *Key Ways Artificial Intelligence (AI) Will Power Integrated Logistics*, Maersk website, May 2, 2023.
13 Kai Shen, Xiaoxiao Tong, Ting Wu, and Fangning Zhang, *The Next Frontier for AI in China Could Add $600 Billion to Its Economy*, Mc Kinsey & Company, Jun 7, 2022.
14 TLME News Service, *Flexport Secure $100m Boost From Chinese Company*, Transport & Logistics Middle East, May 2, 2018.
15 Sinotrans, 2022 Annual Results Corporate Presentation.
16 Daxue Consulting, *Who Can Benefit from Smart Warehouses in China*, Oct 8, 2018.
17 Aaaron Raj, *Alibaba's Cainiao Launches Enterprise Smart Warehouse Solution*, Techwire Asia, Mar 31, 2022.
18 *Maersk to Build First Green and Smart Flagship Logistics Centre in Lin-gang, Shanghai*, Maesk press release, Jan 4, 2023.
19 San Francisco-based Parade is an example of firms that provide this capacity management software.
20 11mmsk, *You shenme banfa neng jiejue siji de kongche fancheng wenti*, on *Zhihu. com*, Feb 2019.
21 John Kingston, *China'sFull Truck Alliance Digital Freight Platform Pulls Back Curtain in Prospectus*, on *Freight Waves*, Jun 1, 2021.
22 John Kingston, *China'sFull Truck Alliance Digital Freight Platform Pulls Back Curtain in Prospectus*, on *Freight Waves*, Jun 1, 2021.
23 Xinhua, *China's Digital Freight Industry Shows Promising Prospect*, on *China Economic Net*, Apr 20, 2023.
24 *China's Transport Authority Summons On-line Freight Platforms to Protect Driver's Rights*, on *Global Times*, Jan 21, 2022.
25 Ding Yi, *Logistics Automation Startup G7 Wins $2.2 Billion Valuation*, on *Caixin Global*, Feb 15, 2022.
26 *Global and China Heavy Truck Industry Report, 2021–2027*, on *ReportLinker*, Dec 11, 2022.
27 Co-author Clifford consulted on this transaction with what at that time was Daimler-Chrysler. He recalls there was the goal to put an Actros engine into an Auman truck to create a hybrid. But this concept was abandoned after trials showed that the sheer power of the Benz engine tore the Chinese truck apart.

28 Anusha Kukreja, *Autonomous Trucks Lead the Way*, on *Deloitte Insights*, Feb 17, 2012.

29 Will Knight, *China's Driverless Trucks Are Revving Their Engines*, on *MIT Technology Review*, Nov 16, 2016.

30 Tu Simple Holdings Inc, *Agreement with Committee on Foreign Investment in the United States*, on *PRnewswire*, May 29, 2024.

31 Inceptio Technology website.

32 Inceptio Technology, *Inceptio Technology Announces New order for Heavy Duty Autonomous Trucks Equipped with Its Truck Navigation Autopilot Feature*, Aug 2023.

33 Kavipriya, *Dongfeng Sharing Granted Autonomous Driving Licenses in Gansu*, on *Telematics Wire*, Dec 18, 2023.

34 Zheng Zhiwei, *Quanguo zhengxie weiyuan Huang Baorong zidongjiashi zhinenghua chanye xu jiaqiang chuangxin zhengce gonggei*, on *Minsheng zhoukan*, Mar 21, 2021.

35 Xinhua, *Dapo chuantong jiaotong yunshuyetai moshi. Shoutiao lvse shuzi zhuanyong gonglu zhengjiasu tuijin*, *from Keiji ribao*, on *Xinhuawang*, Sep 20, 2022.

36 Interview with Paul Lam, BOT Auto, Jun 9, 2024.

37 Interview with Paul Lam, BOT Auto, at Cambridge, MA, Jun 7, 2024.

38 Qiu Quanlin, *DHL Signs Deal with Chinese Drone Company*, in *China Daily*, May 7, 2019.

39 Stolchnew Alexey, Savenkova Ekaterina, *World's Most Powerful Electric Locomotive Shen24 by CRRC for Coal Cargo Service in China*, on *Rolling Stock*, Jan 20, 2023.

40 *Freight trains running at 350 km/h. China takes rail transport to a new level*, on Cargo-partner, 2023.

41 Zhu Yao, Mi Gan, Xieke Li and Xiaobo, Lu, Strategic Plan for China's Air High-Speed Rail Express Freight Network and Its Carbon Reduction Potential, on *Environmental Science and Pollution Research*, 30, 2023.

42 *US Increases Cybersecruity Citing Threat of Chinese Cargo Cranes*, on *The Maritime Executive*, Feb 21, 2024.

43 Fox 13 News Staff, *Rising Concerns over Chinese "Spy Cranes" in Seattle, Tacoma Ports*, on *Fox 13 News*, Feb 26, 2024.

44 Wang Ying, *SIPG Automates Israel's Port in Haifa*, on *China Daily*, Sep 4, 2021.

Chapter 8

Striving for green sustainability

In September 2020, Xi Jinping, when addressing the UN General Assembly, surprised many observers by announcing China's "dual carbon goals": "We aim to have CO_2 emissions peak before 2030 and achieve carbon neutrality before 2060."[1] Here, we examine how addressing the development of China's logistics can play a significant role in achieving these bold targets.

As we have stressed, China's backwardness in logistics presents an obvious opportunity to improve the nation's economic performance. In energetically going after this opportunity, China is not only reducing the proportion of GDP that logistics constitute but is also using this improvement to drive China toward a "higher quality" GDP in terms of its social and environmental impact. As we shall see, logistics contribute heavily to greenhouse gas (GHG) emissions and pollution more generally. Governments, shippers, and logistics firms around the globe are active in striving for technology and approaches that address this pressing issue and which drive toward green sustainability in logistics. China, the world's largest emitter of GHG (though not on a per capita basis – that is the US), is playing a key part in these efforts. This is driven not only by the Chinese government's heavy emphasis on a green transition but also by the fact that it is forced upon China as a participant in the global economy where environmental concerns pervade all walks of life. Today, it is standard for logistics contracts to have language calling for high performance in terms of emissions reduction.

So, the good news is firstly that green sustainability is an integral part of the drive to make logistics more efficient and secondly that China is an active player in addressing climate change, not just in words but also in bold actions. What is less good news is that to fundamentally address GHG emissions from logistics, there has to be a major shift away from the fossil fuels used in goods transportation. Though, as we shall see, there are relatively positive signs that this shift can occur in trucking, it is much more problematic when it comes to shipping and aviation.

There are essentially two routes to addressing the climate warming crisis with respect to logistics. One is to reduce the emissions created by transportation. Below, we explore how that is happening on land and at sea. But before getting

DOI: 10.4324/9781003489115-11

to that, it is important to note that the other route is to radically rethink the supply chain, to shrink demand, to reduce the need for transportation. Under globalization, the world has become highly intertwined. In the winter, consumers in the US and Europe rely on fresh fruit and vegetables from Latin America and Africa, respectively. It is hard to force the consumer to go back to just seasonal local produce in order to reduce the carbon footprint of such trade. In the same way, it is hard to reduce the supply chain links in industrial production, as exemplified by auto production with components moving by rail across the land bridge between Asia and Europe. It is true that in light of geopolitical factors, as well as pandemic disruption, there is a move to reduce supply chain risk through locating production closer to home called "re-shoring" or "near-shoring" (for instance, from China to Mexico) or by making supply chains regional rather than global.

It makes good sense to question the need for certain goods to be shipped across the world in polluting container ships, whether it is reasonable to use airfreight to bring in out-of-season fruit and vegetables. But, given our dependency on the global supply chain that has been painstakingly established over many decades, it is unlikely that it can be dismantled in the medium term. It would be complicated to change consumer expectations and the profitable business built upon then. While it may be difficult to put the genie back in the bottle, it is nonetheless worthwhile to strive for this at least in part. Even though addressing this demand side of the environmental crisis may be an uphill battle since it flies in the face of commercial considerations, it is an important component of our "green" efforts, alongside the other track which is to reduce the damage caused by the current logistics.

Still, for the time being, it is likely that the main focus of government and companies alike will be on achieving "green" goals through reducing the GHG emissions from the various modes of transportation and improving the overall efficiency of logistics.

The Chinese government has energetically embraced the significance of the upgrading of logistics as a key driver of the nation's "green" transition. The five-year national plan for logistics states emphatically:

> Green, low carbon, safe and resilient. The concept of green environmental protection runs through the whole chain of modern logistics development and embraces the sustainable development of logistics.[2]

The Plan sets out a series of approaches to "promoting the development of green logistics." Central to this are efforts to move away from road transportation and to an increase in the proportion accounted for by rail and water. This effort to reduce trucking extends to the international transportation along the Belt and Road, for example, the "green and low-carbon electrified" China-Laos railway which began operations in late 2021. The proposed railway from China to Lao

Cai and onto Haiphong in Vietnam would likewise play an important role in bringing more goods traffic off of the highways.

When it comes to roads, there is a focus on curbing the pollution from diesel engines and moving toward New Energy Vehicles powered by electricity, hydrogen, and biological liquid fuels. This new technology is also to be used on forklifts used in warehouses. Shippers and 3PLs are urged to conduct "energy-saving diagnosis" and to adopt contracts with strict energy requirements. There is a call to "reduce excessive and secondary packaging." The Plan envisages a series of "green logistics hubs and green logistics parks."

For some time now, China's largest logistics firms have energetically taken the "green" agenda on board. Sinotrans states in its annual Corporate Social Responsibility Report that it has;

> implemented the strategy of promoting green development by intelligent logistics, adhered to the path of ecological priority and green development, with strict control on ecological environmental risks... strengthened energy conservation and emission reduction.[3]

In this report, it documents how year-by-year it is reducing the sulfur dioxide, nitrous dioxide, and carbon dioxide emitted from its motor vehicles and ships. The emphasis is on smart technology, on "intelligent logistics," which can use large quantities of historical data to optimize transportation and reduce fuel consumption. The firm pledges to implement multimodal approaches whereby goods are switched from roads to rail, thus reducing the carbon footprint.[4] In 2022, Sinotrans announced its strategic plan for "carbon peaking and carbon neutrality."[5] COSCO Shipping, China's largest shipping concern, which also has a large land-side logistics business, likewise publishes its annual Environmental Social and Governance (ESG) Report[6] in which it maps out how it plans to "improve quality and efficiency to open up a new chapter in zero-carbon."[7] COSCO has set a target of carbon neutrality by 2060 but this lags the more ambitious competitors such as Maersk and CMA. Private Chinese firms have also signed up for the green transition. One of China's largest e-commerce companies, SF Express states its commitment to a "zero-carbon future" and spells out how it will help deliver the UN sustainability goals. It has set a 2030 target for a 70% reduction in the carbon footprint of each e-commerce package. This will be achieved by low-carbon transportation (including moving goods from the roads and air onto rail), "green" industrial parks which have smart and efficient storage and a reduction in packaging used.[8] These three Chinese firms are not only responding to the clarion call from the Chinese government. As firms that are listed in stock markets in Hong Kong, Shanghai, and Shenzhen, they are also complying with regulatory requirements on ESG that come with that status.

Foreign logistics firms active in China also have comprehensive ESG programs that include measures to reduce emissions and address climate change.

UPS has a Sustainability Action Plan that calls for it to achieve "carbon neutrality" by 2050.[9] Maersk is still heavily reliant on highly polluting liner (container) shipping, much like COSCO Shipping. It has set the bold target of net-zero CO_2 emissions by 2040.[10]

Globally, there is widespread skepticism about corporate commitments on ESG, including the "green" aspects. While all major firms are expected to express commitment to ESG, there are reasonable grounds for believing that many companies just pay lip service to this, while continuing in the old way. However, when it comes to logistics firms, we can see that "green" approaches may converge with efficiency and productivity goals, thus in some instances driving toward better profitability not the opposite. That said, when it comes it comes to container ships and air freight that convergence with profitability is not apparent. Nonetheless, the global pressure to reduce GHG emissions is such that the shipping and airfreight companies and those that ship the goods have little choice but to make major changes. The adoption of new clean fuels will inevitably have a cost that will be absorbed within the supply chain and also be passed on to the consumer. The hard truth is that dealing with climate change will have a high price tag, as is the case with massive investment required to achieve the fuel change in container shipping.

Below we proceed to examine to what extent logistics firms in China, both Chinese and foreign, having demonstrated a loud commitment to "green," are now implementing these lofty goals.

Heightened overall logistics efficiency. There can be little doubt that, as the principles of modern integrated logistics are adopted throughout the Chinese economy, thus reducing the economic cost of transportation and storage, there also comes with it a broad-based reduction in the carbon emissions. Technology is playing a big part in this progress whether it is in Transport Management Systems that route goods most efficiently, in online platforms that help make sure there is a back-haul (no empty truck in the return trip), or AI which can anticipate bottlenecks and respond to changing customer needs. Green improvement is integral to all this refinement and optimization of logistics processes.

Ground transportation improvement

As mentioned above, a key element to reducing emissions in logistics is to shift goods onto rail. The creation of China's superhighway network, coupled with the failure of the railways to respond to the needs of the economy, left China over-reliant on long-haul trucking. China is going into high gear to reverse this imbalance, with a strong emphasis by both government and companies on rail containerization and multimodal truck-to-rail, ship-to-rail routes. In addition, the advent of e-commerce has meant a strong demand for domestic China air cargo, which is highly polluting. As documented earlier, new high-speed goods trains are now being introduced to handle long-distance e-commerce traffic.

When it comes to transportation between China and Europe, the challenge for the rail links is that they mainly still use diesel locomotives. Electrification of China-Europe rail is still a long way off. As it stands, one TEU traveling by rail from China to Europe emits 0.7 tons of CO_2, compared to 0.5 tons by sea.[11] Moreover, as we examine below, the carbon intensity of sea cargo is set to fall, due to new fuels and better designed/slower ships. The international rail links look destined to focus on relatively time-sensitive products, and in competition with air cargo. In terms of CO_2 emissions, compared to rail, ocean transportation will remain on par or better in the future. That said we should also consider the geopolitical and other risks of transportation through the Taiwan Strait, the Straits of Malacca, the Red Sea up to the Suez Canal, which may make the land-bridge option a useful way to mitigate risk.

While autonomous-driving passenger cars in China are, as elsewhere in the world, facing serious headwinds due to safety concerns, when it comes to long-haul trucks in China the news is encouraging. Chinese logistics firm Sinotrans is partnering with autonomous driving firm Pony.ai and machinery maker Sany, to produce and test heavy-duty trucks which use sensors, radar, and AI to permit L4 (with a driver still in the cab) autonomous driving (self-driving) in China's superhighways. Pilot programs have accumulated over half a million kilometers of safe driving. It is estimated that by 2030, there will be over 6 million such trucks on China's roads.[12] These trucks not only offer the prospect of safer and more efficient trucking but will also help optimize fuel consumption. But the heart of the issue still remains the propulsion technology itself.

China is, with the US, co-head of the Electric Vehicle Initiative, a multi-governmental policy forum, coordinated by the International Energy Agency. China has already grasped the lead in passenger EVs, using government subsidies and technical innovation to produce lightweight EVs for the mass market at prices much lower than the high-end and much heavier Tesla that originally dominated.[13]

In China, electric-powered light commercial vehicles (LCVs) are already competitive with internal combustion engine LCVs and account for around 6% of such vehicles sold there annually. China's ports are also already adopting battery-powered heavy-duty trucks for short haul around the port and battery-powered cranes. Likewise, battery-powered (and in some cases autonomous or self-driving) forklifts have been introduced in China's latest "smart" warehouses.

Although broad adoption of battery power for long-haul trucks globally has been slow due to cost, weight, and range, it is forecast that 20% of medium and heavy trucks will be battery-powered by 2030 (and with a second even faster scenario reaching 50% in that time frame!). Both of these scenarios would permit the achievement of a net-zero target for heavy-duty trucks by 2030.[14]

In the US, the cost of an EV tractor (for a truck) can be double that of a diesel tractor. But if there are government subsidies, this gap on cost might be bridged.

The bigger issue is range. Almost all EV freight trucks have a maximum of 250 km per charge. That works well for trucks in container yards or for AGVs in ports. But it falls way short of what is needed for long-haul trucking. There is still a long way to go in resolving the cost and range issues.

That said, there are signs that rapid progress may be possible, especially in China, through the improvement of the energy density of batteries (thus permitting longer range and lower weight) and in lowering their cost. Moreover, most of the battery-powered electric heavy trucks in China use lithium-ion-phosphate chemistry batteries (not lithium-ion) which are well suited, from the safety aspect, for battery swapping. Chinese government policy is geared to supporting battery swapping for long-haul trucks, and a number of pilot programs have been launched. Further developments using (lithium-free) sodium-ion batteries, with fewer issues over raw materials not just the lithium supply but the metals used for the anodes, present the prospect of further improving the competitiveness of battery power.[15] Until recently, due to the weight of batteries, Chinese heavy-duty trucks could only drive 100–150 km before needing to recharge. But in response to new government policies and incentives, in 2023 Chinese truck makers Sany and FAW both announced new long-haul battery-powered heavy trucks with a range on one charge of 800 and 500 km, respectively.[16] This kind of range is highly impressive and clearly transformative. Given China's utter dominance in the battery supply chain and in battery-related R&D, it is highly probable that China will come to lead the world in adopting battery power for long-haul trucking.

That said, there are still uncertainties and concerns regarding the pace of battery development to power heavy trucks. Therefore, China is also focused heavily on a radical alternative, introducing fuel-cell–powered heavy-duty long-haul trucks to run across the nation's superhighway network. The major constraint to achieving this is supply of hydrogen to power them. It should be noted that most of the hydrogen used to power fuel-cell engines today is "grey hydrogen" or "black hydrogen" produced from natural gas and coal, respectively. However, the Chinese government has announced a 2025 target of up to 200,000 tons per annum[17] of clean "green hydrogen" (produced through the electrolysis of water using renewable electricity). But things are now moving faster. Sinopec which is one of the two main operators of gas stations across China has set a target of producing 2 million tons of green hydrogen by 2025 and to use that to massively expand China's hydrogen refueling network. Sinopec is constructing two green hydrogen plants which use wind and solar power. They are located in Kuqa, Xinjiang (20,000 tpa of green hydrogen) and in Ordos, Inner Mongolia which will produce 30,000 tpa, with the electrolyzer, which is used to split water into oxygen and hydrogen, fueled by 450 MW of wind and 2,070 MW of solar.[18] The Ordos project, which is said to be the largest such facility in the world, is a strong indicator of how the nation is moving into the hydrogen era and doing it using renewables. The vision of using wind and solar, which is often far from the major areas of population thus making electricity transmission troublesome, to produce green hydrogen for transportation has the potential of being game changer. The Chinese government is also urgently working on the safe transportation of hydrogen and on establishing charging stations along China's highways. There are currently only a few thousand fuel-cell trucks operating in China. In announcing the 200,000 tpa target for green hydrogen, China's top planning body also set a target of 50,000 fuel-cell trucks by 2025, with 1 million by 2023.[19] German firm Bosch is partnering with Chinese truck-make Qingling Motor to produce fuel-cell heavy trucks. They not only have already delivered trucks to a mining company but also have large-scale contracts with COSCO Shipping and China Post Express & Logistics.[20] The Qingling-Bosch truck has a range before refueling of 550 km.[21] The fuel-cell truck developed by Shandong Province's truck firm Sinotruck and engine maker Weichai Power has a range of 600 km and, with over 1,000 orders, is moving into full production. Weichai built its name as high-quality producer of diesel engines for shipping. Hydrogen re-fueling stations have already been built along highways in Shandong.[22] This move into hydrogen is a just one indication of how China, on the back of its measures to combat climate change, is building a whole new industry around green technology.

The green transformation of shipping

Sea freight is under enormous pressure to clean up its act. As a veteran US journalist put it succinctly:

> About 90% of the world's trade is transported by sea. But the cost to the environment is enormous. Every year, those container ships plying the world's waterways spew about 1 billion metric tons of carbon dioxide into the air, which is about three per cent of all greenhouse gas emissions.[23]

Of course, in addition to container ships, there are also bulk carriers, tankers, and general cargo vessels. Those that operate the ships, either as ship owners or as ship leasers, face pressure to reduce and ultimately halt carbon emissions. The pressure comes from multiple directions.

Ultimately, the biggest pressure will be regulatory, whereby mandatory control of emissions will be imposed on shipping. As it stands, it is still on a voluntary basis. The UN International Maritime Organization (IMO) in 2023 established new targets which called for the shipping industry to reduce CO_2 emissions by 40% by 2030 and achieve net zero by 2050. This is to be achieved by new more efficient ship designs and by the adoption of new green fuels.[24] The EU is also moving fast to introduce targets for the reduction in the use of bunker fuel by maritime transport and will mandate that while in European ports, ships have to plug into land-based fuel sources.[25] The International Chamber of Shipping, which represents 80% of the world's shipping firms (and includes China's COSCO), has also pledged to achieve net zero by 2050. However, as mentioned above, COSCO's corporate pledge remains more cautious, set at 2060.

At the COP28 environmental conference in 2023, a coalition of the world's largest shipping firms (but not including China's COSCO) called for the IMO to impose mandatory regulation on greenhouse emissions from shipping, which includes an end-date for when fossil fuel power vessels cannot be brought into operation. Container shipping line CMA CGM noted that it has already invested US$ 15 BN in green shipping. It has invested in LNG propulsion. Though they painted their first LNG vessel green, being LNG, it is not fully green, but certainly an improvement on using bunker fuel. Maersk has pledged themselves to carbon-neutrality by 2040, ahead of the IMO target[26] and has ordered a number of new container ships that are "dual fuel" or "methanol dual fuel." To be clear, these vessels are not hybrid-powered in the sense that a Toyota Prius is. There is only one engine that burns bunker fuel. They are called dual fuel since they are designed so that at a future date, the diesel engine can be ripped out and a new methanol engine can be fitted, so that there is space for new pipes and storage tanks. But on day one, they are still powered on bunker fuel. Maersk has called for a tax on bunker fuel as a way of encouraging the use of new fuels. It is easy to see why fast movers in terms of reducing shipping emissions would like to see more enforcement to make sure that there is an even playing field and that they are not put at an unreasonable disadvantage by dint of acting more swiftly.

Shipping firms also face pressure from large customers such as Ikea, Walmart, and Target which have set their own green targets. These firms are heavily motivated in this by the prospect of regulations mandating levels of carbon emissions permitted in products such as the EU's Carbon Border Adjustment Mechanism. They also receive pressure from their own customers and from their institutional investors such as pension funds. These retail firms state that they are willing to accept higher freight rates as the cost of decarbonization.[27]

China's main container line, COSCO Shipping is the third or fourth largest in the world in terms of container capacity, about equal to CMA CGM and behind Maersk and MSC. It has 1,114 vessels of all kinds. In its Sustainability Report, COSCO acknowledges that it has CO_2 emissions of over 6 MM tons per annum. It sets a target of carbon neutrality by 2060, with an interim goal of reducing emissions by 12% by 2023 (compared to 2019). In response to IMO pressure, it has already reduced its sulfur emissions through using lower sulfur bunker fuel. To address the CO_2 issue, it plans to adopt "alternative fuel and renewable energy (to produce the fuel)." COSCO is initially focusing on methanol. At a cost of nearly US$ 3 BN, it has ordered 12 24,000 TEU container ships with dual fuel including green methanol.[28] Maersk and CMA CGM have 25 and six dual-fuel methanol ships on order respectively, with a middle-range capacity of 9,000–15,000 TEUs.

The thorniest issue in decarbonization of the world's merchant shipping fleet is the question of what type of fuel should replace bunker fuel. LNG, a less polluting fossil fuel is seen as important during the transition (CMA CGM has order 12 LNG-powered vessels) while the shipbuilding underway indicates that methanol will be widely adopted in the medium term. Both Maersk and COSCO have indicated that they favor a transition to methanol.[29] Methanol is produced from biomass (from plants or animals), CO_2 capture, or green hydrogen. Maersk, CMA CGM, and COSCO's methanol ships have one other thing in common: dual fuel. In choosing dual-fuel ships, these firms are hedging their bets, given the huge uncertainty around whether the required quantities of sustainable fuel will be available.

One estimate is that for shipping to achieve net-zero emissions by 2050, there will have to be around US$ 2.4 trillion of investment. Some of this will be used to achieve operational efficiency (digital solutions to optimize speed and routing) and technological sophistication in terms of new hulls and propellers to reduce drag. But US$ 1.7 trillion of that total will be needed for new fuels, for hydrogen production and downstream synthesis, and for the fuel storage and distribution.[30] Maersk has signed a number of agreements to purchase 730,000 tons of green methanol by the end of 2025. One new agreement by Maersk with the Danish firm Orsted will produce 300,000 tons of green methanol from 1.2 GW of onshore wind and solar in the US.[31] China has also invested heavily in using wind farms and solar energy to produce green hydrogen and, downstream E-methanol and ammonia. A number of major investments are being made in addition to the green hydrogen plants in Ordos and Kuqa that we mentioned above. US$ 4 BN is being invested in the Songyuan Hydrogen Industrial Park in Jilin Province which will use 750 MW from wind and 50 MW from solar to annually produce 45,000 tons of green hydrogen, which will be converted into green ammonia and green methanol. The park also includes the manufacturing of electrolyzers and a hydrogen energy research institute. The park will be energy self-sufficient and will not need to be connected to the grid.[32] In late 2023, China's State Power Investment Corporation announced that is investing nearly US$ 6 BN in Heilongjiang Province in establishing a plant that will provide 164,000 tons/year of green hydrogen produced from a 3.5-GW wind farm which will be further processed into green methanol and green aviation fuel.[33] One challenge with regard to China's wind and solar resources is that they are located far from the centers of population. Producing green fuels in such locations may offer an alternative to often inefficient long-distance electricity transmission.

The pace of China's ramp-up of green hydrogen and downstream green methanol and ammonia that it can produce is impressive. But even as significant volumes become available, there are a number of issues. One is the different customers competing for that supply which is likely to be constrained. Those looking to tap into this new supply include fuel-cell trucks requiring liquid compressed hydrogen across the superhighway network. There are shipping companies seeking to shift from bunker fuel to green methanol. And there is the plastics and fertilizer industry looking for green ammonia to replace the current feed-stock that is based on natural gas or coal. The other big issue is transporting these clean fuels to where they are needed. When it comes to shipping, can Singapore which has always been the largest center for bunkering (providing bunker fuel to shipping) transform itself so that it can be a key entrepot for new fuels? The logistics of green fuel distribution for use on land and on the ocean are complex and new, given the volatility of these materials.

The breaking news is the prospect of thorium molten salt reactors (MSRs) becoming a game-changer in terms of ship propulsion. These MSRs, being fueled by thorium rather than uranium, are therefore much safer and do not require water for cooling. The US had originally pioneered this technology but gave it up for in favor of uranium power (related to military use) and a decade or more ago shared information with China which has pushed ahead with MSRs. This technology is technically difficult since the very hot molten salts are highly corrosive, thus requiring advances in materials science that can permit the development of resistant alloys. As it stands, China has already issued a commercial license to a small-scale thorium MSR operating in the Gobi Desert. Then in late in 2023, it was announced that China's Jiangnan Shipyard in Shanghai is building a 24,000-TEU container ship which will be powered by a thorium MSR,[34] the first attempt at this globally. If this proves to be technically viable and operable, then this will be an enormous breakthrough in the drive toward net-zero.

The decarbonization of air freight

This is a very hard nut to crack. Air freight, depending on your sources, results in anything from 22 to 47 times more CO_2 emissions (per ton/km) than container ships. Each year aviation as a whole (passenger and cargo) produces 1 BN ton of CO_2 or about 2.5% of global GHG emissions.

The obvious way to reduce this impact is to reduce the demand for air freight. As discussed above, rail links between China and Europe are competing for business that might otherwise have gone by air freight. Likewise in China's domestic market, there is a realization that e-commerce's reliance on air transport is not healthy, with the result that high-speed rail freight has already been launched. While air cargo is relatively small (140,000 tons or about 1% of world trade compared to ocean shipping which carries 11 BN tons or 90%), this mode of cargo transportation is growing at about 4.8% per annum. Despite its protestations about the need to deal with GHG emissions, Maersk recently acquired an air cargo logistics firm, as part of its goal to diversify away from liner shipping.[35]

There is building pressure to adopt Sustainable Aviation Fuels (SAF) for all aviation, passenger, and cargo. The US Federal Aviation Authority in its Aviation Climate Action Plan has called for net-zero carbon in aviation by 2050.[36] There is intense activity to establish the production of SAF whether it is hydrogen or green methanol (as mentioned above in Heilongjiang). There was a surge of optimism in 2023 when a Virgin Atlantic Boeing 787 airliner traveled from London to New York powered exclusively by re-processed cooking oil, albeit with just Richard Branson and not a full load of passengers. The excitement is of course premature. It is generally accepted that a reliable supply of SAF, in the volumes needed, is at least a decade away.[37]

Meanwhile, the air cargo industry is nibbling away at the issue of decarbonization. There is attention to reducing emissions at both ends of the journey through improved warehousing and ground transportation. There are efforts to use technology to optimize the air cargo routing, so as to reduce fuel usage The air cargo fleet is being radically upgraded from the old MD11s, B747s, and 757s converted from passenger use, as well as from the B 747Fs, designed as a freighter. The new generation of Boeing 777Fs and Airbus 350Fs being introduced have greatly enhanced fuel efficiency. The two-engine B777F has almost the same payload as the four-engine B747-400F but uses 30% less fuel.

There is a high awareness of the impact of freight transportation on GHG emissions and climate change but action to rectify this issue is very much work in progress and, in many cases, real results are a long way away. It is hard to be confident that the ambitious targets can be met. What we do know is that China is taking a leadership role in rolling out the production of sustainable fuels such as green hydrogen, using wind and solar, and downstream products such as green methanol. In China, there will be intense competition from different modes of transportation and industries for new sustainable fuels. It is likely that fuel-cell–propelled long-haul trucking will be realized in China in the short to medium term. The skills China develops in the production and distribution of green fuel and the vehicles themselves will no doubt give China a lead in global markets, just as its passenger EVs are achieving.

When it comes to new fuels for shipping and aviation, there is a strong will globally and in China to make the transition. But in those areas, it will take much longer for the new green era to arrive. The news about thorium-fueled MSRs for container ships may be the breakthrough the world has been looking for.

Notes

1 Matt McGrath, *Climate Change: China Aims for Carbon Neutrality by 2060*, on *BBC*, Sep 22, 2020.
2 *"Shisuwu" xiandai wuliu fazhan guihua (14th Five year Plan, Modern Logistics Development Plan)* issued by the State Council of PRC, Dec 15, 2022.
3 *Corporate Social Responsibility Report 2020*, Sinotrans, 2021.
4 *Corporate Social Responsibility Report 2020*, Sinotrans, 2021.
5 *2022 Annual Report Corporate Presentation*, Sinotrans, 2023.
6 Port Technology Team, *Cosco Aim to be Carbon Neutral by 2060*, on *Port Technology International*, Apr 28, 2022.
7 *Environmental, Social & Governance Report 2002*, Cosco Shipping, 2023.
8 *Zero Carbon Future*, SF Express, 2023.
9 *A Look at UPS's Sustainability Action Plan*, UPS, July 28, 2022.

10 *2021 Sustainability Report*, A.P. Moller-Maersk, 2022.
11 Maria Smotrytska, *China's New "Green Policy" of Sustainable Mobility and Development*, on *Modern Diplomacy*, Feb 8, 2022.
12 Fan Feifei, *Self-Driving Trucks Posed to Overhaul Long-Haul Logistics*, on *China Daily*, Jan 4, 2023.
13 Timur Gül, *Global EV Outlook 2023. Catching Up with Climate Ambitions*, The International Energy Agency, 2023.
14 Daan Walter, Kingsmill Bond, Sam Butler-Sloss, Laurens Speelman, Yuki Numata and Will Atkinson, *X-Chang: Batteries. The battery Domino Effect*, on *RMI (Rocky Mountain Institute)*, Dec, 2023.
15 Timur Gül, *Global EV Outlook 2023. Catching Up with Climate Ambitions*, The International Energy Agency, 2023.
16 Ma Jizhao, *Chinese Electric Heavy Trucks Makers Launch New Longer-Range Vehicles*, on *Yicai*, June 6, 2023.
17 *China Sets Green Hydrogen Target for 2025, To Produce Up to 200K Tonnes Per Year of Green Hydrogen*, on *Hydrogen Central*, Mar 23, 2022.
18 Rachel Parkes, *World's Largest Green Hydrogen Project Now under Construction in China, Replacing Coals-Based H₂*, on *Hydrogen Insight*, Feb 20, 2023.
19 Alan Kirk, *Hydrogen Fuels a Revolution in China Trucking*, on *Asia Times*, Mar 29, 2021.
20 Logan King, *Bosch: A Contract in China for a Fleet of Hydrogen Truck*, on *hyrodrogentoday.info*, July 11, 2023.
21 *Qingling-Bosch Hydrogen Powered Truck Completes It First Trial Operation*, on *China Truck*, Oct 13, 2021.
22 Carrie Hampel, *Sinotruck & Weichai Power Take Orders for 1,100 FCEVs in China*, on *Electrive*, Sep 19, 2022.
23 Jackie Northam, *Shipping Industry Is Pressured to Cut Pollution Caused by Merchant Fleet*, on *NPR*, Dec 1, 2021.
24 *Revised GHG Reduction Strategy for Global Shipping Adopted*, issued by International Maritime Organization, July 7, 2023.
25 *Fit for 55: Deal as on New Eu Riles for Cleaner Maritime Fuel*, statement by European Parliament, Mar 23, 2023.
26 *Shipping CEOs Join Forces to Accelerate the Decarbonization of the Global Maritime Transport*, issued by MSC Line, Dec 1, 2023.
27 Peter Jameson, Camille Egloff, Ulrik Sanders, Mikkel Krogsgaard, Dustin Burke, Michael Tan, Eshen Hegnsholt, Erik Nyheim, *Global Shipping's Net-Zero Transformation Challenge*, Boston Consulting Group, Sep 24, 2021.
28 *COSCO Orders 12 Ultra-Large Green Methanol Containerships for $2.9BN*, on *The Maritime Executive*, Oct 28, 2022.
29 Confidential interview by Paul G.; Clifford with shipping expert, London, Feb 5, 2024.
30 Peter Jameson, Camille Egloff, Ulrik Sanders, Mikkel Krogsgaard, Dustin Burke, Michael Tan, Eshen Hegnsholt, Erik Nyheim, *Global Shipping's Net-Zero Transformation Challenge*, Boston Consulting Group, Sep 24, 2021.
31 Plamena Tisheva, *Orsted to Develop Big Power-to-X Project in US to Supply E-methanol to Maersk*, on *Renewables News*, Mar 10, 2022.
32 Leigh Collins, *China's Largest Green Hydrogen Project – a $4bn, 640 MW Ammonia/Methanol Facility - Begins Construction*, on *Hydrogeninsight*, Sep 28, 2023.
33 *China's SPIC Plans $5.9 Billion Investment Turning Green Hydrogen into Fuel*, on *Reuters*, Dec 11, 2023.

34 Can Emir, *China Has Revealed the 'World's Largest' Nuclear-Powered Container-ship*, on *Interesting Engineering*, Dec 27, 2023.

35 Aurora Almendral, *Shipping Giant Maersk's Shift into Airfreight Is Undermining Its Green Ambitions*, on *Quartz*, Nov 5, 2021.

36 *Working to Build a Net-Zero Sustainable Aviation System by 2050*, issued by Federation Aviation Authority, Dec 13, 2023.

37 Aurora Almendral, *Shipping Giant Maersk's Shift into Airfreight Is Undermining Its Green Ambitions*, on *Quartz,* Nov 5, 2021.

Chapter 9

Logistics as a lifeline

COVID-19 and other natural disasters

COVID-19 and China's logistics – a positive yet untold story

As the initial COVID-19 outbreak epicenter, China's logistics networks endured immense pressures yet also led to responsive solutions helping stabilize worldwide supply chains. China's pandemic timeline and policy approaches differed considerably from that of other nations, which suffered from complicated impacts on global shipping. We shall see that in many ways, despite the enormous global supply chain disruptions during the COVID time frame, China's logistics system – particularly the efficiency and resiliency of its ports – acted as a stabilizing force and as a lifeline for the global logistics network.

COVID-19: High-Level Timeline and Global Responses. The early months of 2020 marked a turbulent period for China's logistics networks. As the initial epicenter of the outbreak, China implemented the world's swiftest and most aggressive virus containment measures and lockdowns which also coincided with customary Lunar New Year factory closures.

These necessary actions caused significant ripples for supply chains dependent on China's production. The impacts quickly spilled over globally as manufacturing productivity and exports plummeted even more than normal for the New Year. As China brought the outbreak under control domestically and restarted its economy, other nations began to face surging COVID cases. Countries across North America, South America, Europe, Africa, and elsewhere experienced waves of lockdowns, travel limits, quarantines, and other infection-control policies that echoed many of China's initial policy responses. In these countries, factory productivity declined, and ports and other logistics services faced worker shortages.

As the waves of COVID-induced disruption shifted from a supply-side issue in Asia to a demand-side issue in the Americas and Europe, nearly everyone was anticipating a catastrophic and long-lasting collapse in demand for global transportation, similar to the experience with the SARS pandemic in 2003, but at a much larger scale and scope. Demand for both ocean and airfreight plummeted

DOI: 10.4324/9781003489115-12

as US imports from China tumbled 31.4% in February 2020 with Chinese factories closed and ports operating at lower capacities. The World Container Index slumped 15% from late February to late March 2020 and manufacturing productivity hit all-time lows, with China's manufacturing Purchasing Manager's Index (PMI) falling to 35.7 in February 2020 from 50.0 in January.[1]

However, this collapse in demand was short-lived, and in late 2020, the combination of rebounding demand for ocean and airfreight along with the new COVID-induced capacity constraints to each of these global supply chains set the stage for global supply chain chaos with China playing a role in shielding the global logistics networks from catastrophic failure.

Focus on Ocean Freight. The demand for ocean freight in and out of China in terms of Twenty-foot Equivalent Unit (TEU) volume fell rapidly in he first two quarters of 2020. Ocean carriers reacted to these volume declines by reducing capacity through "blanked sailings" (that is with skipped ports). Globally, ocean container carriers reduced the total number of port calls by 5.8% in Q2, although this decline was only 1.9% of East Asia ports which consist primarily of Chinese ports.[2] These blanked sailings took capacity out of the market in order to match supply with decreased demand and thereby keep ocean freight rates stable.

In the latter half of 2020, consumers in Europe and North America increased their spending on goods, driven by two key factors. First, governments provided fiscal transfers to consumers, boosting their purchasing power. Second, lockdowns around the world prevented people from spending on services, leading to a shift in consumer spending toward products. This surge in demand for consumer products, predominantly manufactured in China, led to a substantial increase in cargo demand. In fact, China saw its port vessel calls increase in 2020 by 2.1%[3] and for the full year 2020, the number of containers handled by China's ports actually increased 1.2% over 2019[4] despite a contraction in Q1 and Q2.

With demand for ocean shipping from China to the rest of the world growing again in late 2020 and accelerating into 2021, the global supply chain had a new challenge to contend with – port congestion driven by impacts from COVID. While both Chinese and destination ports suffered from congestion, their causes and the magnitude of their impacts varied tremendously. As we shall see, the Chinese ports typically had short acute bouts of congestion that were cleared quickly with the resumption of normal service. Whereas the congestion in destination ports in the US and Europe built over time until a combination of factors overwhelmed these ports and kept them gridlocked for the duration of the pandemic.

The largest ports in China – Shanghai, Ningbo, and Yantian – did indeed suffer from congestion and vessel delays due to COVID. In fact, the impact of the lockdowns on these ports was much more severe than that of the lockdowns in the US or Europe on their port operations. However, the Chinese ports were able to quickly resume normal operations and clear the backlog of containers thereby causing only temporary disruptions to the global logistics network.[5] As an example, in April 2022, the port of Shanghai deployed over 20,000 staff in a "closed loop management" structure so they could operate without risk of port shut-down during the two-month Shanghai-wide lockdown.[6]

By contrast, the ports in the US began to develop congestion in late 2020 which remained high until the Q3 of 2021 when it skyrocketed. In fact, but the end of 2021, vessels were sitting far offshore as berthing delays stretched into weeks.[7] A headline describes the situation as "the floating traffic jam that freaked us out," referring to how in October 2021 "more than 50 enormous vessels bobbed" at anchor, "marooned off the twin ports of Los Angeles and Long Beach" (California).[8] Although the number of vessels waiting outside these ports did begin to decline in early 2022, the ports remain congested and the ports on the east coast of the US, mainly Savannah and New York, saw commensurate increases in vessels waiting.[9]

While ports were congested in the US, Europe, and Asia, the ports in East Asia (mainly in China) exceeded 50% terminal congestion for only two weeks throughout the entire COVID crisis. Meanwhile, ports in Europe breached the 50% threshold in early 2021 and peaked at over 90% congested, and the North American ports (mainly in the US) crossed 50% in the 2nd half of 2021 and peaked at 80% congestion.[10]

In early 2022, when congestion was near its peak, analysis from freight forwarder Kuehne + Nagel indicated 80% of shipping delays were concentrated at American ports rather than in China.[11] Although Chinese ports did have a large number of vessels waiting at port at any time, the majority of these ships were small feeder vessels and the average waiting time was often 1-3 days, whereas the US had very large vessels waiting 7-12 days for Los Angeles, Long Beach and 6-7 days for Savannah.[12]

In addition, China created a control center to implement improvements in its customs clearance processes to minimize delays for both exports and imports. For example, for exports, China customs implemented a no-stop, no-check, toll-free policy for vehicles transporting emergency supplies. For imports, China Customs updated policies for faster clearance, minimum-interference customs control, certification services, and market access processes. Both export and import customs offices operated 24 hours per day seven days per week.[13]

In the second half of 2022, two new dynamics began to untangle the congested global ocean freight logistics network. First, demand for consumer and industrial goods leveled off and then began to decline back toward pre-COVID levels. The resulting reduction in container volumes allowed the ports to work their way out of their congestion issues by early 2023. In addition, carriers began taking delivery of large new containerships that they had ordered in the earlier phases of the COVID crisis. This additional capacity, along with softening demand rebalanced the supply-demand structure and brought ocean freight rates back toward pre-COVID levels by the end of 2022.

While congestion impacted both Chinese ports and destination ports, the resilience of the Chinese ports ensured that the global supply chain disruption did not develop into a full-blown supply chain catastrophe.

Focus on Air Freight. When COVID-19 emerged on the global stage in early 2020, a surge in demand for Personal Protective Equipment (PPE) became urgent. Most of this vital equipment, including ventilators, originated from China, sparking an unprecedented demand for airfreight services to ship these critical supplies worldwide.

Unfortunately, this surge in demand coincided with a dramatic reduction in available airfreight capacity. Traditionally, approximately 50% of long-haul airfreight capacity was provided in the cargo holds of wide-body passenger aircraft.[14] However, due to the global response to COVID-19, which included travel restrictions, particularly concerning China and travelers from China, many airlines were forced to significantly reduce or entirely cancel their long-haul passenger flights.

This had a knock-on effect as the belly space in these passenger aircraft, which was essential for air cargo, was suddenly unavailable. The removal of nearly half of the air cargo capacity from the market created an acute capacity crunch. Rates soared, reaching anywhere from three to four times the normal transportation rates overnight. Even for companies willing to pay these exorbitant rates, securing air cargo capacity was not guaranteed, leaving many shippers struggling to find space for their shipments.[15]

To address this challenge, some airlines ran passenger aircraft without passengers simply to provide much-needed belly capacity, particularly to transport PPE. Some airlines even converted their passenger aircraft into makeshift cargo carriers, known as passenger-freighters or p-freighters.[16] While these options provided some additional capacity to the market, they came at a significantly higher operating cost. While these approaches helped during the early stages of the pandemic when the demand for PPE was at its peak, they were not a sustainable long-term solution.

As the year progressed and the demand for PPE shipments by airfreight diminished, countries were able to stock up on their inventories and transition new orders to ocean freight. However, the situation did not fully return to normal as consumer demand in the US and Europe picked up in late 2020, keeping heavy pressure on diminished airfreight capacity as the belly space in passenger aircraft remained unavailable.

Throughout 2021 and into 2022, this dynamic persisted. Demand for airfreight surpassed historical levels due to heightened consumer spending on products, while capacity remained constrained, with freighters serving as the primary source of air cargo capacity. Long-haul passenger flights had not yet fully returned to the market.

As the world gradually reopened, the two factors that had driven the high demand and prices in airfreight began to subside. Firstly, consumers shifted their spending from products back to services, moderating the demand for Chinese exports. Secondly, airlines reintroduced some passenger capacity back into the market, as people regained interest in traveling. Over time, many long-haul wide-body passenger planes returned to service, providing belly cargo space that had been scarce during the height of the COVID crisis.[17]

Toward the end of the COVID era, airfreight rates had stabilized, trending back toward 2019 levels. However, the dynamic was somewhat different than it was in 2019. Although many long-haul passenger flights returned to the market, they had not yet reached their 2019 levels. This discrepancy has been particularly noticeable in long-haul passenger flights between China and the US, which remain significantly lower than pre-pandemic levels.

Throughout the COVID-19 pandemic, the Chinese aviation sector in concert with international providers of air freighter services kept the world supplied with the goods that they needed, albeit at much higher freight rates than normal. And once again, China air exports led the way in the recovery in 2023 with volumes strongly growing year-over-year compared with the rest of the world.[18]

Other natural disasters

On May 12, 2008, a massive 8.0 magnitude earthquake hit Wenchuan and surrounding areas in China's Sichuan Province, killing 69,000 and injuring 374,000. A further 17,000 remained missing. 15 MM people were displaced and a total of 46 MM affected. It brought down complete mountainsides, with farmer's homes crushed by huge boulders. Along river valleys, roads were obliterated, with the occasional truck protruding from the rocks. The terrain was mountainous with many Tibetan and Qiang minorities in the higher areas cut off from the medical services located in the valley floor.[19] Aftershocks brought further landslides and death to the residents and those organizing the rescue. 34,000 km of highways were destroyed. Roads and telecommunications were cut.

After some initial delays, help poured in. On the superhighways, there were never-ending columns of military vehicles bringing in troops and supplies. Military helicopters were deployed to get access to the remotest villages. As the days and weeks passed, so the mission moved from search and rescue to relief and rebuild. In a way that few other countries are able to, China mobilized the whole nation to help. 19 of China's provinces in East and Central China were each allocated, matched up with, one of the 18 "affected" counties in Sichuan, where they deployed rescue crews, medics, psychologists, construction firms, building materials suppliers – and the logistics to support all this. Once China had made an initial need assessment, it quickly welcomed international assistance with material and experts being flown in from all over the world, including from Taiwan.

In the four years after the earthquake, RMB 146 BN was invested in reconstruction, involving whole new towns. The World Bank observed: "One of the most astonishing aspects is the speed and efficiency with which the Chinese government was able to mobilize government agencies, the private sector and the population at large."[20] Research comparing the "humanitarian aid logistics" after the 2008 Wenchuan earthquake with that after the Haiti earthquake (2010, 250,000 dead) shows that China's performance was far superior to that of Haiti.[21] However, given our knowledge of Haiti's governance (or lack of it), this may not come as a surprise. There is a sizable body of Chinese academic articles addressing ways to analyze the experience from the handling of emergencies. Its economists are actively learning from the 2008 earthquake in order to "improve the emergency relief," for instance with respect to optimization the location of warehousing and the allocation of relief supplies.[22]

Earlier in 2008 China had already suffered a brutal series of heavy snowstorms that swept across central and south China, for which it was acutely unprepared. Over 200,000 homes were destroyed by the weight of the snow. Roads and railways and electricity were disrupted. More recently, the tally of natural disasters continues. In 2020 alone, 138 MM Chinese or about one-tenth of the population were affected by natural disasters with a direct economic cost of RMB 370 BN.[23] In the Summer of that year, unusually heavy rains, which are likely related to climate change, created disastrous floods across central and Southern China, affecting 63 MM people. In 2021, severe flooding hit Henan province, devastating its capital city Zhengzhou. In 2022, Southern provinces Guangdong, Guangxi, and Fujian suffered their heaviest rainfall since 1961, resulting in landslides and flooding. In late 2023, North and Northeast China suffered heavy snow and record-breaking temperatures of low as minus 47 °C, forcing the authorities to implement emergency relief measures. These increasingly severe natural disasters are putting pressure on the government to constantly improve both their forecasting and their rapid emergency response logistics.

Notes

1 Monique Giese, *Troubled Waters for the Shipping Sector*, KPMG, June 22, 2020.
2 Athanasios A. Pallis, *COVID-19 and Maritime Transport: Impact and Responses*, UNCTAD, Mar 23, 2021.
3 *COVID-19 and Maritime Transport: Navigating the Crisis and Lessons Learned*, UNCTAD, June 15, 2022.
4 *Statistical Communiqué of the People's Republic of China on the 2020 National Economic and Social Development*, National Bureau of Statistics of China, Feb 28, 2021.
5 Greg Miller, *Shanghai Lockdown Is Not Causing Global Supply Chain Chaos (Yet)*, on *Freightwaves*, Apr 21, 2022.
6 GT staff reporters, *Shanghai Port Sees 80% Recovery in Container throughput Despite Epidemic Drag; Port Efficiency Edges over US*, on *Global Times*, May 16, 2022.
7 Greg Miller, *Only 8 Ships Waiting Off Southern California — But 41 off Savannah*, on *Splash247*, Aug 30, 2022.
8 Peter S. Goodman, *The Floating Traffic Jam That Freaked Us Out*, in *New York Times*, June 2, 2024.

9 Peter S. Goodman, *The Floating Traffic Jam That Freaked Us Out*, in *New York Times*, June 2, 2024.

10 *Sea-Intelligence Spotlight*, issue 558, Apr 4, 2022.

11 Just2bruce, *New TEU Waiting Days Indicator Highlights the Severity of Global Container Congestion*, on *Splash247*, Jan 20, 2022.

12 Gill Plimmer and Harry Dempsey, *The Waiting Game: Where Are the World's Worst Port Delays?*, on *Financial Times*, Oct 15, 2021.

13 *COVID-19 and Maritime Transport: Navigating the Crisis and Lessons Learned*, UNCTAD, June 15, 2022.

14 Flexport Editorial Team, *A Perfect Storm: How the Impact of COVID-19 Has Driven Airfreight to Historic Levels*, on *Flexport*, Apr 17, 2020.

15 Katherine Barrios, *The Effects of Coronavirus on Air Cargo*, on *Xeneta*, Feb 14, 2020.

16 *COVID-19 and Its Impact on the Air Freight Shipping Industry*, on *Conqueror Freight Network*, June 4, 2020.

17 *The Current State of Air Cargo Capacity*, on *Accenture*, Nov 13, 2023.

18 *WorldACD China Special Report: Directional Rebalance*, on *World ACD*, Dec 15, 2023.

19 Co-author Paul G. Clifford was a member of Cisco System's Wenchuan Earthquake Committee and worked in the affected areas to bring remote medical and education networks.

20 Vivian Argueta and Paul Procee, *Four years On: What China Got Right When Rebuilding after the Sichuan Earthquake*, on *World Bank Blogs*, May 11, 2012.

21 Anthony Beresford and Stephen Pettit, *Humanitarian Aid Logistics: The Wenchuan and Haiti Earthquakes Compared*, in *Relief Supply Chain Management for Disasters: Humanitarian Aid and Emergency Logistics*, in Gyöngyi Kovács, Karen M. Spens, Ed: *Relief Supply China Management for Disasters: Humanitarian Aid and Emergency Logistics*, Published by Information Science Reference, 2012, pp. 45–67.

22 Jiaxin Geng, Hanping Hou, and Shaoqing Geng , *Optimization of Warehouse Location and Supplies Allocation for Emergency Rescue under Joint Government-Enterprise Cooperation Considering Disaster Victims' Distress Perception*, (Beijing Jiaotong University), published on *Sustainability*, Sep 23, 2021.

23 Jiaxin Geng, Hanping Hou, and Shaoqing Geng, *Optimization of Warehouse Location and Supplies Allocation for Emergency Rescue under Joint Government-Enterprise Cooperation Considering Disaster Victims' Distress Perception*, (Beijing Jiaotong University), published on *Sustainability*, Sep 23, 2021.

Chapter 10

The global footprint

The Belt and Road, ports, and air cargo

The Belt and Road Initiative

China's Belt and Road Initiative (BRI) means different things to different people and provokes a wide range of reactions. For some, including us, it is primarily an international expression of China's economic rise, while for others, it is perceived as China's neo-imperialist program. But when we bore down to a more practical level, we find that logistics is a critical element to the BRI as it enables and enhances its fundamental flows of trade and investment.

The BRI, also known within China as One Belt and One Road (OBOR) (*yidai yilu*), takes its name from recent efforts to revitalize the ancient trade routes from China on land across central Asia (The Silk Road) and by sea through the Indo-Pacific. It has become China's official mode of engagement not only with Asia and Africa but also with Latin America (Argentina for instance), the Caribbean, and Europe into the Balkans. Although Xi Jinping is given credit for coining the term BRI in 2013, its origins are to be found in the earlier policy of encouraging China firms to "go out" or "go out into the world." Currently, 151 nations are affiliated with the BRI through Memoranda of Understanding with China. A further eight are considering joining.

There are indeed distinct political dimensions of the BRI as a vehicle for projecting China's geopolitical power and influence globally. But there is an essential core dimension to it related to economic and business-driven goals. The BRI's fundamental nature is as an international expression of China's industrial and technological rise.

From the outset, one element of the BRI has been China's goal of locking in supplies of strategic minerals through the investment in resources such as bauxite and lithium, and with that trade flows back to China. With regard to trade flows from China, the BRI has also served as an export outlet for areas of primary industry and consumer goods manufacturing where an unbalanced development surge created domestic overcapacity. But today, it has far transcended that role.

China is exporting the engineering skills that it has developed and fine-tuned through its own massive domestic infrastructure upgrade program. These skills

DOI: 10.4324/9781003489115-13

range from the construction of airports, railways, ports roads, bridges to cellular network infrastructure. Beyond the project construction stage, China is also exporting management skills, for instance in running ports such as at Piraeus in Greece, which we discuss below. China is making direct investments along the path of the BRI in manufacturing industry such as electric vehicles in South Africa and mobile phones in Ethiopia.

At the heart of the BRI's trade, construction, and direct investment lies intense logistics activity. When Xi Jinping talks about the BRI, he constantly refers to "connectivity," or goods flow, transportation, and logistics. In a major speech in 2017, he stated, with regard to the BRI, that:

> Infrastructure connectivity is the foundation of development through coop- eration. We should promote land, maritime, air and cyberspace cooperation, concentrate our efforts on key passageways, cities and projects, and connect networks of highways, railways, and sea ports…We should improve transre- gional logistics networks…[1]

But not all is well in the BRI. There is evidence that it may have become overex- tended and that it is coming under severe financial stress. One Chinese firm that ventured into diamond mining in Zimbabwe was kicked out of that country with the result that it defaulted on the bonds that it had used to finance its big push.[2] Chinese banks have become much chastened by the fact that they loaded up BRI host countries, such as Laos, Sri Lanka, and Zambia, with debt that cannot be easily repaid. Faced with this reality, China recently declined to provide financ- ing for a Chinese railway project in Uganda with the result that the project was transferred to a Turkish firm. There is international pressure on China to speed up its efforts at loan restructuring and debt relief.[3]

About a decade ago, analysts were quite bullish about the BRI. The World Bank predicted that the BRI would increase trade flows, cut the costs of global trade, and add to the GDP of participating nations.[4] The mood has changed. But despite global concerns over the BRI and China's own reevaluation of cer- tain aspects of this program, it still remains a core element of China's foreign trade and investment, central to the nation's interests whether commercial or geopolitical. On the trade front, it also presents a useful hedge against Western de-coupling and a decline in China's earlier role as the "factory of the world."

In light of the headwinds the BRI is facing in Africa and elsewhere, China recently put greater emphasis on the BRI in Southeast Asia. In 2020, China led the formation of the Regional Comprehensive Economic Partnership (RCEP) which is the world's largest free trade area. It includes the nations of the Asso- ciation of Southeast Asian Nations (ASEAN) as well as China, Japan, South Korea, and others. It is quintessentially a trade agreement between countries many of which have different and often conflicting political systems and agendas. Within ASEAN, Laos and Cambodia are extremely close to China, one might even say client-states, dependent on China for their financial and economic sustenance. Below, we document the freight rail links between China's Kunming into Laos and Thailand. But even Vietnam, which for good historical reasons, remains cautious about too close an embrace with Beijing, enjoys, under the RCEP, growing trade and investment links with China, even while cozying up to the US. China's logistics industry looks set to play a key role in the S.E. Asia dimension of the BRI.

China has recently stepped up its efforts to give the appearance that the BRI is an equal partnership with the participating nations, a "win-win." There is undoubtably strong evidence that China's aid has a positive impact on the host nations, whether it is with railway and port construction in East Africa, or creating the mobile telephone infrastructure which can bridge the urban-rural digital divide, for example in Angola. But BRI was initiated by China, serves China's commercial and political goals, and most critically is financed by China. Though China is today more prudent about the credit risk they take on as they lend to projects in the participating countries, there remains an array of funding sources. This includes the Asia Infrastructure Investment Bank (in which China has a large role), China's US$ 40 BN Silk Road Fund, its sovereign wealth fund (China Investment Corporation), China Development Bank (loans beyond five years), China Export-Import Bank (low-interest concessionary loans), and its state commercial banks.

Xi Jinping defined BRI "connectivity" in terms of a series of transportation corridors. Each one involves investment in infrastructure, by land, sea, and air, and developing logistics businesses that can enhance the efficiency of the flow of goods across it.

The 21st Century Maritime Silk Road (*21 shiji haishang sichou zhi lu*) is a term first coined by Xi Jinping in October 2013. It is also referred to as the Belt as in OBOR. This Indo-Pacific sea corridor, which was first in use around 200 BCE, today goes South to Singapore and Indonesia then north to Thailand, Sri Lanka, Pakistan, and East Africa and then up to Djibouti and the Red Sea and through the Suez Canal to the Mediterranean and Europe. Along the Belt are a series of deepwater ports where China has a presence and is creating logistics hubs such as in Myanmar, Pakistan (linking to a land corridor from Xinjiang in Western China), Sri Lanka, Djibouti, and Greece (Pireaus). Goods are carried by both Chinese and foreign shipping (container ships, bulk carriers, tankers, and general cargo vessels). From the Southern Europe hub at the port of Piraeus (Greece) and the Central and Eastern European hub in Trieste (Italy), there are rail links into all parts of Europe. The port of Valencia in Spain is also doing its best to attract Chinese business. As we discuss later, China's firms are also investing heavily in ports in Northern Europe, for example in Hamburg.

With regard to the *BRI's ground transportation*, be it by road or by rail, the reference to the ancient Silk Road is really shorthand for a series of modern-age land bridges, mostly between China and Europe. Although six transportation corridors were envisaged initially, today at least 35 have been designated as such. Below, we examine some of the most consequential.

Two factors make some of these corridors complicated. The first is Russia's invasion of Ukraine, which has put pressure on finding routes that do not pass through Russia. German automakers are said to have stopped moving components and parts to China by rail. Logistics providers such as Maersk and DHL have also avoided rail through Russia. Some logistics providers are offering war insurance to their customers, as a way to allay concerns.[5] The second is the fact that in the railways in Russia, in the countries which were part of former Soviet Union (such as Kazakhstan and Belarus) and former client states (such as Mongolia) have a gauge of 1,520 MM which is wider than the standard gauge of 1,235 MM elsewhere in the world, thus requiring the transfer of goods/containers from one railcar to another.

China-Mongolia-Russia Economic Corridor. Agreed to by the three countries in 2016, this corridor is in the process of being built on the basis of two rail routes out of China. This corridor has been important for the increased China-Russia trade since the Ukraine War began. One route is from the Beijing/Hebei region across Inner Mongolia, to Mongolia, and into Russia's Siberia. The second takes a more northerly route from Harbin in Heilongjiang, through Inner Mongolia to Manzhouli and into Siberia. Both of the routes involve transferring the goods on-and-off different gauges. These routes from China connect into the Eurasian Land Bridge, which provides rail links from the Russia Far East through to Europe. Inevitably, the Ukraine war has deterred foreign shippers from relying on these routes. This loss of traffic volume may have in part been offset by the increased China-Russia trade in the wake of the Ukraine war.

The New Eurasian Land Bridge is a new corridor, which takes a more southern route, traveling through China's Xinjiang to the Kazakhstan border at Khorgos and at Dostyk (across the border from China's Alashankou). Khorgos, which has two parts one in China and one in Kazakhstan, is hailed as the largest "dry port" in the world. Given the change in rail gauge, cranes lift the containers onto new wagons. The line passes on to Western Russia and to Belarus, where cranes are again deployed to move the containers onto Polish wagons. While global shippers are rerouting away from this route due to the Ukraine conflict, it is likely that the reduction in traffic, as with other routes mentioned above, may in part be compensated for by the recent increase in China-Russia trade.

The *China-Central Asia-West Asia Economic Corridor (CCAEC)* links China with Turkey. It has the benefit of not entering Russia. It passes through Almaty in Kazakhstan and onto Turkmenistan on the shores of the Caspian Sea. There is talk of China building a bridge over the Caspian. But for now, by land, there is no alternative to going North through Russia or through Iran to the South. So far, the solution has been to use ships to carry the containers across the Caspian to Baku in Azerbaijan, and then onward through Georgia to Turkey and the newly completed Marmaray Tunnel under the Bosporus and into Europe.

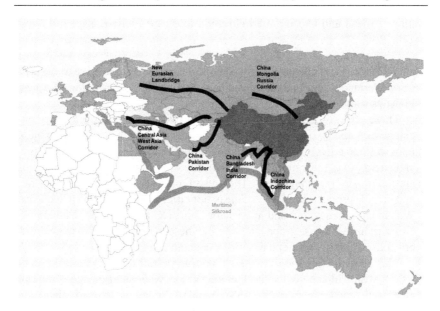

Figure 10.1 Trade flows and the BRI.

China is spending over US$ 60 BN to construct the *China-Pakistan Economic Corridor (CPEC)*. It entails a massive overhaul of Pakistan's infrastructure, in power generation, rail, roads, and ports. The new port being built by China in Gwadar will be connected to Kashgar in China's Xinjiang region by an upgraded Karakoram highway and ultimately by a new rail link. The CPEC is viewed as valuable since it can provide an alternative route for oil to be transported into China, thus mitigating the risk that hostile powers might apply a chokehold in the Straits of Malacca.

The 1,035-km *China-Laos Railway*, linking Kunming in China with Vientiane in Laos, was opened in late 2021. Laotian exports to China have included fruit and rubber.[6] In 2022, regular cargo trains began services from Chongqing to Vientiane, halving the former travel time and cutting the costs by two-thirds. Then in late 2023, the "New land-Sea corridor," linking Thailand and China via Laos by rail, was inaugurated. Freight trains have been launched linking Rayong (on the Gulf of Thailand) to Chengdu in China and Nong Khai (just across the Mekong River from Laos) to Chongqing. The trains carry frozen seafood and fresh fruit such as durians into China and industrial products (such as sodium sulfate) back to Thailand. The goods from SE Asia also find their way by the China-Europe rail links to Russia, Poland, and Germany.[7]

How local government took the lead on China-Europe rail freight. Local city governments in central and Western China, driven by the desire to foster local economic development, create jobs, and generate fiscal revenues, initiated and continue to lead and execute the bold trend to create China-Europe rail hubs, revealing;

> a reincarnated and enlarged role of the local Chinese state relative to the central government and market mechanism leading to the formation of a new logistics state.[8]

These city government efforts are supported by their respective provincial government and also by central government (which has invested in these hubs in three cities). But it is local government that demonstrated the vision and energy to get this moving. The majority of the large China-Europe hubs are intermodal (containerized). They also typically go beyond just logistics and include production bases. All the major cities in central China (Changsha, Wuhan and Zhengzhou) and in Western China (Xi'an, Chengdu, Chongqing, Urumqi) have China-Europe rail hubs and these in turn are linked to the Eastern coastal cities. This trend has major economic significance.

This spatial expression (of the China-Europe rail hubs) is logically consistent with China's goal of accelerating the development of major interior cities and enhancing their roles in stimulating the less developed inland and border regions.[9]

A powerful example of this trend is the role played by the government of Xi'an, a city in Northwest China with a population of 13 MM and the capital of Shaanxi Province. In ancient times, then called Chang'an, it has been capital of Tang Dynasty (618–907 AD) and served as the key Chinese entry point into the Silk Road along which goods passed on their way to central Asia and beyond. So, it was fitting that Xi'an would seek to re-create that pivotal logistics role through the China-Europe rail routes. With strong support from the provincial government, Xi'an city government established a new entity which not only built and now operates a logistics park covering 120 km² with space for private companies and bonded warehousing but also runs China-Europe freight trains. The location of the logistics park outside the crowded old city of Xi'an has permitted the emergence of production facilities in addition to the storage and transportation. Xi'an has become China's largest China-Europe rail hub, outpacing other cities out West such as Chengdu and Chongqing. Its freight trains head out on 15 rail routes across Russia and Central Asia to numerous cities in Europe such as Duisburg, Hamburg, Kuovola (in Finland), Riga, Budapest, Moscow, and Istanbul. On these rail routes, the Xi'an government works closely with the central government China Rail Express which controls the rail infrastructure and with foreign firms such as DHL, Deutsche Bahn, and Nippon Express which place orders for space on the trains. It has forged links with coastal cities such as Shanghai, Xiamen, Lianyungang, Ningbo, and Qingdao, so that containerized cargo, including from South Korea and Japan, can travel from seaports into Xi'an and on to Europe.[10]

The businesses running the international rail links. Above we highlighted some of the main rail corridors that have been developed as part of the BRI. Here, we provide examples of how businesses are taking advantage of this new infrastructure.

The choice of whether to put goods on a train from China to Europe rather than on a ship or aircraft has to do with a variety of factors: the time sensitivity, the cost, and the cost in proportion to the value of the product. The rail transit time from China to Europe (even including the issues with rail gauge or crossing the Caspian Sea by ship) is about half that by container ship. It may be two weeks compared to four weeks (Beijing-Duisburg, 10,300 km) or in the case of the Yiwu-London link, 20 days versus 40 days. The serious congestion at European container ports during the COVID-19 pandemic also highlighted the reliability of train links. But the cost/efficiency of the largest container ship with 24,000 TEUs compared to an Asia-Europe train with 40–100 40 ft containers is hard to challenge if time is not critical. But for some types of shipper and goods, the China-Europe rail links are competitive against sea and air. These links can be "green-friendly" since they are 95% less polluting than air cargo.

While sea freight still accounts for around 90% of China-Europe trade by weight and 60% by value, there is a trend toward China-Europe rail freight. This is in part because it is significant in strategic geopolitical terms. Firstly, it reduces China vulnerability to sea transportation. A Taiwan crisis would put at risk the shipping lanes that carry China's imports and exports. Further disruption could be exercised through the US and its allies using the chokeholds of the Straits of Hormuz (petroleum passing through the Persian Gulf) and the Straits of Malacca (between Indonesia and Malaysia). The enormity of this impact can be seen through projections that war over Taiwan would reduce global GDP by 10% or US$ 10 trillion, while something short of that, a blockade of Taiwan, would lop 5% off the world economy.[11] While the China-Europe rail routes can hardly fill the gap left by disrupted sea lanes, this nonetheless serves to highlight the important strategic and national security risk mitigation role that the land bridge plays for China. Secondly, it also fosters trade and investment with the nations along the routes of the rail corridors. While it is thought unlikely that the proportion of goods carried by rail between China and Europe can expand much beyond 2%–3% of the total volume, that is still part of a large pie and remains a fast-growing and significant business. Its origins can be found in JVs between Chinese, Russian and Kazakhstan government interests which in 2011 began to operate trains between China and Duisburg, called to Yu-Xin-Ou route, running from Chongqing to Kazakhstan, Russia, Belarus, Poland, and on to Germany. The number of trains in both directions between China and Europe on all routes grew from just 17 in 2011 to 15,183 in 2021, when they carried 1.46 MM TEUs. There are at least 73 routes linking 50 cities in China with 92 European cities in 21 countries plus a number of others in Central Asia.

As may be expected, the China State Railway Group Co. (China Rail) plays a central role in the China-Europe rail links, principally through its subsidiary China Railway Express (CRE) also known as China-Europe Railway Express. In establishing CRE, China's top planning group, National Development and Reform Commission (NDRC), and China Rail consciously set out to "create a well-known logistics brand with international competitiveness." CRE is billed as being 20% the cost of air cargo, and 25% faster than sea. Another explicit goal of the government for CRE is to reduce CO_2 emissions compared to air and road.[12]

From its establishment in 2011 to the end of 2022, CRE's accumulated China-Europe business was 65,000 trips, 6 MM TEUs, and freight worth US$ 300 MM. In 2022, the number of CREs freight trains passing along different routes in and out of China was as follows:

Alashankou (Kazakstan border) 6,211 freight trains
Korghos (straddles China's Xinjiang and Kazakhstan border) 7,068
Erenhot/Erlian (on China-Mongolia border) 2,477
Manzhouli (China/Inner Mongolia border with Russia) 4,818
Suifenhe (in China's Helongjiang Province, border with Russia) 884[13]

CRE offers full containers or LCL (Less-than-Container Load) service, plus refrigerated and open-top containers. It has 18 routes running on a weekly or monthly basis. The longest route is 13,052 km from Yiwu (known as the "World's Capital of Small Commodities" in Zhejiang) and Madrid, which takes 22 days. This route also has some of the longest trains, each carrying 82 40 ft containers, with a total length of 560 M. The trains on the other routes are mostly 40–46 40 ft containers in length.

Examining CRE's routes, we get some insight into the goods that are carried, for instance:

- Chongqing-Duisburg. To Europe: auto parts, mobile phones. From Europe: auto parts, red wine, cosmetics
- Chengdu-Lodz (Poland). From China: IT products from Sichuan and the Pearl River Region of South China
- Yiwu (Zhejiang)-Madrid. From China: small consumer products – toys, tools, home decorations, kitchen utensils, festive decorations, etc.
- Zhengzhou-Hamburg. From China: clothing, handbags, LED lights
- Suzhou-Warsaw. From China: laptops, tablets, LCD screens, hard drives, and semiconductors
- Wuhan-Czech Republic. From China: notebook computers made in Wuhan
- Baoding-Minsk (Belarus). From China: autos, clothing, and household appliances
- Xining (Qinghai)-Antwerp (Belgium). From China: Tibetan rugs and oysters
- Guangzhou-Moscow. From China: electronic products

- Qingdao-Moscow. From China: household appliances, rubber, and machinery
- Changchun (Jilin)-Hamburg. From China: auto parts and textiles.
- Chengdu-Vienna. From China: electronics, LED lights[14]
- Xi'an-Ghent (Belgium). From Chengdu in China: China-built Volvo XC60s, From Ghent to China: Belgium-built Volvo XC90 and V40 hatchbacks.

China's state-owned logistics firm Sinotrans plays an important role within the broader CRE picture. Through rail hubs in Guangzhou, Shenzhen, Dongguan, and Changsha and partnerships with local CRE entities, it operates a series of international rail routes. Their accumulated volume is 8,600 trains and I MM TEUs, of which China-Europe routes account for 7,300 trains and 830,00 TEUs. Sinotrans stated that in 2023, they delivered 17.6% of CREs China-Europe business. In 2021, they dispatched their first train from Changsha (Hunan) to Minsk (Belarus) loaded with over 700 tons of construction machinery parts (from Hunan firms such as Sany), textiles, and electronics.[15] Sinotrans has been an active participant in the China-Laos railway corridor, with a multimodal (truck to rail) route from Thailand to Laos and into China in Shenzhen.[16]

Foreign firms have been quick to enter this sector. Germany DB Cargo is aggressively addressing the opportunity. It has formed Trans-Eurasian Logistics with China's and Russia's railways to operate the China-Duisburg route. DB intends to expand their capacity on their routes (currently ten) from 200,000 TEUs to 500,000 TEUs per annum by 2025. Its major rail routes from China pass through Manzhouli to Siberia and into Kazakhstan (at both Khorgos and Dostyk/Alashankou).[17]

Finnish firm Nurminen Logistics has also pioneered China-Europe rail freight creating links between Helsinki (linking to Narvik in Norway) and multiple cities in China such as Suzhou, Hefei, and Chongqing. In May 2022, in response to the Soviet invasion of Ukraine, it launched a regular Trans-Caspian service between Chongqing and Helsinki which avoids Russia, Belarus, and Ukraine. For much of its route, this rail takes the path of the CCAEC mentioned above, including crossing the Caspian Sea. Later on, its route also crosses the Black Sea into Romania.[18]

The China-Laos Railway is proving to be a valuable linkage from Southeast Asia to the China-Europe land bridge. DB Schenker uses trucks to bring goods from Thailand, Myanmar, Malaysia, Vietnam, and Cambodia up to the rail head in Vientiane, from which the railway carries them to Kunming in China and onward into central Asia and to Europe. The railway to Kunming takes two to three days compared to five days by truck.[19]

Ports construction and management

At the heart of China's BRI is the deployment internationally of skills and knowledge developed and fine-tuned in the course of its breakneck development over the last four and a half decades. In this respect, seaport construction and operations stand out as hugely successful.

Many of China's ports were built by China Harbor Engineering Company (CHEC) the civil engineering giant that focuses on marine engineering, dredging, and land reclamation. CHEC, with an annual turnover of around US$ 30 BN, is now deploying its expertise globally, operating in 100 counties from Angola to Argentina, from Bangladesh to Cameroon. It has a US$ 880 MM contract for the new port in Doha, Qatar and a US$ 930 MM contract to upgrade Israel's second largest port, Ashdod.

China is also exporting the deep experience it has developed in managing ports. On the back of Israel's decision to privatize its ports, Shanghai International Port Group, which manages Shanghai Port, has a 25-year contract, which began in 2021, to operate the new Haifa port, Israel's largest.[20] Israel has worked hard to allay the concerns of the US which has a naval installation there.

China's shipping line COSCO operates Piraeus Port, the largest port in Greece and in the Eastern Mediterranean, through a 67% stake in the Port Authority, acquired after Greece privatized its ports. For COSCO, this is a key entry port into Southern Europe for goods it transports, such as white goods and electrical appliances from Haier and Hisense, two large-scale Chinese firms based in Qingdao, Shandong Province. COSCO is proud that an independent shipping index ranks Piraeus as 9th of the top ten ports in the world, just behind New York-Newark and Hamburg. (Shanghai was ranked third globally, ahead of Hong Kong, Dubai, and Rotterdam).[21] This ranking is based mainly on the quality of services provided but also takes into consideration the port's scale and throughput.[22] It is no exaggeration to say that so far China's operation of Piraeus has likely proved to be a boost to Greece's GDP and an excellent entry gate for Chinese goods. In 2019, Xi Jinping stated that the port was evidence that the Belt & Road Initiative is "not a slogan or a tale, but a successful practice and brilliant reality."[23]

However, COSCO's expansion of Piraeus port with a passenger terminal for cruise ships, and auto import terminal and new warehousing has been blocked by the Greek government after it was disclosed that COSCO had dumped dredged material into nearby fishing grounds. Despite this wrinkle, the Pireaus Port still looks like the kind of win-win that is often talked about but rarely achieved.

COSCO also has a controlling interest in ports at Zeebrugge and Valencia, plus minority holdings in seven other ports in Europe and the Middle East, such as Rotterdam, Antwerp, Genoa, and Port Said. COSCO's port acquisitions now include Hamburg. The mood in Europe recently turned more hostile toward China and the German government came under great pressure to halt this acquisition. In the end, the deal was pushed through since the German authorities are competing with Antwerp, Rotterdam, and Zeebrugge which all can handle the largest container ships and seek to be primary gateway for Chinese exports to Northern Europe. But the compromise was that COSCO holds only 24.99% stake in the Tollerort terminal in Hamburg Port, a stake less than the 35% it originally negotiated and under the 25% threshold when, under German law, a minority investor gains the ability to block resolutions. Moreover, this is only one of three terminals in Hamburg. COSCO has no operating control and the existing IT systems remain in place. Unlike in Piraeus, the Hamburg Port Authority remains firmly in the hands of the city government. There are clear benefits for both parties. Hamburg gets a leg up when it comes to increasing its goods flow, while COSCO has an assured "safe haven" for its container ships and a hedge against the kind of congestion that occurred during Covid-19.

The Chinese state-owned firm China Merchants has a controlling interest in a port in Sri Lanka and minority shares in seven ports such as Dunkirk, Marseilles, Istanbul, and Tanger. China's Qingdao Port has invested in Genoa. The Hong Kong-based firm Hutchison, which many consider now to be a proxy for China, has long been a major player in the world's ports including owning and running the Port of Felixstowe in the UK.

China's extensive network of port operations around the world attracts considerable controversy. Some point to those investments as a precursor to a chain of military bases or at minimum of heightened political influence. There are indeed examples of China's international port expansions that are troubling. In Sri Lanka, Chinese firms built this new port of Hambantota, which is second only to Colombo's port. To do this, Sri Lanka took on massive loans from China which it has found impossible to repay. The outcome is that China Merchants has obtained 70% of a joint venture that runs the ports and a 99-year operating lease. This may be the product of simple bad judgment by China or, as some like to portray it, cynical "debt-trap diplomacy." China Merchants is investing US$ 2 BN to develop this port into a logistics hub. The development includes an LPG and bunkering storage facility. The bunkering (fuel for ships) could be helpful to China in giving its navy extra reach.

Also raising concerns is China's involvement in developing Gwadar Port in Pakistan. In 2014, China launched its CPEC project, which allocated US$ 62 BN to link Kashgar in China's Xinjiang region, through the Karakoram Highway down to Pakistan and ultimately to Gwadar Port. Gwadar Port has three berths and one roll-on roll-off terminal (for autos). A Chinese firm, China Overseas Port Holding, was awarded a 40-year port operations contract. The port has also set up a Free Zone (tax-free area) covering over 2,000 acres. The Chinese operator is taking 91% and 85% of the gross revenues of the port and zone respectively, to recoup its investment.

So far, China has only one overseas military base, in Djibouti, which sits in a highly strategic location on the Horn of Africa, which guards vital sea routes and is useful as a place to combat the pirates and sea terrorists that plague that region. The US (with 4,000 troops), France, Italy, the UK, and Japan also have military bases there. But the China presence is broader. It built the US$ 3.4 BN railway that links land-locked Ethiopia's Addis Ababa with Djibouti's Doraleh port which is the largest deepwater port in East Africa. Djibouti then kicked Dubai-based port and logistics firm DP World out of the management of that container terminal and gave China Merchants a 23.5% stake to run it. DP World has alleged that the Chinese government pressured Djibouti to achieve this and the case is being litigated in Hong Kong. Early in 2023, it was announced that China is investing US\$ 1 BN in constructing a Spaceport in Djibouti.

Notwithstanding certain cases that reveal how China's geopolitical goals and even its military goals can be intertwined with the commercial aspects of China's international ports activity, the evidence points strongly to the fact that the commercial aspects dominate. This global reach through port construction and management is at heart an international expression of the skills China has fine-tuned during its economic reforms and domestic infrastructure makeover. The global network of ports that China is contributing to forms part of the sea passage of the BRI along which China's goods, services, skills, and investment are flowing from Asia to Africa, the Middle East, and to Europe. It is primarily market and trade-driven.

International airfreight

China's national logistics plan specifically highlights the "shortcomings" of the nation's international air logistics industry. China was late to enter this business and remains in catch-up mode.

When it came to international airfreight, it was China Eastern (partnering with shipping firm COSCO) that put its toe into the water in 1998, forming China Cargo Airlines. It initially had one fuel guzzling MD-11 freighter. The firm was headed up by a celebrated and feisty senior pilot from China Eastern. Shortly later, Air China formed its cargo subsidiary Air China Cargo followed by China Southern and later Hainan Airlines.

Two decades ago, these state-owned airlines wrestled with the economics of establishing freight-only routes using freight aircraft. Demand for the transportation of high-value goods was still nascent. They also had the alternative of using the belly cargo of their passenger planes, domestically and internationally. Today China Eastern, Air China, and China Southern still have the belly cargo capacity of their passenger fleets – today 600, 488 (plus 130 on order), and 640 passenger aircraft, respectively. In building their air cargo business, they also faced the issue that traditionally belly cargo has been something of an afterthought with scant thought to the pricing and service required. It took time for them to learn how to run a profitable air cargo business which was clearly differentiated from the core passenger business.

Today, strong demand for high-value air cargo has finally arrived. Products that are carried by air include food and perishables, apparel, pharma, consumer electronics, semiconductors, and livestock. To this, we can add the rapid growth of e-commerce. To address this burgeoning demand, China's large state-owned airlines have beefed up their international airfreight capability. Air China Cargo has two main hubs in Beijing and Pudong (Shanghai) with a fleet of fuel-efficient B777Fs and also some B747Fs, plus converted A330s on order. They have eight cargo flights to Europe a week, to places such as Amsterdam, Zaragoza, and Copenhagen, plus five flights per week to the US (Los Angeles, Chicago, and JFK). Alibaba's logistics firm Cainiao has taken an equity share in Air China Cargo, to help ensure access to international and domestic air cargo routes. China Southern has 17 B777Fs, operating from Pudong and Guangzhou to routes across the globe.

Hong Kong-based Cathay Pacific, now partly owned by Air China, has a strong history in air cargo, now delivered through its recently rebranded Cathay Cargo which has 20 B747 freighters and operates out its hub at Hong Kong airport. Cathay Cargo has pioneered ship-air intermodal transportation. In nearby Dongguan (on the Mainland), China's export goods are palletized and prepared for customs clearance and then air shipment, before being transported by water to the airport in Hong Kong. Cathay Cargo has also been granted certification to carry lithium batteries in special containers. They have experience in carrying live horses, given the importance of horse racing in Hong Kong.

Taiwan has direct air links to the Mainland and its two major airlines are players in air cargo. China Airlines has 21 air freighters (B 747s and 777s), while EVA has eight B777 aircraft with eight more on order.

A number of global purely air cargo firms fly into China. For instance, Atlas Air, the world's largest operator of B747 freighters provides wet leases (aircraft, crew, maintenance, and insurance) or dry leases (without crew members) to the Chinese e-commerce-focused firms SF Group and Cainiao. So, Atlas supplies the aircraft (and sometimes the crew) which are then operated by these Chinese firms under their own operating licenses and landing rights. Atlas's subsidiary Polar Air also has a large fleet of Boeing air freighters and flies to Shanghai. It provides services for a number of foreign logistics providers, such as DB Schenker, Expeditors, Kuehne + Nagel, as well as to DHL which has bought an equity share in the firm.

But, it is the three global so-called "integrators," (i.e. integrating pick-up and delivery with the air transport) UPS, FedEx, and DHL, which dominate air cargo and have developed a strong presence in China. Later in Chapter 14, we shall look at how DHL operates within the domestic China logistics market. Here, we confine ourselves to China's international air cargo business.

UPS, FedEx, and DHL have adopted a hub-and-spoke approach to air cargo. They each have one main global hub: UPS in Louisville (KY), FedEx in Memphis (TN), and DHL in Leipzig, (Germany). UPS has 200 flights to China weekly, into its Shenzhen and Shanghai hubs. Through a joint venture with China's SF Group (which we discuss later), it is providing SF with international air cargo routes. FedEx that has its Asia-Pacific hub in Guangzhou's Baiyun Airport and its North Asia hub in Shanghai has more than 300 flights from China weekly.

As is typical of these foreign air cargo carriers, FedEx has achieved access to China's domestic air cargo network through working with local Chinese airlines, such as the cargo arm of Okay Airways that has a fleet of B 737 freighters. DHL has its North Asia Hub in Shanghai and its Central Asia Hub in Hong Kong. It also has other air cargo "gateways" in China such as in Wuxi, Jiangsu which has a route to Leipzig.

The services provided by UPS and FedEx into China are delivered by their own aircraft fleet while DB and DHL operate through a mixture of their own fleet and of aircraft owned by airlines in which DHL has invested such as Aerologic (formerly with Lufthansa). What is striking about the air cargo fleets of these three integrators is that their early start in the business means that they have large a number of legacy aircraft such as MD-11s and B747s that are only gradually being replaced with more fuel-efficient B777 freighters.

As an indication of the importance of having one's own captive air transport capability amid strong demand for air cargo, German 3PL, and freight forwarder DB Schenker have leased air freighters that operate from Beijing, Shanghai, and Zhengzhou to Hong Kong and Chicago. As mentioned earlier, K+N has signed long-term charter agreements with Atlas.

Notes

1 Xi Jinping, *Work Together to Build the Belt & Road Initiative*, in Xi Jinping, *The Governance of China*, edited: State Council Information Office, publisher: Foreign Languages Press, Volume 2, 2017, p. 560.
2 Paul G. Clifford, *The China Paradox: At the Front Line of Economic Transformation*, De Gruyter, 2022, pp. 159–166.
3 Paul G. Clifford, *Making Sense of China's Belt & Road Initiative*, on *The Pacific*, Apr 26, 2023.
4 Norbert Meyring, *China's Belt+Road Initiative and the Global Chemical Industry*, in Reaction. Chemicals Magazine, on *KPMG's Insights*, 2019.
5 Ji Siqi, *What Is the China-Europe Railway Express, and How Much Pressure Is It under from the Ukraine crisis?*, on *South China Morning Post*, Mar 6, 2022.
6 Huaxia, *China-Laos Rail Freight Tranport Sees Significant Expansion in 2023*, Xinhua on *China.org.com*, Sep 25, 2023.
7 *All Abord: China's Rail Freight Trail Blazers Historical Route to Thailand, Breaking New Ground in Cross Border Cargo Collaboration*, on *Thaiger*, Nov 20, 2023. *Thailand and China Launched the First Cargo Rail Link from Nong Khai to Chingqing via Laos on Friday*, on *The Nation*, Dec 29, 2023.
8 Xiangming Chen, *Reconnecting Eurasia: A New Logistics State, the China–Europe Freight Train, and the Resurging Ancient City of Xi'an*, on *Eurasian Geography and Economics*, Apr 2021.
9 Xiangming Chen, *Reconnecting Eurasia: A New Logistics State, the China–Europe Freight Train, and the Resurging Ancient City of Xi'an*, on *Eurasian Geography and Economics*, Apr 2021.
10 Xiangming Chen, *Reconnecting Eurasia: A New Logistics State, the China–Europe Freight Train, and the Resurging Ancient City of Xi'an*, on *Eurasian Geography and Economics*, Apr 2021.

11 Hong Tran, *Expect Chinese Economic Retaliation against Taiwan after the DPP's Presidential Victory*, on *the Atlantic Council*, Jan 25, 2024. Liliana Oleniak, *China's invasion of Taiwan could cost global economy $ 10 trillon – Bloomberg*, on *MSN*, 2024.

12 Zhiping Liu, Di Liu, and Qiumin Liao, *Can the Opening of China Railway Express Reduce Urban Carbon Emissions; A Difference-in-Difference Analysis in China*, on *Environmental Economics and Management*, Col. 10, 2022.

13 *Graphics; China Railway Express, the Modern Silk Road*, on *CGTN*, June 28, 2023.

14 *China Rail Express*, on GoodHope Freight corporate website, 2024.

15 Xinhua, *Freight train Leaves Changsha to Minsk*, on Global Times, May 23, 2021.

16 *Sinotrans Annual Report 2022*, published by Sinotrans 2023.

17 *The New Silk Road Is Booming. New DB Cargo Subsidiary to Increase Rail Freight Transport between China and Europe*, on *DB Website*, Nov 26, 2021.

18 J. Bachmann, *Nurminen Logistics' New Southern Trans-Caspian Route, Train Departed from Chongqing*, on *New Silkroad Discovery*, May 11, 2022.

19 Ryan Finn, *DB Schenker Leverages China-Laos Railway to Expand Cross-border Logistics Services*, on *Logistics Manager*, Dec 26, 2022.

20 *Israel Opens Chinese-Operated Port in Haifa to Boost Regional Trade Links*, on *Reuters*, Sep 2, 2021, and *New Haifa Port Constructed by Chinese Company Begins Operation*, statement by State Council of PRC, Sep 2, 2021.

21 GTP Editing Team, *Piraeus among Top Global Ports in 2022 Shipping Index*, on *GTP* (Greek Travel Pages), July 20, 2022.

22 *Xinhua-Baltic International Shipping Centre Development Index Report (2022)*, on website of *Baltic Exchange*. 2023.

23 *Where to from Here?*, on *The Economist*, Sep 9, 2023.

Chapter 11

China's logistics intertwined with the rest of the world

As we explained earlier, we are bullish about the growth of China's logistics in the Chinese domestic market. However, we are less optimistic or confident about logistics in the global markets since that arena comprises three threads or narratives that present varying degrees of unpredictability and significant challenges and risks for commercial participants be they Chinese or foreign.

Firstly, there is the geopolitics around China role's in global economy. With globalization, jobs migrated from developed countries to China (The Factory of the World). Some seek to use tariffs or other measures to bring slow China's exports in order to bring back those jobs and to reduce dependency on China. Secondly, there is globally a widespread trend toward putting up barriers to products developed in China such as solar cells and electric vehicles (EVs) on the grounds that they present unfair competition due to subsidies from the Chinese government. Thirdly, the Belt and Road Initiative is facing some headwinds that are having an impact on the logistics that help make it function.

Geopolitics, technology war, and "decoupling"

As we come to look at China's international logistics, it is first useful to come to some conclusion as to how sustained and long-term China's role in the global economy may be. There is much talk about the need to reduce the risk of over-reliance on China's manufacturing. How likely is it that this talk will result in action, either a decoupling or even some modest "de-risking"? Were this to happen it, what would be the impact on the flow of goods from China and on the related logistics industry.

When China's economic reforms began in the early 1980s, its initial takeoff was, to a great extent, driven by US and European businesses shifting much of their basic, low-value–added manufacturing or product sourcing to China which offered low wages rates, a relatively well-educated workforce coupled with government incentives and subsidies to help things along. China became the "Factory of the World," producing goods that were labor intensive or which (like die casting or leather tanning) were dirty and polluting. It should be stressed that all

DOI: 10.4324/9781003489115-14

along China has been able to rely on its still expanding domestic market demand as a hedge against a weakening of export markets. In that sense, it does not resemble heavily export-oriented nations such as South Korea.

The design aspect of products remained in the West, while the actual production or the final assembly was done in China. Firms such as Nike (sports gear), Liz Claiborne (garments), and Mattel (toys such as the Barbie doll) provided drawings, technical supervision, and final quality inspection to Chinese firms which made the product for the Western markets. Pharmaceutical firms have become heavily reliant on China for the final production of generics as well as for active ingredients.[1] Suppliers of medical devices and consumables share the same dependency and the associated risk.

Large US retailers such as Walmart and Target have built large and effective operations, including logistics, around sourcing from China. Apple's iPhones ("Designed in California") are all manufactured offshore, principally in Mainland China by the Taiwan firm Foxconn which has 12 factories in China. Assembled in China is more accurate. China gains a small (albeit rising from the 3.6% reported in 2018) proportion of the value of the iPhone from the assembly work and some components (such as casing and batteries). But most of the assembled components (such as chip sets) come from the US, Japan, South Korea, and elsewhere. Likewise, Cisco Systems has the manufacturing of its routers and switches done by others, such as by Foxconn, in China.

All this "offshoring" has fostered a mammoth need for global logistics both inbound and outbound. Lower value goods travel on container ships, while iPhones travel by air. Apple uses cargo planes, each of which can carry 450,000 iPhones from China to the US.

But with this shift of manufacturing to China has also come heightened supply chain risk. In the rush to lower the cost of goods, mitigation of this risk was often left as a footnote. Recently that has changed dramatically. Trump imposed a 25% tariff on US$ 200 MM of goods from China. Then, there was the Covid-19 pandemic that disrupted the supply chain and related logistics: Foxconn's largest iPhone plant in Zhengzhou, central China was closed and also suffered labor unrest. On top of this, the heightened tension between the US and China, and with it the concern over Taiwan's future and potential threats against foreign firms, has thrown into perspective the risks associated with too much dependency on China's manufacturing.

Apple repeats its mantra of "in China for China" and its CEO Tim Cook visits China regularly to meet with top leaders including Xi Jinping. But in its relationship with China, Apple is having to thread the proverbial needle. Though its iPhone sales in China are facing severe competition from Huawei's Mate Pro, China still represents an important part of its global revenues. But at the same time, Apple is diversifying some of its global production away from China. In 2020, China accounted for 60% of its total global production but since then that proportion has been falling steadily. Foxconn, which does much of Apple's outsourced production in China, is looking to shift some of its production to Vietnam and Mexico.[2] Logistics are changing and adapting in response to these trends.

Many US politicians have been screaming for a massive economic decoupling from China, to mitigate these risks and to bring jobs back to the US. The US government brought in the CHIPS and Science Act as a way to provide incentives to semiconductor firms to build wafer fabs in the US, on the condition that they scaled back their role in China. There are also concerns about China's industrial overcapacity resulting in the dumping of products in the US, prompting the US government to place 100% tariffs on imported Chinese EVs.[3]

Although the Biden administration repeatedly disavows the "containment" of China's rise, its actions are perceived by some, including China, as indicating the opposite. The US argues strongly that it wants to avoid a total decoupling and encourages the notion of US-China collaboration such as on climate change. Yet much of the US approach seems to see to be focused not just on competition with China but on also on an adversarial posture. The US government has reinforced restrictions on trade and investment where there are national security concerns and where domestic industry is seen to need protection from unfair Chinese trade practices.

It is not only China that is in the crosshairs of these geopolitical forces. Multinational corporations (MNCs) have to take steps to react to this new world. But a key factor is that while the US and other Western governments run on a 4–5-year election cycle, large MNCs think longer term - 10–20 years out. While these global firms are now painfully aware of the risks surrounding heavy reliance on China and have been forced to diversify to some extent, it still takes a lot to pull down the supply chain structure that has functioned so well over half a century. It is hard to challenge the momentum and to turn a large ship around.

The idea of reshoring (bringing it back to the US) or nearshoring (bringing it back to countries such as Mexico) remains a high priority. But the issue is that it is easier said than done. There are three reasons for this.

Firstly, reshoring or nearshoring is not the only way to diversify away from China and mitigate the potential for supply chain disruption. Most global manufacturers prefer to implement a partial "de-risking" away from China by sourcing from and manufacturing in other Asian locations such as India, Bangladesh, Vietnam, Indonesia, and Malaysia. But even those new sources present issues. India's poor transportation infrastructure and local government-based bureaucracy create barriers to this diversification. Foxconn abandoned its plans for a US$ 19.4 BN wafer fab joint venture in India. Malaysia's high-tech island of Penang is now running out of space. Vietnam lacks the talent pool of highly trained STEM (science, technology, engineering, and mathematics) people that China can provide. (China is said to have 25% of the world's STEM talent).

Secondly, the global supply chain has taken decades to design and establish. This includes identifying, qualifying, and developing Chinese suppliers and partners. It entails building a complex eco-system of components, as we see from the complexity of the iPhone. To make all this work requires a resilient and well-integrated logistics system and processes. As mentioned earlier, there is also the question of local skills, resources, and infrastructure which China can promise and on which other countries may struggle to deliver.

And there is another good reason why the decoupling or de-risking will not happen rapidly or comprehensively. It is the domestic China market itself. Walmart imports around 20% of its products from China, at a cost of more than USD 30 BN annually. There was some talk of it diversifying its sourcing to India and away from China. Walmart moved quickly to scotch those rumors. The reason is that in addition to being its major supplier, China is also one of its largest markets: over 400 stores in China with annual sales of US$ 15 BN. It needs to defend that market presence. Likewise, Apple does not only rely on China for its manufacturing. The China market annually accounts for US$ 74 BN, or 20% of its sales.

A useful data point is The American Chamber of Commerce in Shanghai's annual business report. Started in 1999, it has served as a barometer of the sentiment of foreign investors in China. The results of its 2023 survey presented a mixed picture. On the one hand, 31% (compared to 25% in the previous year, albeit in the wake of Covid-19) of the respondents were increasing investment in China in main due to China's market potential. 40% still expected revenue growth in China to outstrip their global growth over the next 3–5 years. But, on the other hand, only 68% of the firms said they were profitable in China, well down on previous years. Only 52% were optimistic about their next five years in China, the lowest level since the survey began. 22% were decreasing their China investment compared to the previous years, due to geopolitical tensions and slowing China growth. 40% (compared to 34% the year before) were planning to redirect investment away from China and mostly to Southeast Asia. It said that "pessimism among our members in logistics, transportation, warehousing and distribution stems from growing domestic competition and softness in US-China trade, both in exports and imports."[4] Among MNCs, much of their China risk mitigation involves thinking about sourcing (and with that also logistics) on a more regional basis, rather than globally.[5] It is hard to deny that the pattern which prevailed for decades is now changing. As the CEO of VW put it, "the ecosystems in the West and China are growing apart. That means we have to clearly adapt to the situation."[6]

For the Netherlands firm Philips, China is the second largest market after the US and generates around 15% of its revenues. In China, it has 8,000 employees, five production facilities, and a particularly strong position in medical equipment such as CT scanners and ultrasound machines. But it also has relied heavily on imports to supply the China market. Recently though, due to the fragility of the supply chain and increasing trade tensions, it has focused in China on increasing the proportion of locally made products from 48% in 2022 to 75% in

2023, and ultimately to 90%. As Philips put it, "Before we were all seeking the optimal global supply chain efficiency...Now you need to source, manufacture and deliver much closer to your end markets."[7]

Undoubtably, the enthusiasm of foreign traders and investors working with China is waning for many good reasons. Perhaps, it is inevitable that as China rises and gets stronger it has less-and-less need to welcome the foreign presence. As discussed above, China's concept of "dual circulation" is putting increased emphasis to its domestic economy. Around one quarter of China's population remains to be urbanized, leaving room for plenty of further growth. On top of this, in most sectors, China has developed its own crop of "national champions" that are able to compete at home and on the world stage. While it is surely premature to say that this is "China's century," the advent of innovation and quality performance amongst Chinese firms is sending ripples across the world.

China's own objectives will also shape the evolution of global trade. The new trade relations forged through the BRI, the fact that China exports more to SE Asia than it does to the US, and that 40% of its exports are to nations or territories with which it has Free trade Agreements, could all be viewed as a signal that China is accepting that globalization is under serious threat and that a bifurcated world economic order is most likely.[8] These new relationships are certainly a smart hedge against the scenario of rapid and large-scale decoupling. But the evidence is that China's would prefer a sustained globalization. At heart, it wants to participate in the broader, truly global economic order. But, as a fast-rising, major player, it wants to take its full seat and, to certain extent, on its own terms. The WTO is moribund and not functioning these days. But our view is that China would like to see the WTO's role in arbitrating global trade issues revived, rather than facing bilateral sanctions from the US or the EU. It is keen to see revisions to the post-WW2 so-called Bretton Woods "rule-based order" which was designed by the US to largely benefit the US. This challenge from China will inevitably create trade friction. But it is clear that China has no intention of abandoning the broader global economy and shrinking back into its more compliant trade partnerships.

What this means for China's international logistics is firstly that trade flows and logistics demand between China and the world will likely not grow in the way they did over recent decades. Secondly, Chinese logistics firms, whether state-owned enterprise (SOEs) or private, will likely play a more prominent role in China's international logistics, through expertise upgrading, smart international acquisitions, and government support. Thirdly, even if China's trade flows with the world take a hit, there will be sectoral adjustments that favor areas such as China-Europe rail routes. Finally, China is still in a strong learning mode in logistics and there will be plenty of opportunity for foreign providers to participate, as long as they can carve out their competitive niche and find a productive way to partner with the Chinese side.

Japan and South Korea trade and investment in China

Below, we delve further into the geopolitical tensions and risks that threaten trade and investment between China and the US and the EU which is by far the largest part of global trade. However, before that, we should note the very strong and long-lasting economic embrace between China, on the one hand, and Japan and South Korea, on the other, which, even with a potential worsening of global geopolitics, may offer a significant degree of continuity and sustainability for the Asian logistics industry. Japan's annual bilateral trade with China and accumulated foreign direct investment (FDI) in China is around US$ 371 BN/year and US$ 160 BN, respectively, while for South Korea, the figures are around US$ 274 BN/year and US$ 70 BN.[9]

South Korea's FDI in China has rocketed since diplomatic relations were established in 1992. In 2014, the China-South Korea Free Trade Agreement was signed. Such was the flourishing of South Korean trade and investment relations and the geographic proximity that many South Korean firms such as Samsung would describe China as "our second domestic market."[10]

The investments made by Japan and South Korea in China have been wide-ranging. They include basic process manufacturing, for example in flat glass (such as Asahi Glass in Dalian) or in PVC (LG Chem in Tianjin). In the auto industry, firms such as Nissan, Toyota, Honda, and Hyundai/Kia) have all established a strong manufacturing presence, as have consumer electronics giants such as Hitachi, Sony, Toshiba, Samsung, and LG. While the process and auto industry investments tend to rely heavily on local domestic China logistics for inbound raw materials and components and for outbound distribution, the electronics industry remains highly globalized and reliant on cross-border logistics, with high-value components such as semiconductors being shipped into China, often by airfreight.

Is China-US "decoupling" real? It's complicated

In 2018, the trajectory of US-China trade was at an unprecedented high: US imports from China reached a record US$ 538 BN, making up 21.5% of total US imports, with a strong growth of 22% from 2013 to 2018.[11] But from 2018 through to 2022, imports from China receded in each intervening year, recovering only to 2018 levels of US $536 BN by 2022,[12] reducing China's share to 16.5% (US Census Bureau). Such a swift reversal in trade volumes spurred in-depth analysis and debate on its causes.

This dip coincided with pivotal shifts in US trade policy. Specifically, the US initiated a 25% tariff on US$ 34 BN of Chinese imports by July 2018, which expanded to encompass US$ 50 BN by August 2018.[13] The scope of the tariffs continued to grow: US$ 200 BN by September 2018, intensifying with a 25% increase by June 2019. By September 2019, tariffs covered an additional US$ 100 BN of China's US-bound exports.[14]

Alongside these policy shifts, terms like "friendshoring," "nearshoring," and "decoupling" entered the trade vernacular, indicating a re-evaluation of supply chain strategies.[15] This sentiment was further amplified by increasing US-China strategic tensions and national security concerns.

Interpreting the decline in US imports from China – three perspectives

The Structural Shift: Advocates of this perspective perceive the import decline as an enduring transformation of supply chains, veering away from a China-centric approach. Evidently, corporate earnings calls indicate a trend: mentions of "friendshoring" and "reshoring" increased from 25 per quarter in 2017 to 150 in early 2022.[16] This argument suggests tariffs triggered companies to revisit and restructure their traditional supply chain models. Analysis of the evolution of US imports by trading partner does show unmistakable trends for China's decline and the rise of other countries such as Vietnam and Mexico.[17]

Supporting this viewpoint, China's share of US imports decreased by 5 percentage points from 2017 to 2022. Meanwhile, countries like Vietnam and Mexico amplified their contributions, each accruing over 2 percentage points.[18] Additionally, US FDI initiatives in China fell by over half from 2017 to 2022.[19] Instead, the investment focus shifted to Vietnam and Mexico, especially for goods vulnerable to US tariffs. However, the data on full reshoring to the US itself remains elusive.

The Tariff-Induced Rebasing: The decline in US imports from China over recent years cannot be discussed without acknowledging the substantial tariffs introduced by the US starting in July 2018. Data suggests a clear correlation: products hit with a 25% US tariff experienced a decline that was 56 percentage points greater than products that weren't targeted from 2017 to 2019, and those facing a 10% tariff weren't far behind, with a 36% greater decline.[20] These significant drops suggest that the tariffs were the primary contributors to the change in trade dynamics.

Moreover, the timing of these declines aligns neatly with the implementation of tariffs. Products on the so-called List 3, which faced 25% tariffs in September 2018, saw a marked decrease in exports by the end of that year. Likewise, the announcement of List 4 tariffs in August 2019 preceded a significant dip in the subsequent months.[21] ·

Piecing this together, it appears the tariffs led to a one-time shift or "rebasing" of trade. The interpretation from this perspective is clear: as long as these tariffs are in place, we might expect trade to stabilize at this new, lower level, rather than continually decline.

The Complicated Perspective: This view combines the complexities of the decline, integrating both one-time policy-induced rebasing and long-term structural alterations. For instance, sectors like semiconductors, auto parts, and machinery saw immediate downturns post-tariffs. However, for industries like apparel, intrinsic shifts due to rising Chinese labor costs were already underway, preceding the tariffs. There are huge disparities between industries, with tariff-affected sectors facing steeper declines, while non-tariffed sectors maintained growth.[22]

In fact, the import of many products has surged from China over the last five years, particularly for products where China holds a dominant position, such as laptops and monitors, phones and smartphones, video game consoles, and toys.[23]

In conclusion, it's evident that the meaningful downturn in US imports from China over the recent five-year stretch cannot be attributed to a single cause. The situation is, undoubtedly, complicated. Dissecting the data, we find patterns and divergences across industries, stemming from a few important drivers: US trade policy shifts and the imposition of tariffs on a selection of Chinese imports, China's evolving economic positioning and the associated rise in labor costs, and sector-specific variances in competitiveness and import alternatives. More time will need to pass in order to determine the specific impacts of each of these factors. What is apparent is that we are *not* witnessing a complete decoupling; rather, a strategic reconfiguration is in motion.

Notes

1 The White House, *Executive Order on American Supply Chains*, Feb 24, 2021
2 Gene Munster speaking on *Here's What Apple CEO Tim Cook's Visit to China Means for the Company and Stock*, on *CNBC*, Mar 27, 2023.
3 Announced by the Biden Administration, May 14, 2024.
4 *China Business Report 2023*, survey published by The American Chamber of Commerce in Shanghai, 2023.
5 Interview with David Bovet, Aug 21, 2023.
6 Oliver Blume, cited in *Notable & Quotable* on *The Wall Street Journal*, Sep 21, 2023.
7 Toby Sterling, *Philips CEO: China Business, Supply Chain Undergoing Major Change*, Reuters on *MSN Business*, 2023.
8 James Kynge and Keith Fray, *China's Plan to Reshape World Trade on Its Own Terms*, on *Financial Times*, Feb 26, 2024.
9 Jaeho Hwang, *The Continuous But Rocky Developments of Sino-South Korean Relations: Examined by the Four Factor Model*, on *Journal of Contemporary East Asian Studies*, Aug 9, 2021.
10 Paul G. Clifford, recollection from consulting to Samsung on China.
11 US Census Bureau, *Trade in Goods with China*, https://www.census.gov/foreign-trade/balance/c5700.html#questions.
12 US Census Bureau, *Trade in Goods with China*, https://www.census.gov/foreign-trade/balance/c5700.html#questions.
13 Chad P. Bown *Four Years into the Trade War, Are the US and China Decoupling?*, on PIIE(Peterson Institute for International Economics), Oct 20, 2022.
14 Chad P. Bown, *Four Years into the Trade War, Are the US and China Decoupling?*, on PIIE (Peterson Institute for International Economics), Oct 20, 2022.
15 *What Is "Friendshoring"? Western Policymakers Want to Move Supply Chains to Friendly Countries*, on *The Economist*, Aug 30, 2023.

16 Laura Alfaro and David Chor, *Global Supply Chains: The Looming "Great Reallocation,* Jackson Hole Symposium, Aug 2023.
17 Laura Alfaro and David Chor, *Global Supply Chains: The Looming "Great Reallocation,* Jackson Hole Symposium, Aug 2023.
18 Laura Alfaro and David Chor, *Global Supply Chains: The Looming "Great Reallocation,* Jackson Hole Symposium, Aug 2023.
19 Laura Alfaro and David Chor, *Global Supply Chains: The Looming "Great Reallocation,* Jackson Hole Symposium, Aug 2023.
20 Alessandro Nicita, *Trade and Trade Diversion Effects of United States Tariffs on China,* UNCTAD, Nov 5, 2019.
21 Alessandro Nicita, *Trade and Trade Diversion Effects of United States Tariffs on China,* UNCTAD, Nov 5, 2019.
22 Chad P. Bown, *Four Years into the Trade War, Are the US and China Decoupling?,* on *Peterson Institute for International Economics,* Oct 20, 2022.
23 Chad P. Bown, *Four Years into the Trade War, Are the US and China Decoupling?,* on *Peterson Institute for International Economics,* Oct 20, 2022.

Chapter 12

Taiwan

The logistics gray rhino

The term "Gray Rhino" was coined in the book of the same name[1] meaning "a highly probable, high impact yet neglected threat." The term has been widely used within China and quoted by even the most senior Chinese business and political leaders including Xi Jinping.[2] The gray rhino in the case of China logistics is the issue of Taiwan. It is not our role in this book to take positions on geopolitics or potential trade sanctions or military conflicts. That said, we do believe that there is a high probability of some sort of crisis over Taiwan (which might well fall far short of a full invasion by the Mainland) which would have high impact on China's logistics sector, the logistics in the South China Sea, and logistics throughout the entire world.

There are grounds for believing that a blockade of Taiwan would be China's preferred way to tighten the noose on Taiwan, since it would not represent an outright declaration of war and might not provoke a full response from the US.

As one analyst has observed:

"[Given the world's reliance on Taiwan's semiconductors,] if Beijing blockages the island for more than 14 days, it would have devastating effects on the global economy as Taiwan would run out of power..." [And moreover] "the Taiwan Strait... carries half of the global goods traffic... If Xi were to position his army there, everything would come to a standstill."[3]

The Taiwan flashpoint: its history and context

For those who focus on Supply Chain Risk Management, no area is more critical than that of Taiwan risk. The issues surrounding Taiwan present a multidimensional threat to global flows of goods. The Island of Taiwan, which is separated from Mainland China by 180 km of the Taiwan Strait, has an area just slightly larger than Belgium but with a population of 24 MM. Despite its undetermined diplomatic status and absence of full statehood, it is the 21st-largest economy in the world, similar in size to that of Poland or Switzerland and the 16th largest trading territory in the world.

DOI: 10.4324/9781003489115-15

Its history makes it a flash point in US-China relations. In 1949, in the final stages of the civil war between the insurgent Chinese Communist Party (CCP) and the Republic of China (ROC) (led by the Guomindang Party), the ROC forces fled to Taiwan, while the CCP established the People's Republic of China (PRC) in Beijing. Since then, China has continuously vowed to take back Taiwan (the mantra is "we shall certainly liberate Taiwan"), but at a time of its choosing. So far it has not tried to do so and claims, while building up its military forces, a preference for "peaceful reunification."

In 1979, in order to normalize its relations with Beijing, the US recognized the PRC and derecognized the ROC but refused to acknowledge PRC sovereignty over Taiwan. (And in 1982 the US went further in stating that it would not pursue a "two China policy.") However, in 1979, the US Congress passed an act that provided for continuing non-state-to-state relations with Taiwan and military support, in terms of weapons, munitions, and, today, some advisors. The Taiwan and US governments established informal offices in each territory. The US thus created a diplomatic work-around for the issue, often referred to as a "strategic ambiguity." China is left guessing as to what extent the US would intervene in the event of a Mainland invasion or blockade of Taiwan.

In recent years, the China Mainland has stepped up the pressure on Taiwan using political pressure and military threats to undermine a trend in Taiwan toward "independence," that is something more like full nationhood. China has ordered its military to be ready by 2027 to fight to take back Taiwan, though it is unclear that it intends to do so. In turn, the US has pushed back against China's increased bellicosity toward Taiwan.

Many Taiwanese would prefer that the status quo with China, which has stood for the last 50 years, continues to prevail. However, there is little doubt the status quo itself has evolved, so that things today are more heavily weighted in favor of China. Likewise, despite its tough talk, there are grounds for believing that the Mainland would like to see the status quo continue for quite some while, firstly, since it brings it great economic benefits and, secondly, because the military solution would derail China's rise.

Notwithstanding these views on the status quo, the risk of US-China conflict over Taiwan remains extremely high. For Taiwan, there is the risk that China would invade, blockade the Island, or take many smaller measures to strangle it. There is of course uncertainty as to what steps the US might take or whether the US electorate would accept the nation going to war over this issue. But all of these scenarios, plus an additional one of accidental conflict, caused by a miscalculation on either side, would leave Taiwan – its economy, its trade, and its logistics – in great hazard. That hazard would of course extend to trade and logistics routes elsewhere in Asia.

Given its relatively small population, Taiwan is heavily dependent on foreign trade which in 2022 was over US$ 900 BN (total export and imports). China accounted for 25% of that trade, followed by the US with 16%. In 2022, its exports of US$ 480 BN accounted for 60% of GDP. 35% of those exports were semiconductors. TSMC, Taiwan's largest semiconductor fab (or foundry) until recently accounted for as much as 92% of the world supply of high-end logic chips of 10 nm or smaller. But it is thought that firms such as South Korea's Samsung are catching up.

Since the 1980s, Taiwan has been a heavy investor in Mainland China, with the accumulated amount being around US$ 190 BN. Heavy concentrations of Taiwan-owned firms appeared across China, for instance in Kunshan, a Jiangsu city on the border with Shanghai Municipality which early on saw the opportunity to attract Taiwan capital and entrepreneurs. Hiring Taiwan-born managers became a popular way for Western investors to move toward localization, as an alternative to using Mainland people or Singaporeans (which presented more culture friction with the Mainlanders). For much of the 1980s, goods had to travel between China and Taiwan via Hong Kong, Macau, or South Korea. The big breakthrough came with the Three Connections (*santong*) permitting direct links for mail, ground trade, and aviation, which were implemented in steps over several decades.

The perfect example of the intimate economic embrace between Taiwan and the Mainland is Taiwan's largest firm Hon Hai Precision (more commonly known as Foxconn), an electronics contract manufacturer with an annual turnover of around US$ 200 BN. Foxconn has 12 factories in mainland China, assembling products for firms such as Apple and Cisco Systems. In China, it has expanded its footprint from the initial presence in Shenzhen to inland locations such as Zhengzhou, where labor is in better supply and cheaper. Going inland also pleased the Chinese government. But Foxconn's founder Terry Gou in 2023 became, for a short while, a contender in Taiwan's presidential elections. The Chinese government announced that it would investigate Foxconn's Mainland accounts, thus sending a not-very-subtle message to Mr. Gou that he should abandon his candidacy (which he did) since it diluted the chance of the opposition parties (which China favored) winning.

Just as factors related to political power and control led China's party-state to clamp down on Jack Ma and Alibaba, even at the expense of the economy, so Beijing likewise feels bound to turn the screws on Terry Gou and Foxconn. One Taiwan politician, no friend of Gou, but who himself has faced abuse from Beijing, sounded a warning bell calling on China to "take good care of and cherish" Taiwanese firms that have created jobs and made a "big contribution to China."[4]

The geopolitical forces at play in Taiwan are threatening the intimate Taiwan-Mainland economic partnership. A Taiwan economist put it this way: "We have entered the age of deglobalization, where global supply chains are replaced by regional ones." He added that Taiwan firms "can no longer use China as a main production base because their foreign customers demand them to be in South-East Asia, Mexico and elsewhere."[5]

The potential impact of Taiwan risk on firms such as Apple, which relies heavily on TSMC for its chips and on Foxconn for its iPhone assembly, cannot be underestimated. The Rand Corporation, which is in part funded by the US Department of Defense, did some scenario planning around a situation whereby China uses semiconductors as a way to coerce Taiwan. It concluded that a disruption of the semiconductor supply chain in Taiwan would pose a major national security challenge. None of the scenarios, whether severance of supply or a slower process which allowed some time to find alternative supplies, were deemed attractive. The advice provided to the US government was to do its utmost to incentivize TSMC to diversify away from Taiwan.[6] The CHIPS and Science Act (passed by Congress in 2022) is already seeking to do that, with US$ 53 BN in loans and tax credits, but provided on condition that the recipient restricts its supply to and R&D cooperation with Mainland China. To assuage the US concerns, TSMC has pledged to invest US$ 40 BN in Phoenix, Arizona. However, work on that wafer fab has been behind schedule and faces issues including cultural friction.

Based on the experience of recent decades, there is a strong argument that the economic interdependency between Taiwan and the Mainland has been a key factor in preventing conflict between the two territories. A counter to that view would also be that things have changed under Xi Jinping and that China's ratchetting up of its warlike rhetoric will make cross-strait trade and investment, along with the related logistics, more complex and precarious. Wherever one falls philosophically in this debate, it is undeniable that the Western firms that are so reliant on these supply chains are bound to take note and to "de-risk" accordingly but proportionately.

As we lay out in detail below, beyond the disruption that a Taiwan crisis would bring to Taiwan trade and to Taiwan-Mainland trade, we can also add its impact to broader trade routes and logistics in Asia. As any invasion, blockade, or tightening of the noose by the PRC on Taiwan, coupled with the inevitable response from the US, Japan, and Australia, would see a rapid suspension of container shipping and air cargo routes in the vicinity of Taiwan. China's role as the Factory of the World would risk being negated or unmined. Japan and South Korea's trade with Europe and the Middle East would be severed. Supplies of oil and natural gas from the Middle East to Japan would be interrupted.

Taiwan supply chains and semiconductors

Taiwan itself is a massive node in the global supply chain, particularly in the realm of critical high-performance semiconductors. The semiconductor's physical manufacturing occurs in facilities known as "foundries" or "fabs." These fabs are mainly located in Taiwan, China, and South Korea, with Taiwan having nearly 64% of production share globally.[7]

Fabs are enormously costly and time-consuming to build, with new fabs likely to require US $5–$15 BN and 18–24 months to build. The US has been attempting to rebuild its own semiconductor fab facilities, but even after several years of concerted US government intervention, there still have been only a few groundbreakings in the United States. In the near term and likely in the medium term, there will be only limited replacement for Taiwan semiconductor manufacturing capacity.

China's nine-dash line and the South China Sea

The geographic scope of logistics disruptions as a result of a Taiwan crisis would be in or around the South China Sea. The two specific areas that would be in play would likely first be the air and ocean areas around Taiwan itself. This would likely include the waterway between Taiwan and the Philippines, which is the major trade route for east-westbound commercial vessels. The second geographic area that would be in play would be the rest of the South China Sea within

LARIS KARKLIS/THE WASHINGTON POST

Figure 12.1 China's nine-dash line.

the Nine-Dash Line (see above) as depicted on Chinese maps to delineate what China asserts is its sovereignty.[8] In particular, areas surrounding the shoals in the Spratly Islands (Nansha in Chinese) and the Paracel Islands (Xisha) that are now home to Chinese military bases would also likely be in play. In particular, the Spratly Islands which are located in the southern portion of the South China Sea are variously occupied by the PRC, Taiwan, Vietnam, the Philippines, and Malaysia and are claimed in their entirety by China, Taiwan, and Vietnam, while portions are claimed by Malaysia and the Philippines.[9] Despite China asserting its claim to the waters within the Nine-Dash Line, so far the reality has been that China has not enforced that claim and international shipping passes through that area without requesting permission from China. Of course that could quickly change.

These two regions when combined constitute a very large geographic area. It is home to a very large amount of commercial traffic. Through it transits an estimated equivalent of 5% of the world's GDP, or over US$ 4 trillion.[10]

Some estimates predict staggering potential impacts as a result of large-scale disruptions or closure of trade through the South China Sea. An extreme case whereby maritime traffic would be rerouted south of Australia could result in a contraction of one-third of its GDP for Taiwan itself, up to 22% for Singapore, and a 10%–15% GDP impact for other nations within the South China Sea such as Vietnam, Malaysia, and the Philippines.[11]

The stakes are extremely high.

Ocean freight and the Red Sea analogy

A timely analogy for the dramatic impact on ocean freight in the South China Sea as a result of a Taiwan crisis is what is currently happening in the Red Sea. In December 2023, the Houthi rebels based in Yemen created a significant security crisis for ocean shipping passing through the Red Sea and into the Suez Canal.

That crisis did not start all at once but was a gradual ramping up of tensions and of quasi-military actions which slowly created a crisis for ocean shipping. The Houthis began small isolated attacks on commercial vessels attempting to transit through a narrow Strait that links the Red Sea to the Gulf of Aden and the Indian Ocean. Initially, these attacks were small in scope, often not damaging the vessels or endangering the crew. And initially, these attacks were targeted at a small subset of ocean vessels that were deemed to have connections with the enemy according to the Houthis. In those early days, the shipping patterns through the Red Sea were largely unchanged. Vessels took additional precautions but the transits themselves remained. Then over time, the attacks grew more frequent they began hitting actual targets and causing actual damage, and the scope of vessels that were targeted greatly expanded beyond the initial stated target vessel profile.

At that point in time in late December 2023, many ocean carriers began to rethink transiting through the Red Sea since the risk had by then been elevated and expanded to many different types of vessels. These were no longer highly targeted but broad-based attacks – everyone was at risk. In late December 2023 and in January 2024, different types of ocean vessels and different ocean carriers themselves made very different decisions. First, the bulk vessels and the fuel tankers largely continued to transit through the Red Sea. Although they did adopt better security and tactical measures, they chose not to reroute around Africa which was the alternative routing. While there continued to be some attacks on bulk and tanker vessels these were relatively few on a percentage basis and the individual companies making individual choices on charters did a cost-benefit calculation realizing that the additional cost of going around Africa plus the additional inventory holding costs attributable to the fuel exceeded the potential risk of continuing to transit in the Red Sea. As a result, most fuel tankers and bulkers continued their transit.

Ocean container companies were different. Each container company had its own view of the situation and these strategies changed from week to week or even from day to day. Some carriers very quickly shifted all of their traffic from Red Sea transits to transiting around Africa. For a typical container vessel, this would add 10–15 days onto their voyage and up to US $4 million of additional operating costs. This also would cause their customers, the shippers, to have their shipments delayed by these 10 or 15 days.

Therefore, this was not an ideal situation for the container carriers, given the higher cost and a lower level of service. Notwithstanding these concerns, several carriers including Maersk and Cosco quickly decided to route all of their traffic around Africa. Other carriers viewed things on a case-by-case basis, sometimes rerouting around Africa while with other vessels sticking to the Red Sea. In some cases, they changed the routing while in transit and there were cases where vessels were coming from Europe to Asia and had transited the Suez Canal and entered the Red Sea only to stop and reverse course back through the Suez Canal, back through the Mediterranean and around Africa, causing a tremendous delay and extra cost. And then there was one ocean carrier, CMA CGM who continued to transit through the Red Sea throughout the crisis. This French carrier was relying on French Navy support to protect its vessels through the most dangerous portions of the journey. In addition, a few small opportunistic carriers jumped in to fill the gap in the market. Shadowy carriers such as Chinese-owned Sea Legend Shipping are offering "ultimate care for crew, cargo and vessel with high-security level" for direct Red Sea transits.[12]

Rerouting in the case of a disruption in the South China Sea would first be through the Lombok Strait in Indonesia and then to the east of the Philippines, or in the case of a much more widespread disruption an actual rerouting to the south of Australia.

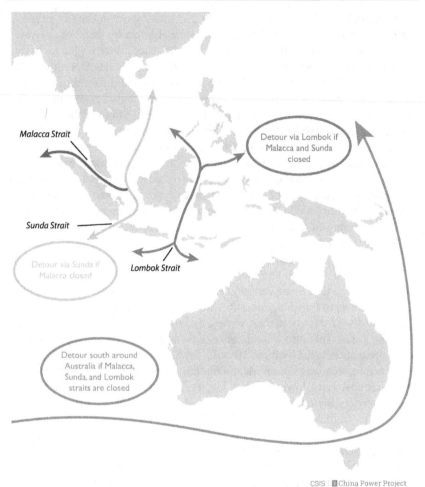

Figure 12.2 Possible re-routing.

So, the three main lessons from the Red Sea crisis of late 2023–2024 were these: First, maritime crises can develop over time. It does not happen overnight and the situation tends to start at a modest level and then escalate gradually and often in unpredictable ways. Second, different types of ocean carriers, for example fuel carriers bulk carriers and container carriers, will choose different strategies at different times since their financial decision-making and risk profiles are different. Third, even among a common class of carriers such as container vessels, the decisions vary tremendously from one company to another company.

A crisis in the South China Sea may unfold in a similar way. The intensity of the risk will change and escalate over time. It may not immediately entail a dramatic shift from the South China Sea fully open to all commercial traffic to one that quickly becomes a closed route. While, as a Taiwan crisis takes shape, and there is a decrease in traffic through the South China Sea, the specific choices on whether to re-route are likely to depend heavily on the judgment of different shipping companies operating different kinds of vessels.

Airfreight and the Russia–Ukraine War analogy

In the event of a Taiwan crisis, airfreight would be significantly less impacted than ocean freight. To understand the implications and the scenarios around airfreight our best starting point as an analogy is the Russia-Ukraine War. Russia began is invasion of Ukraine in 2014. But, in 2022, after Russia expanded its attack to the whole of Ukraine, the US and other NATO nations imposed a series of financial, economic, and logistics sanctions on Russia.

In addition, logistics companies themselves, in this case major airlines, took independent decisions with respect to how to deal with the conflict between Russia and Ukraine at a company level. The first thing that all air carriers did was to reroute their aircraft outside of Ukrainian airspace. This was a visceral issue for air carriers given that Malaysian Airlines Flight 17 had previously been shot down by unknown actors along the Russia-Ukraine border in July 2014.[13] The initial impact of these flight re-routings around Ukraine was relatively minimal, with a little extra flying time and a little additional fuel cost.

However, once the Western nations imposed transport sanctions, Russia closed its airspace to all aircraft other than Russian aircraft and those of selected other allies. As a result, nearly all airfreight had to reroute completely around Russia. This had a small impact on freight coming from certain parts of Asia to North America that still transited through Alaska or over the North Pole to Europe. But the bigger impact was Asia-to-Europe flights since these flights have had to reroute not only around Ukraine but also around all of Russia. This new routing added significant extra flying time, the results of which were twofold.

First, the direct impact was greater fuel cost which was translated into higher freight rates for all shippers from Asia, primarily China and Japan, to Western Europe. The second impact was capacity reduction due to the dramatic increase in the amount of flight time between Asia and Europe. In total, there was a 22% reduction in airfreight capacity on the East Asia to Europe trade lane due to the Russian invasion of Ukraine.[14]

This capacity reduction occurred at a time when airfreight was already constrained due to factors related to COVID, primarily the near absence of long-haul passenger plane belly space for cargo. As a result, freight rates further increased and the pressure on freighters in particular remained extremely high.

Another factor that drove airfreight rates higher was a further reduction in capacity from Russian-owned freighters. The fleet of Russian air freighters owned by the AirBridgeCargo Airlines and its parent Volga-Dnepr Airlines comprised 41 aircraft, mostly widebody freighters. These companies were subject to sanctions and all these freighters were no longer able to operate outside of Russia.[15] Air carriers who had been chartering those aircraft and freight forwarders who had been contracting directly with them had to scramble for additional capacity elsewhere. And the largest cargo aircraft in the world the Antonov AN-225 "Mriya" was destroyed in its hangar in Ukraine during the early months of the war.[16]

While this reduction in capacity was not nearly as dramatic as the initial reduction in capacity due to COVID back in early 2020, this was a significant reduction at a time of a 10% capacity deficit and with airfreight global rates up 2.5–3 times above pre-pandemic levels.[17] Airfreight capacity remained constrained until mid-2023 when belly capacity began returning to a meaningful level globally.

What lessons do we learn that we can apply to a crisis in Taiwan? We would likely see a similar dynamic – initially air carriers would divert around Taiwan at quite a distance to ensure the safety of their aircraft. The carriers would stop commercial airfreight service to Taiwan, thereby cutting the island off from airfreight for exports and imports. The rerouting of aircraft would drive additional fuel costs and additional time delays similar to the experience with Russia and Ukraine. However, overall, it would likely cause only a moderate reduction in global airfreight capacity and the increase in freight rates might be modest.

The impact on China's logistics networks

The Red Sea and Ukraine analogies provide a good framework for understanding the types and magnitudes of disruptions to international oceans and airfreight that might result from a Taiwan crisis. However, there is no perfect modern analogy for the impact a Taiwan crisis would have on China's international logistics network.

China is both the world's largest exporter and the world's largest importer. Historically, it imported mainly energy and raw materials and then exported finished consumer goods. However, now China also dominates trade in intermediate manufactured goods both inbound and outbound. Basically, if there is a product in this world, then China is either a leading importer or exporter of that product, or both. The vast majority of these imports and exports travel by ocean freight and would be significantly disrupted by any Taiwan crisis.

As noted above, one report projects that complete closure of the South China Sea could result in major contractions in the GDP for Taiwan, Singapore, Vietnam, Malaysia, and the Philippines.[18] But that same report shows less than a 1% negative impact on China's overall economy. Why?

Firstly, the overall Chinese economy is so large, diversified and with future growth potential that even a large volume foreign trade disruption that would create a 10%–15% impact elsewhere would have a much lower impact on China on a percentage basis.

Secondly, while China does have ports, mainly in Hong Kong and in Guangdong, which are vulnerable to a crisis in the South China Sea basin and around Taiwan, they have many large ports further north such as in Ningbo, Shanghai, Qingdao, Tianjin and Dalian that are potentially outside the immediate crisis zone. While China-Europe rail links could not fill the gaps in sea and airfreight resulting from a Taiwan crisis, they provide some alternative capacity that China can use to partially hedge these risks.

Notes

1 Michel Wucker, *The Gray Rhino: How to Recognize and Act on the Obvious Dangers We Ignore*, St. Martin's Press, MacMillian Publishers, 2016.
2 *Xi Says China Should Make Contingency Plans for "Black Swan" and "Grey Rhino" Events*, on *Reuters*, Jan 29, 2021.
3 Alexander Gorlach, *Xi Jinping's Clever Play – How Maritime Blockades Could Paralyze Taiwan and the World*, on *Focus Online*, May 24, 2024.
4 Kathrin Hille, *Taiwan Presidential Frontrunner Blasts China over Foxconn Probe*, on *Financial Times*, Oct 24, 2023.
5 Kathrin Hille, *'Like It Was with Jack Ma': China Puts World's Largest Apple Supplier in Its Crosshairs*, on *Financial Times*, Oct 26, 2023.
6 Bradley Martin, Laura H. Baldwin, Paul DeLuca, Natalia Henriquez Sanchez, Mark Hvizda, Colin D. Smith, N. Peter Whitehead, *Supply Chain Interdependence and Geopolitics Vulnerability. The Case of Taiwan and High-End Semiconductors*, The Rand Corporation, 2023.
7 *Taiwan's Strategic Role in the Global Semiconductor Supply Chain*, on *Dimerco*, Oct 10, 2023.
8 *China Sovereignty Claims in the South China Sea 2012*, Perry-Castañeda Library Map Collection, China Maps.
9 *Spratly Islands*, on *The World Factbook*, Jan 31, 2024.
10 Lincoln F. Pratson, *Assessing Impacts to Maritime Shipping from Marine Chokepoint Closures*, in *Communicationa in Transportation Research*, Vol.3, Dec 21, 2022.
11 Kerem Coşar and Benjamin D. Thomas, *The Geopolitics of International Trade in Southeast Asia*, National Bureau of Economic Research, Nov 2020.
12 Cichen Shen, *Mysterious New Chinese Carrier Emerges to Capitalise on Risky Red Sea Trades*, on *Lloyd's List*, Jan 23, 2024.
13 Olga Razumovskaya, *Ukraine Fully Closes Airspace after Malaysia Airlines Flight 17 Crash*, on *Wall Street Journal*, July 18, 2014.
14 Damian Brett, *NE Asia-Europe Capacity Drops More Than 20% Due to Ukraine Crisis*, on *AirCargo News*, Apr 12, 2022.
15 Eric Kulisch, *Sanctions Squeeze Russian Carrier Volga-Dnepr, Air Cargo Capacity*, on *Freightwaves,* Feb 28, 2022.
16 Jack Guy, *World's Largest Plane Destroyed in Ukraine*, on *CNN*, Feb 28, 2022.
17 Eric Kulisch, *Sanctions Squeeze Russian Carrier Volga-Dnepr, Air Cargo Capacity*, on *Freightwaves,* Feb 28, 2022.
18 Kerem Coşar and Benjamin D. Thomas, *The Geopolitics of International Trade in Southeast Asia*, National Bureau of Economic Research, Nov 2020.

The key players

Profiles and case studies

Chapter 13

China's own logistics titans and trailblazers

Third-party logistics providers (3PLs) or firms that deliver modern integrated logistics are a new breed or species of company. But distinctive as they are, few are newly created and most have their own history and DNA. Globally, we see how 3PLs have emerged from a wide range of backgrounds, such as from freight forwarding (Kuehne + Nagel, DB Schenker, Expeditors) ocean shipping (Maersk, DP World), trucking (C.H. Robinson, J.B. Hunt, XPO), Express mail (DHL, UPS, FedEx), and warehousing (Americold). A smaller number have emerged as start-ups (such as technology-centered firm Flexport). In China, we can observe that there is the same range of DNA or backgrounds. But the remarkable difference in China is that these firms have emerged more recently and rapidly, and out of a highly fragmented marketplace, compared to what has occurred on the global scene.

What is striking about the Chinese scene is the recent explosive growth of e-commerce and with that related logistics companies that are essentially start-ups designed for a specific purpose and without the baggage of legacy assets. Some of these newly emerged firms have also extended beyond e-commerce. A good example of this is how e-commerce firm SF (Shunfeng) has carved out a strong niche for itself in cold-chain logistics.

Figure 13.1 China's 3PLs come from disparate backgrounds.

DOI: 10.4324/9781003489115-17

The other major participants are state-owned enterprises (SOEs) that come from a background deeply rooted in the legacy of the centrally planned economy – culture, capabilities, and assets – which have shaped these transformed businesses. It would be easy to simply portray their inherited legacy as essentially negative. It is true that they were left with vast quantities of poor-quality warehousing that was utterly unsuited to the needs of modern logistics. They suffered under the burden of a fragmented organizational structure that could not deliver an integrated logistics solution. They had to work with the remains of the dismantled centrally planned economy, which was an overcomplex, multitiered distribution system with separate warehousing and transportation units at each level. The old SOE corporate culture obstructed the development of a management style based on putting customers, first, on executives being adaptive and capable of taking the initiative to ensure a strongly customized and responsive logistics service.

That said, these old-style firms also enjoy some significant advantages. Perhaps, the largest benefit from their historical legacy is the strong support from Chinese party-state. Around the turn of the century as China's reforms deepened, the government strongly encouraged these firms to embrace Western business theory and practice, empowering them to hire expensive foreign consulting firms to assist them in this process. Following a thorough diagnostic which often laid bare the unsustainability of the existing business, they were able to develop a robust long-range development plan. On the back of that, they could break free of government subsidies and recapitalize themselves through a stock market listing. However, as these old firms re-invented and modernized themselves, they have turned out to be nowhere agile or creative enough to match the emerging e-commerce logistics firms.

In this chapter, we do not seek to provide an exhaustive portrayal of all the main Chinese logistics players but instead provide contrasting examples of how Chinese firms entered the 3PL business from different backgrounds. We shall not be shy about presenting financial analysis where it sheds light on the nature and performance of the firms we profile. But we try to avoid the kind of dry, formulaic, numbers-driven focus that one could expect from a stock analyst, in favor of an approach which also places emphasis on the "softer" aspects such as the firm's historical legacy, the quality of the management team, and, behind the scenes, the role of China's party-state.

Sinotrans: a story of successful SOE transformation

Sinotrans Limited 中国外运股份有限公司

Date established: 1950. HQ: Beijing

Ownership: State-owned, stock-market listed. *Owners*: Since 2017 part of state-owned China Merchant Group. Ultimate owner is China's State Assets Management Administration

Stock market listings: Hong Kong (2003), Shanghai. *Market cap*: HK\$ 37.07 BN
Management: Chairman: Feng Boming, President: Song Rong
Turnover (2022): RMB 108.8 BN (US\$ 16.2 BN). *Net Profit*: RMB 4.2 BN (US\$ 0.6 BN)
Employees: 34,000

Early life. Sinotrans' history dates back to 1946 when it was established to handle the trade between "liberated areas" (that is areas captured and controlled by the Chinese Communist Party (CCP) during the civil war against the Republic of China) in North East China, close to the Soviet Union. In 1953, it became China Land Transportation Company and in 1955 was merged with a sea transportation entity to form *China National Foreign Trade Corporation*, also known as *Sinotrans*, based on the name that was used for telex messages. It was one of a series of foreign trade corporations (FTCs) set by China after 1949 as it established a Soviet-style centrally planned economy and, as such, reported to China's foreign trade ministry. But Sinotrans played a very specific role among these FTCs, serving as their one and only freight forwarder for foreign trade, booking space on ships and handling the necessary paperwork at the border. As a freight forwarder, its services stopped short of the actual provision of transportation (whether by ownership or by sub-contracting). So, for decades, Sinotrans enjoyed on a total or near monopoly over China's international freight forwarding.

The economic reforms; a painful restructuring. It is easy to see how, after the economic reforms that began in 1978, the end of Sinotrans' monopoly and opening up of the Chinese market to competition – first to local firms and later to foreign ones – came as a serious shock to Sinotrans, forcing it to rethink and to restructure. As the reforms unfolded, Sinotrans was already changing incrementally, adding its own transportation capabilities (not only trucking but also its own shipping line) and its own warehousing. But in the late 1990s, as China approached World Trade Organization (WTO) accession and with it heightened international competition, Sinotrans was in poor shape to face the new challenges. To its credit, it had already created a new "contract logistics" division that positioned itself as a 3PL, serving Chinese shippers and a handful of MNCs active in China. But more radical steps needed to be taken.

In its transformation, Sinotrans benefited from two key factors, strong government support and a top-notch and open-minded management team. Seen from the government's point of view, Sinotrans was the obvious candidate to play the role of a future "national champion" in modern logistics. Its existing strength in freight forwarding could readily be extended into fully fledged logistics. The encouragement and facilitation from China's party-state opened up the path to Sinotrans' restructuring and rebirth.

Earlier, in discussion of how Chinese logistics firms dealt with the legacy of central planning, we discussed the role of Sinotrans' Chairman Luo Kaifu in driving change in the company. At the operational level was Yu Jianmin, in his 30s – half the age of Luo – who headed up the newly created "logistics department" which was to be the crucible out of which the new Sinotrans 3PL business would emerge. He had already worked for Sinotrans in Europe, where he developed an affinity for Western culture and the good life (he gained a private flying license). Back in China, he was carving out an entirely new business line, providing integrated modern logistics to both emerging Chinese manufacturers and also to a handful of multinationals that were entering China. Within what was a rather conservative firm, he brought charisma, vigor, and a mercurial style to his marketing. He became much feared by competitors who witnessed how he was able to convince the shippers and capture contract after contract. He reported to Zhang Jianwei, who would become the first President of the stock-market–listed Sinotrans. Now in his early 40s, he had studied English at China's Foreign Trade University and had recently received an EMBA from the China Europe Business School in Shanghai. Although he was conventional in his loyalty to the CCP and temperamentally cautious, he nonetheless perceived the value in Yu Jianmin's flourishing new business line and put his heart and soul into creating the new, restructured Sinotrans that would finally be recapitalized through the stock market listing.

Between 1997 and culminating in its listing on the Hong Kong stock market in early 2003, Sinotrans embarked on a complex and at times painful restructuring. At that time, the firm had a profit margin of only around 2% and net cash flow, after capital investment, was negative. As a first stage, the firm was corporatized with the adoption of board management and Western accounting practices. The firm's 36 provincial-level branches across China appeared to a powerful national network but was in fact a series of separate legal entities that only paid lip service to head office directives. Below the provincial level, there were a further over 500 lower level subsidiaries. It took complex legal changes and negotiations to change this into a more unified structure that could deliver 3PL services across China in a seamless fashion.

At that time, diagnostic analysis guided the firm to select businesses which had a strong financial future while de-emphasizing those that were sinking in a mire of losses. Sinotrans had 1,600 trucks, most of them over seven years old and needing to be replaced. It had 500 warehouses with a capacity of 3 MM m^2 but these were general purpose and often in a poor state of repair.

It was decided that Sinotrans would focus on the core businesses of freight forwarding (sea, air, and rail), the shipping agency business (handling ships needs in port), and integrated logistics solutions (something they aspired to and which they were still learning how to do). The transportation assets, warehousing, and intra-China container shipping would be retained not as stand-alone businesses but only to the extent that they supported the core businesses. Moreover, trucking, warehousing, and shipping were to be left in the *unlisted* part of the firm, permitting the listed part to be asset-light but still with access to those assets as required. That said, the listed part did own some key container yards near the ports and also went on to make investments in some warehousing and logistics hubs that were deemed to be strategic assets. It was well known that shippers greatly valued access to high-quality warehousing.[1]

However, not all the analysis conducted during the restructuring process was acted upon. Sinotrans' shipping business was subscale and uncompetitive. Over four years, it had lost more than US$ 100 MM and was projected to continue to remain loss-making. It owned 41 ships, of which 26 were bulk carriers and 9 were container ships. It had just a 4% share of the shipping business within China and a miniscule part of the global market. But the decision was taken not to shed this business at that time.[2] There were limits to the number of bold moves Sinotrans could make. It took until 2021 for Sinotrans to offload its shipping business which was absorbed by its then parent China Merchants. At that time, the fleet had shrunk to 19 owned ships and 13 chartered vessels.

At the time of the stock market listing, large numbers of staff were redundant to the needs of the new firm or were on the books even though semi-retired. As part of the firm's restructuring, the excess workforce was paid compensation and removed. Attention was paid to selecting the optimal degree of asset-intensity so that it was relatively light but still assured tight control of the services being delivered. There was a focus on certain types of logistics specialization that could give Sinotrans an edge, for instance inbound auto logistics. Selling approaches were centered on offering customized solutions rather than just low cost.

As mentioned above, for the impending Hong Kong listing which happened in 2003, a new entity was created into which the most viable businesses were injected, while the "bad assets" were left in the parent holding company pending their dissolution or possibly future injection into the listed firm, if and when they were turned around and deemed viable. At the listing in Hong Kong, only 42% of its equity was publicly traded. The remaining 58% was restricted stock owned by the parent state-owned entity which in turn was 100% owned by the Chinese state (through SASAC). In 2022, the Chinese government ownership remained a controlling one but slightly reduced to 53%.

It is also interesting to note that both Deutsche Post (parent of DHL) and UPS invested in the new Sinotrans entity at listing. At that time, Sinotrans was the main Chinese logistics firm that foreign logistics firms were required to partner with. Much earlier in 1986, DHL had formed a 50/50 JV with Sinotrans for cross-border express logistics. In 2003, shortly after the listing, UPS formed a similar JV with Sinotrans. Although the UPS venture was short-lived, the DHL one has endured, as has Deutsche Post's shareholding in Sinotrans.

In 2017, the Chinese party-state embarked on a bureaucratic process of consolidating state transportation firms. COSCO was merged with China Shipping. China Merchants, a conglomerate spanning shipping and finance, was merged with Sinotrans. Sinotrans was essentially brought under a much larger entity.

It was a merger forced on Sinotrans and not of their choice. At the time, Sinotrans employees felt demoralized.[3]

As it turned out, Sinotrans retained its proud brand. China Merchants' logistics assets were injected into Sinotrans, making it China Merchants' primary logistics platform. Over one year after the merger Sinotrans' revenues grew by 10%, ahead of market trends.

A new corporate culture. When in 1999, Sinotrans embarked upon its transformation into a modern corporate entity capable of delivering modern integrated logistics up to global standards, a key challenge it faced was that of changing its corporate culture. Its old deep-rooted SOE culture was not all negative or unsuited to the modern age. Sinotrans was in official language a "large SOE" but unlike COSCO for instance, not an "especially large SOE." Although it was under central government control, it still enjoyed a degree of autonomy and was not interfered with that much. Salaries were not high but there were good benefits which included company housing. Company buses left on the dot at 5 PM taking employees back to various parts of Beijing. Working long into the evening was rare. The leadership was approachable and would eat breakfast and lunch alongside the rest of the staff in the canteen. There was of course a clear hierarchy not just in terms of corporate roles but also with regard to the CCP which exercised strong influence through its Party Committee, its Secretary, and its Disciplinary Committee within the firm. But compared with some larger SOEs, the CCP played a relatively low-key role and was less inclined to halt business operations for days while a political campaign was underway. There was an earthy camaraderie across ranks. Outsiders (including foreigners) could drop by for a chat without an appointment.

Still, in many other respects, the SOE culture was a heavy burden that stood in the way of the firm's transformation. Fortunately, in the open atmosphere of the economic reforms, the ghosts of the past could be identified and confronted.

Under the traditional SOE culture, leadership was autocratic. Endless meetings and consultation with employees presented the impression of consensus but this was largely fake. The emphasis was on continuity and not change. There was a strong aversion to risk-taking. The firm was inward-focused not customer-oriented. When it came to financial objectives, the emphasis was on revenues not on profits. Under the notion of the "iron rice bowl," employment was for life if you played your cards well, and individual performance was undervalued. Asset-intensity was seen as a pure positive, not as a potential balance sheet burden. Maintenance of employment was a core objective, a virtue in itself. The goals of the party-state were paramount and trumped the firm's strategy. Now, we do not have a dog in the race. We are not prescribing what is best for China. But it was the Chinese themselves that at this moment in history determined that the old economic model, including the corporate governance and culture described above, had to be transformed if China were to be able to compete effectively in the world economy it so earnestly wished to join.

So Sinotrans, like many other SOEs, embarked on the path of culture change. During its restructuring prior to stock market listing, it still exhibited some of the old style of leadership with regard to laboriously building broad consensus before taking a decision. That said, there was a new bolder and more decisive approach. While key managers were consulted, the top executives moved with purpose to make the business and organizational changes even when painful or controversial. The focus was on the external environment and on customer needs. There was a move to a more entrepreneurial frame of mind, a willingness to take a degree of acceptable risk, and to be responsive to market shifts. In terms of commercial objectives, there was shift away from mainly revenue growth toward a frame of mind that pays attention to profits, return-on-investment, and "shareholder value." The changes in the firm's corporate culture were critical to breaking free from the stifling legacy of central planning.

Building the new business. As discussed earlier, over recent decades, Sinotrans has used its scale and deep pockets to invest heavily in developing its own proprietary IT systems using integrated digital platforms to link it to shippers and outsourced service providers, to link all functions from sales and marketing to service delivery (transportation and warehousing management, optimization, and tracking), regulatory compliance and billing. An entity created for the further development of its Y2T.com logistics platform is successfully raising private equity funding. This digitalization will surely help Sinotrans compete with the emerging private Chinese logistics firms that are broadening their appeal from e-commerce fulfillment and delivery to logistics more broadly.

In terms of business mix, when Sinotrans was listed in 2003, it was still essentially just a freight forwarder. The nascent 3PL business was tiny and not material to the company's finances. In 2022, Sinotrans' revenues were over RMB 109 BN, six times the level in 2003. But freight forwarding still accounted for 64% of its revenues. This includes sea, air, and rail freight forwarding, plus related stored and terminal facilities. As discussed above in Chapter 10, a key aspect of its fast-growing rail freight forwarding business is the numerous dedicated routes rail routes provided by Sinotrans from China, across Russia and Central Asia to Europe and also from South China into South East Asia. This is essentially an extension of the freight forwarding business. Sinotrans makes a commitment to China's railways for a certain amount of rail space (a whole train or part of it) and then markets and sells this space to its customers. Sinotrans leaves the train operations to the railways.

E-commerce accounts for only 5% of Sinotrans' revenues and 95% of that are cross-border e-commerce, in part attributed to the DHL partnership.

Logistics have grown to be 25% of revenues and 29% of net profit. This part of the business is dominated by contract logistics (75% of this segment) while project, chemicals, and cold-chain logistics (14%, 9%, and 2%) make up the rest.

Contract logistics is the classic 3PL business, based on long-term contracts with shippers of goods such as fast-moving consumer goods, consumer electronics and white goods, pharma, and auto. Project logistics is used to refer to moving large items of capital equipment such as turbines for hydropower. Logistics, as a whole, show a net profit margin of 3%–4%, with the exception of cold-chain logistics which is loss-making. The implication is that given Sinotrans' lack of scale and its poor performance in cold chain it has little chance of challenging cold chain specialists in China such as SF (see below).

Future trajectory. Looking ahead, Sinotrans has distinct advantages given its prominent position on rail links across the China-Europe rail bridge. Geopolitical tensions and threats in the South China Sea, Taiwan Strait, and the Red Sea all make sea routes more vulnerable. There are already cases of liner shipping firms choosing the Cape of Good of Hope over the Suez Canal. All this increases the competitiveness of rail freight to Europe (even with the complication brought on by the Russia and Ukraine War).

Unlike COSCO which has a series of ports management projects across the globe that can help extend its logistics reach, Sinotrans, despite being internationally focused in the past, is not as well positioned in terms of actual capabilities and asset overseas. To create that capability, Sinotrans has been active internationally, making acquisitions (KLG Group in Eurrope), forming JVs (in Saudi Arabia), and establishing and staffing new logistics entities (in Singapore).

Sinotrans has inevitably been hit by the weakness of international trade. In mid-2023, its freight forwarding was down 15%, compared to the previous year. However, revenues from the logistics business, largely reliant of the domestic China market, were only marginally down and profitability was up substantially. As Sinotrans Chairman Feng Boming puts it, the firm is adjusting to the "new development pattern which focuses on the greater domestic circulation and features positive interplay between domestic and international circulation." He explained in more detail that markets along the Belt & Road can help to counterbalance the weakness of demand in the US and Europe, stating that they shall "capture the business demands of emerging economies, emerging regions and third countries, and continue to expand emerging markets such as Southeast Asia and the Middle East."[4]

One can argue that, through its evolution into a 3PL, it has become a well-balanced firm that sits astride both the international market and the domestic Chinese market. It is a strong 3PL player in the Chinese market, threatened less by foreign competitors (unlike the story two decades ago) but more by private Chinese logistics firms. But while Sinotrans remains a major force in China's fast changing domestic market, competing strongly against newly emerged firms, it is hard to see it becoming an international titan among 3PLs.

COSCO Shipping Logistics – life under the shadow of a shipping giant

---

COSCO Shipping Logistics & Supply Chain Management Co. 中远海运物流供应链有限公司

Date established: 2003. HQ: Beijing

Ownership: State-owned. Part of COSCO Shipping group. Ultimate owner is China's State Assets Management Administration (SASAC)

Management: Jiang Kai, President

Turnover: Not published.

We have profiled above the extent to which 25 years ago the time was ripe for Sinotrans to evolve into a 3PL. At that same time, it was not nearly as obvious that China's largest container line the China Ocean Shipping or COSCO (since 2017 called COSCO Shipping) could or should create a fully fledged logistics firm. However, due to strong leadership and careful strategic thinking, they succeeded in transforming its land-based capabilities and assets into a modern integrated logistics business.

The background. COSCO bore little resemblance to humble Sinotrans. It was then and remains a massive shipping firm. Today, it has over 1,100 vessels, of which 510 are container ships (with a capacity of 2.9 MM TEUs). As an "especially large SOE," its Chairman/CEO and Party Secretary are both appointed by the CCP Organization Department (and not by state organ SASAC). Back at the turn of the century, Sinotrans was still located in a run-down office block in Northwest Beijing where all staff including senior management waited an eternity for a lift to get up to their offices. In contrast, COSCO was moving into their massive new office complex, on Chang'an Boulevard, just opposite the central bank, the People's Bank of China. The building was known to be the most expensive new office building in Beijing, featuring only imported materials and fittings. The COSCO senior executive floor featured massive, well-appointed offices. In the basement, guests were hosted by COSCO at a pricy seafood restaurant which was owned by COSCO. There was no small touch of hubris around all of this. COSCO was at that time led by charismatic leader Capt. Wei Jiafu, a former container ship captain. As Chairman he would host visiting foreign dignitaries as if he were a Minister (in fact his status in the Chinese nomenklatura accorded him Vice Minister status.). As such a meeting drew to a close, he would pose for photographs shaking hands. With the guest still in the room, he would call his PR head in and dictate a message on the high significance of the meeting. He and his firm were flattered to be the subject of Harvard Business School case studies.

In 2001, he led a massive 50th birthday party for the firm which spent over USD 1 MM, including dancers emerging from a giant birthday cake.

For a while, COSCO diversified rashly into real estate, building large high-end apartment blocks in Beijing. It also moved into shipbuilding, establishing its own shipyards. Its core shipping business was periodically rocked by sagging shipping rates, brought on by global recession or by a self-inflicted oversupply of container ship capacity. At times, as it recorded repeated losses in its listed entities, there was the threat of being de-listed in Hong Kong. To mitigate the risk that poor financial performance would trigger default on its bank loans, COSCO refinanced, replacing its group of foreign bank lenders with a group of Chinese bankers which were much less likely to call a default and pull the plug on the firm's debt.

Despite this grand but rather flawed background, the remarkable emergence of COSCO Logistics is a heartening and positive story. It took vision in the top leadership coupled with hard work at the operating level to rethink the landside of their business with the result in December 2003. COSCO Logistics was finally established as a stand-alone logistics firm, with 3PL written into its "scope of business" on its official business license.

Before examining how COSCO Logistics business started out and has evolved, it is useful first to examine the extent to which the new firm had to forge a new corporate culture and with that the appropriate talent and workforce that fit the new business.

Culture change and new talent. The culture of its existing shipping business was of necessity highly regimented and rigid, much akin to the discipline you might find in the army. This entailed a centralized top-down command structure designed to enforce strict adherence to a set of procedures which ensured the safe operation of the ships and a predictable and highly standardized level of customer service.

Even in the COSCO parent company, there was a recognition that things needed to be shaken up. COO and board member Gao Weijie, a modern-thinking executive who had represented COSCO in the UK decades before just as containerization was beginning, sought to soften the rigid layers of authority by encouraging staff to email him directly with suggestions.

The first CEO of the newly created COSCO Logistics was Ye Weilong, just in his late 30s, who was able to make his voice heard in the powerful shipping company into which he reported, while downstream he juggled the many tasks related to building a new and dynamic team and setting the tone for creating long-term client relationships for the new contract logistics business. The team Ye built proved to be loyal and long-lasting: Two of them, Jiang Kai and Ma Xiaodong, are today President and SVP, respectively.

When it came to reforming the culture, the emphasis was on creating a mind-set that embraced logistics solutions tailored to the specific needs of individual customers and which permitted a high degree of adaptation in the course of delivery, as conditions dictated. To help break with the old COSCO culture, the decision was made to locate the new logistics firm in a very modest office building, a far cry from the lavish head office block. The creation of the new corporate culture in turn required the re-training of existing staff and the recruitment of new talent. A powerful illustration of COSCO Logistics' commitment to change is the way that in 2003 it went about hiring staff for the newly created logistics subsidiary. The stated guiding principle of this procedure was to support the "transformation" of the firm's management team through a selection process which was "open, fair, competitive and selected the best." The positions of general manager (GM) and two deputy general managers (DGMs) for two new business units – the Contract Logistics and the Project Logistics Departments – were opened up through external advertising. COSCO incumbents in these roles had to re-apply for their jobs and to compete against external candidates in a series of formal meetings where they made presentations and answered questions from a panel of COSCO executives (plus one external consultant[5]). To qualify for this final selection, there were a series of criteria which included an age band, years in the logistics business, and English ability. There was no explicit requirement that the candidate be a Chinese (PRC) citizen or a party member. As it ended up, the external candidates included some Hong Kong people. The detailed evaluations of the presentations were heavily weighted on "creativity" (30%) followed by logical thinking (20%), speaking, and communications skills language ability and adaptability. This efficient process resulted in the two GMs being the current incumbents, with several of the DGMs coming from the outside, which seemed a logical way to bring in fresh look to the team while still maintaining continuity.

Creating a cohesive business. In 2003, COSCO logistics portrayed itself in this way:

- Head office in Beijing, eight regional companies across China, 300+ operations locations, five rep office overseas.
- 1.7 MM m^2 of warehousing and container yards.
- Nine dedicated rail container routes.
- 1,300 trucks (of which 850 were tractor-trailers and 134 had GPS).

It looked very much like a firm that was strong in warehousing and trucking. But the goal was to transform its market position so that it became a 3PL. The key to this was first to define its core business, which were two existing businesses – shipping agency (providing for the needs of ships while in port) and sea freight forwarding – plus at that time the aspirational modern logistics. Once that core business was clearly defined, the other businesses, the warehousing, trucking, rail, and air freight, were defined as "supporting businesses" for the core businesses. The growth, staffing, and strategic direction of these supporting businesses were all tied to the extent that they addressed the needs of the core businesses and the clients they served. Having begun with a set of disparate businesses with often conflicting goals and priorities, there was now a framework for a cohesive and coherent strategy, something which served COSCO Logistics very well in the decades to come.

Sector/client focus. From its inception as a logistics firm, COSCO put strong emphasis on the fast-growing and highly profitable areas such as auto logistics (both inbound and outbound) and IT/telecom equipment. Also enjoying strong profitability was "power logistics," that is related to the movement of large items of capital equipment such as boilers and turbines for power stations, which required specialized trucking and thus had high barriers to entry. But they were also to find strong volume, though slimmer margins, in logistics relating to consumer electronic and white goods logistics where they became China's leader. In 2003, the firm handled 8 MM units of such products. It built a strong relationship with Qingdao Haier which was to blossom as that firm became a major exporter. COSCO displayed a healthy balance which combined a focus on delivering high-quality specialized services in a few selected areas, while keeping its eyes on new opportunities such as pharma and chemicals.

20 years ago, COSCO was able to deal with ordinary non-hazardous chemicals. But they were already setting their sights on creating a capability to handle hazardous liquid and gas chemicals that would prove to be highly profitable. They correctly perceived that there could be a high return in this area which required complex licensing (facilitated by COSCO's strong government ties) and professional and technical skills, all of which played to COSCO's strengths. Today, COSCO is pre-eminent in chemical logistics in China with seven hazardous chemicals bases across the country including in Chongqing deep in the interior, covering a total of 200,000 m². The basic services encompass warehousing, transportation, international freight forwarding, and multimodal solutions. In addition, they provide value-added services such as chemical filling and tank cleaning and repair.

COSCO has 1.8 MM m² of warehousing across China. Much of this is used for bulk commodities such as grain, chemicals, and nonferrous metals. Its auto logistics business in the domestic market remains strong with SAIC, FAW, Chang'an, Mercedes-Benz, and BMW, among their customers.

However, other branches of COSCO's logistics business remain strongly linked to international sea trade. While it has a strong cold logistics capability, its 100,000 m² of refrigerated warehousing is concentrated at China's ports, related to foreign trade in meat, aquatic products, fruit, pharma, and cosmetics.

COSCO's strategic direction in logistics is strongly focused on delivering international solutions for Chinese firms, such as Qingdao-based consumer appliance producers Haier and Hisense, through harnessing the COSCO groups growing global network of ports investments, including in Piraeus (Greece), Rotterdam, Hamburg, Valencia, and Bilbao. The firm is also mitigating the risk implicit in the sea routes by developing rail freight routes from China to Europe and to SE Asia. It has invested heavily in developing a rail terminal in Khorgos on the Kazakhstan side of the border with China.

For all its efforts in creating a strong role in domestic China logistics, it remains the case that COSCO's logistics arm remains heavily reliant on its massive shipping line parent (annual revenues of US$ 55 BN) The parent positions itself as a "global digital supply chain operator and investment platform with a core focus on container shipping." The stated value proposition for its customers is "end-to-end integrated whole-process logistics services."[6] The emphasis is on creating "synergies" from shipping to port terminals and to freight forwarding. Although this certainly implies a shift from overreliance on plain vanilla liner shipping, the logistics business still relies on the sea-borne aspect of trade for much of its impact and raison d'etre. There is no doubt that COSCO Logistics has carved out a strong reputation for itself as a 3PL. But, longer term, it is hard to see it emerging as a global force, unless it manages to build its own brand and step out of the shadow of its shipping parent.

China Logistics Group – making sense of a fragmented legacy

China Logistics Group 中国物流集团有限公司

Established: 2021, through the merger of China Railway Materials Group and four subsidiaries of China Chengtong Holdings: China National Materials Storage and Transportation; CTS International Logistics; China Logistics; and China National Packaging.
HQ: Beijing. *Ownership*: State-owned. SASAC 38.9%. China Chengtong 38.9%. Remainder by China Eastern, COSCO Shipping, China Merchants
Management: Chairman: Li Hongfeng, CEO: Liao Jiasheng
Registered Capital: Target of RMB 200 BN by 2025
Turnover: Target of RMB 280 MM (US$ 41 BN) by 2025

In Chapter 2, on the history of China's logistics, we documented the path from the planned economy to a more market-driven approach. A central player in that story was the former Ministry of Domestic Trade, which, with its multilayers of countless warehouses and trucking companies, dominated domestic goods distribution. As that ministry was dissolved and the old structure of central planning fell away, a massive infrastructure was left behind. Some of that morphed into private firms. Some simply melted way, leaving land for shopping malls.

But there did remain a significant legacy of warehousing which was substandard and looking to be repurposed. Once the fossilized Ministry of Railways was finally dissolved and merged into the Ministry of Transportation, there were also significant residual legacy assets in the rail sector. These issues were addressed by the formation of China Logistics Group (CLG) in 2021. COSCO Shipping and China Merchants (parent of Sinotrans) through taking an equity share in the formation of the new company, indicated their willingness to share in the future of that firm, presumably through outsourcing storage and transportation to it.

The newly created China Logistics Group's vision is "to become a world-class modern logistics group company with global competitiveness." Clearly that remains highly aspirational. The firm indicated its true core capabilities as:

- Land area – 24 MM m^2
- Warehousing – 4.9 MM m^2
- Yards – 3.5 MM m^2
- Dedicated rail routes – 120
- Future delivery warehouses – 40
- Trucks – 3 MM[7]

The company offers a full range of logistics specializations from manufacturing, Fast moving consumer goods (FMCG), cold chain, and hazardous goods. But there is little evidence that so far that, post-merger, its multiple subsidiaries and their diverse and fragmented assets and services have been melded together into anything that resembles a coherent corporate entity. It will take time to weed out the unneeded assets and staff, to create a sustainable, integrated business that can meet the needs of an increasingly demanding set of customers.

After six months of intensive post-merger integration of assets and staff, CLG did announce a bold five-year plan which set a 2025 revenue target of US$ 41 BN with a net profit of just under 3%. But while it expressed the goal of becoming one of the Fortune Global 500, serious doubt has been cast on whether this can be achieved. As one Chinese logistics specialist points out, CLG's "main business is still just traditional logistics." He further explained that CLG lacks any advantages in the fastest-growing segments of digital, express, and cross-border logistics that are dominated by Cainiao, SF, and JD. Nor is CLG well positioned in shipping logistics, freight forwarding, customs clearance, and air freight where the "old brands of COSCO, Sinotrans and the four large airlines" rule the roost. When it comes to M&A as a path forward for CLP, it is pointed out the CLG does not generate the profits needed to support this nor is it in a position to raise funds by other means. This commentator thought that, as an alternative, CLG might be able to rely on a continued bureaucratic "free allocation" of assets to the business by the government's SASAC[8] which supervises state assets. But he concluded wryly that such a process is no substitute for letting market forces take their course. Even though CLG might receive some benefit from this assistance, at the end of the day:

> Constantly acquiring some state-owned logistics enterprises by means of free asset allocation, it is just that this way of building cannot be understood as market-oriented behavior. In this way, even if a number of enterprises are integrated [into CLG], they do not have strong market competitiveness, and they are just pile of stacked up wooden blocks.[9]

We can acknowledge that the formation of CLG is a major step in the right direction. It shows a path forward for China to shake off its legacy of a highly fragmented and dysfunctional warehousing and goods transportation system. But we have vivid memories of inspecting countless units of substandard warehousing, damp and windy, untidy and poorly run, with poor security and the high risk of theft. We also recall underpowered, overladen trucks with just a tarpaulin to shield the goods from the elements. How much of that legacy remains at the core of CLG? Despite its bold vision to be a global giant, one is bound to question whether it has the ability to catch up and transcend the limitations of "traditional logistics."

Evolution of Cainiao: Alibaba's transformation in logistics

Cainiao Smart Logistics Network Ltd 菜鸟网络科技有限公司

Date Established: 2013. *HQ* Hangzhou, Zhejiang
Ownership: Private. Parent is Alibaba. Has filed for stock listing in Hong Kong
Management: CEO: Shen Guojun
Turnover (2022): US$ 7.9 BN. Net profit: US$ 0.6 BN
Employees: 20,000

The early 2010s marked a watershed moment when Jack Ma, Alibaba's founder, unveiled a pioneering idea to address China's persistently inefficient logistics systems. Amid the exponential growth of e-commerce, Ma envisioned a logistics network that would not only serve Alibaba's growing customer base but also meet a broader national imperative. In 2013, Cainiao Network was formed as a joint venture, with founding shareholders Alibaba, department store owner

Intime Group, conglomerate Fosun Group, leisure company Forchn Group, and five Chinese logistics companies YTO Express, SF Express (SF), ZTO Express, Yunda, and Shentong Express.

Ma's vision for Cainiao was dedicated to meeting Alibaba Group's logistics vision of fulfilling consumer orders within 24 hours in China and within 72 hours anywhere else in the world,[10] a simple yet daunting goal, given the state of China's logistics sector at the time. This vision laid the groundwork for Cainiao's unique three-tier model, which we will elaborate upon below. It also sparked the incorporation of big data analytics, aimed at optimizing supply chain efficiencies.

Domestically, the company created a strong foundation by building automated sorting centers at key logistical nodes within China. These were not typical sorting centers; they were sophisticated automated operations. These centers served as the backbone of Cainiao's physical infrastructure, setting the stage for the nationwide delivery network. The company also invested in a fleet of dedicated delivery personnel, equipped with digitally connected devices that aided in real-time package tracking and reporting. They also rolled out smart lockers in highly populated urban centers.

Cainiao's domestic operations also relied on strong partnerships with other express delivery services, effectively creating a massive collaborative, tech-driven China-wide express delivery ecosystem.

Simultaneously, Cainiao was ahead of the curve in recognizing the value of actionable data. With a delivery force armed with digital devices for real-time tracking, the company was quick to employ big data analytics for improved routing, peak demand prediction, and inventory optimization. These proprietary algorithms became the cornerstone of Cainiao's digital capabilities. Data analysis was not just an auxiliary function; it was an integral part of the operation, enabling a tight integration of physical and digital assets which distinguishes Cainiao from competitors.

By 2015, the payoff was evident. Cainiao's multipronged strategy had triumphed, making 24-hour delivery a reality across hundreds of Chinese cities. The model was agile enough to accommodate ongoing changes: Cainiao continued to refine its operational efficiency, adopting drones, autonomous vehicles, and state-of-the-art robotics in its warehouses, as well as embracing green initiatives like electric delivery vehicles and sustainable packaging.

Fast forward to 2022, Cainiao's physical and digital sophistication reached new heights, capable of dealing with staggering volume. This became particularly evident in the past several years' Singles Days, where Cainiao processed an astronomical 1.3 billion delivery orders, compared to an already impressive average of 100 million on any regular day.[11]

Cainiao's revolutionary three-tiered business model represents a massively flexible approach to logistics, combining operational control, geographic reach, and volume scalability, especially when compared to global logistics giants.

At the foundation of Cainiao's structure is its owned and operated network, which serves as the backbone of its logistics operation. This setup allows Cainiao to exercise significant control over its logistics chain, ensuring high levels of service and efficiency. The operations in major cities throughout China and the links between them are typically part of this Cainiao-owned operation.

The second tier consists of partnerships with major express carriers like ZTO, Yunda, YTO, STO, Best Express, and SF. These collaborations allow Cainiao to expand its pickup and delivery reach significantly. They also serve a critical role during peak demand periods, offering Cainiao the agility to scale operations quickly, ensuring that service levels remain consistent even when the system is under stress.

Lastly, the third tier, featuring Cainiao Guoguo and Cainiao Post, takes flexibility and scalability to a new level. These platforms are designed to handle the vast and diverse delivery needs of an entire nation. Cainiao Guoguo taps into the "gig economy" (based on freelance workers) to provide flexible last-mile delivery options, while Cainiao Post digitalizes community service centers, creating a decentralized network of parcel hubs that can rapidly adjust to market needs.

Cainiao's foray into global logistics operations began with clear aspirations for international coverage and new levels of expedited delivery. As early as 2015, Alibaba and Cainiao publicly set an audacious target for 72-hour global delivery, setting the stage for a series of strategic moves aimed at achieving this ambitious goal. The first significant enabler of this aspiration was the opening in 2020 of an eHub in Kuala Lumpur, Malaysia, providing a heavily automated, data-driven sorting center designed for rapid cross-border shipping and final mile distribution.

Following the successful launch in Kuala Lumpur, in 2021, Cainiao opened another eHub in Liege, Belgium, to service the European market. These two eHubs are not isolated operations; rather, they are vital nodes within Alibaba's Electronic World Trade Platform, a global initiative aiming to make it easier for Small and Medium Enterprises (SMEs) to participate in global trade.

Cainiao's global operations have grown impressively over time, with eHubs, extensive air charters, and more than 500 logistics partners integrated into their network. As of early 2022, Cainiao handled a daily average of over 4.5 million cross-border packages.[12] While their 72-hour global delivery target still remains aspirational, Cainiao is also committed to delivering value for money. Their cost-efficient solutions, such as ten-day delivery for just US$ 5 to 20 countries and 20-day delivery for US$ 2 to 50 countries,[13] illustrate the company's ambition to provide options for either rapid or affordable global shipping.

Their investments in strategic eHubs and building of extensive partnerships are a testament to a larger vision that is beginning to set a new global standard in logistics efficiency and speed.

In FY 2023, Cainiao's revenues reached an impressive US$ 11.3 BN, with US$ 8.1 BN generated from clients beyond Alibaba,[14] underlining its independent market influence. Leveraging big data, IoT, and machine learning, Cainiao distinguishes itself from traditional logistics providers and even global giants like UPS and FedEx. Its uniquely flexible three-tiered business model enables the firm to adapt to market demands, with owned networks ensuring control, partnerships granting reach, and crowdsourced platforms providing unprecedented scalability. As it expands globally, Cainiao is a disruptive force that is resetting global logistics standards.

JD Logistics – an approach which contrasts with that of Cainiao

---

JD Logistics 京东物流集团

Established: in 2007 as internal fulfillment arm of e-commerce firm JD.com. In 2017 became stand-alone logistics business.
HQ: Beijing. Ownership: Private. 2021 listed in Hong Kong. Parent is JD.com, China's largest on-line retailer
Management: Chairman: Richard Liu (Liu Qiangdong)
Turnover (2022): RMB 137 BN (US$ 20 BN) 40% for JD.com and 60% for external customers. *Net loss*: RMB 1.1 BN (US$ 0.16 BN)
Employees: 258,700

JD.com, the parent company of JD Logistics (JDL), is one of China's e-commerce giants, comparable to Alibaba. A private firm, it was founded in 2004 by Liu Qiangdong and by 2022 had revenues equivalent to US$ 152 BN. It is listed in Hong Kong (with a market cap of HK$ 268 BN) and on Nasdaq. Walmart has a 12% equity share in the firm giving it and its Sam's Club access to the JD platform. Tencent, China's leading social media firm, considered getting into e-commerce but decided against that, in part due to the high capital investment in the logistics that would come with it. Tencent has taken an 18% equity position in JD.com, bringing important linkages through its WeChat (*Weixin*) platform. JD.com started off with a focus on consumer electronics but now covers every segment of the market including consumer appliances, fresh produce, and imported goods. In order to ensure quality and avoid fake goods, it has been willing to take title to the products and accept inventory risk. It has successfully expanded its business from Tier 1 and 2 cities to lower tier cities, counties, and rural areas.

JD.com's path to profitability is one of "low margin, based on high inventory turnover."[15] To achieve that:

> JD's integrated model enables it to be more efficient than competitors and be profitable at lower gross margins. JD accomplishes this feat by replacing layers of the traditional retail supply chain with <u>technology and scaled logistics,</u> [emphasis added] which allow it to undercut the competition. The result is that, similar to Walmart or Costco, operating at low margins is a huge barrier to entry, and a strength - not a weakness.[16]

Just as with Walmart in the US, JD.com, through operating its own highly efficient in-house logistics, has been able to drive down costs, with that improvement in part being passed on to customers.

JD.com's stated value proposition is "genuine products at low price, quality guaranteed, on-time delivery, easy to purchase." The ontime delivery dimension is achieved through its subsidiary, JDL, which we profile here.

It is said that shortly after JD.com was established, "70% of customer complaints involved delivery service, since China's logistics infrastructure was essentially nonexistent."[17] In 2007, JD.com took the decision to invest heavily in establishing its own internal logistics capability and today JDL handles the bulk of JD.com's fulfillment. This gave it an advantage over Alibaba which had been hesitant about doing so and only in 2013 established Cainiao, its in-house logistics firm. As of 2018, JD was delivering "90%+ of direct retail orders within 24 hours, an unfathomable achievement in markets outside of China."[18] In 2017, JD began providing logistics to external customers which now account for 60% of its US$ 20 BN of annual revenues. JDL is experiencing double-digit revenue growth. It has 362,000 staff engaged in both warehousing and transportation/ delivery. Complementing its strong organic growth, JDL is also active in M&A. In 2022, it spent US$ 1.4 BN to acquire the Shanghai-based Deppon (*Debang*) Logistics which brings a strong China-wide network of transportation LTL and full truckload, delivery, and warehousing. Working closely with JD.com's technology subsidiary, JDL is pioneering the use of completely robotic warehouse automation, autonomous trucks, drone delivery, and the use of AI to optimize the operations.

JD has made a virtue out of being, through JDL, highly integrated down to and including the "last mile." This contrasts with Alibaba and Cainiao which were happy to rely on others for the transportation and delivery. One former Alibaba executive, writing in 2015, argued that JD's approach allowed them to "control the customer experience from end-to-end."[19] The idea behind this is that through this complete ownership of the supply chain, they can exercise a high degree of control and so ensure top-notch service. But this competitive advantage may be more perceived than real. Chinese e-commerce firms today have leapfrogged the rest of the world in terms of building a comprehensive IT platform that seamlessly links it not only to suppliers and customers but also to outsourced logistics providers. This technology permits strong connectivity to external parties and strongly mitigates the risk of the supply chain breaking down or being compromised. This way of operating may well make JD's focus on owning everything redundant and a burden.

The newly listed JDL explained their operations in terms of "six synergized and digitally integrated logistics."[20]

At the core of the business is the Warehouse Network. This comprises 1,500 of its own warehouses plus so-called "cloud warehouses" provided by third-party providers under JDL's Open Warehouse Program, resulting in an aggregate 30 MM m^2 of floor space. The Open Warehouse Program was specifically directed at providing capacity for external customers that is other than JD.com. An example of JDL's adoption of new technology is its Intelligent Logistics Park in Kunshan, Jiangsu on the border with Shanghai, which it claims to be the world's largest of its type. Its automatic sorting center has 80 sorting lines, 10,000 sorting robots, and with, they say, a sorting accuracy rate of 99.99%. It is said to be five times more efficient than traditional sorting methods. It has a capacity of *4.5 MM packages* per day. Using this new park, JDL can now provide same- or next-day delivery for a population of 200 MM in East China.[21]

Connecting the warehousing and the local e-commerce delivery stations is the Line Haul Network which comprises 210 sorting centers and long-haul transportation. As with the warehousing, the sorting centers have a high degree of automation, for instance through various kinds of robots. On the transportation side, this network has 7,500 in-house trucks (plus outsourced capability), 300 rail routes (many already high speed), and 1,000 air cargo routes.

The final step in reaching the consumer's door is carried out by the Last-Mile Delivery Network which comprises 7,800 delivery offices with staff of 200,000. These offices are also open day and night for consumers that wish to pick up the packages themselves. JDL also has 50,000 lockers sites at apartment blocks and office building where packages can be deposited for pickup. Both Alibaba/Cainiao and JDL decided early on that they wished to be vertically integrated with an end-to-end service that it owned and operates. As we shall see below, Cainiao does achieve some of this capability through partnership and stock crossholdings with firms such as ZTO Express. JDL is purer in this approach that controls everything and does not share aspects of the business process with external partners, and with that accepts the need for a more asset-heavy business model.

JDL has also carved out a niche for itself in handling home appliances and furniture, through its Bulky Items Logistics Network. Unlike other logistics providers who only provide the transportation and delivery, JDL provides an integrated package including the assembly and installation of these goods. JDL is also a player in cold-chain logistics with a network of refrigerated warehouses both for food and pharma. JDL's capability is rounded out by a Cross-Border Logistics Network which comprises bonded warehouses in China, other warehouses overseas, and chartered freight flights. To gain additional reach in Europe, JDL has formed a strategic alliance with Geopost, Europe's second-largest package delivery firm, owned by La Poste, which is in turn part-owned by the French government. Having invested heavily in their own warehousing in Europe, this new linkup means that goods from these warehouses can now achieve same-day delivery in Germany, Netherlands, France, the UK, Spain, and Poland.[22] JDL already has three warehouses in California.

But as a stand-alone business and since 2021 listed on the Hong Kong stock market, JDL faces a high degree of scrutiny and questions about its profitability. Before it being spun off, the logistics business was mainly in the red, due to the heavy investment in creating a logistics network across the nation. In 2019, there were claims that the logistics costs were falling and that the business had reached breakeven. But shortly before the listing the evidence showed that it was still loss-making. While before being integrated into JD.com, it could legitimately exist as simply a cost center that supported the broader e-commerce business. But once on its own, JDL was obliged to demonstrate to its investors a path to profitability. With its continuing close role as the fulfillment arm of JD.com, this was bound to be complicated and fraught with conflicts of interest. For instance, does its continuing close relationship to JD.com mean that it will be constrained from working with competitors of JD.com? This was a question asked at the time of its listing in 2021. In being spun-off, it would have been tidier if there had been a clearer break with its parent. But, as it stands, that relationship will inevitably create difficult choices. Fortunately, JDL has since 2017 been providing 3PL services to external customers and these (60% of revenues today) may provide the higher margins and an end to the red ink.

In 2021, when it came to its stock listing, JDL was losing money, while other major express delivery companies were already profitable. But, at that time, commentators were quick to stress that JDL was forecasting a China's logistics market of US$ 3 TRN by 2025 and has pledged to spend heavily to strengthen their market position as a leading technology-driven integrated logistics provider to address this opportunity and was therefore not over-focused on short-term profitability. JDL's stated goal is to continue to grow rapidly in order to consolidate their leadership in what they correctly characterize as a still highly fragmented China's logistics market.[23]

SF Express (SF) – China's answer to FedEx

SF Express (Shunfeng) （顺风速运）

Established: 2003 (in Shunde). *HQ*: Shenzhen
Ownership: Private. Listed 2017 in Hong Kong. *Market Cap*: US$ 23 BN
Management: Founder and Chairman: Wang Wei
Turnover (2022): US$ 40 BN. Net Income: US$ 0.92 MM
Employees: 177,000

SF was founded by Wang Wei who today remains Chairman of the firm. It is one of many stories in China of self-made wealth. Born in Shanghai in 1970, he was from the age of seven brought up and educated in Hong Kong. But he did not go to university but instead began working in factories in Shunde, a city across the border on the muddy South side of the Pearl River within easy ferry reach of Hong Kong. Manufacturing activity was leaving Hong Kong for places such as Shunde. But Wang observed how difficult it was to get samples to buyers in Hong Kong and so began his courier service, initially with six people. Today, he has a net worth of around US$ 20 BN and his firm, with revenues of US$ 40 BN, is one of the largest logistics firms in China and the world.

SF, which in many respects resembles US firm FedEx, is on an extraordinary growth path with revenues growing annually at around 30%, while it maintains a net profit at over 2%. In 2022, it had over 11 BN shipments. Their declared recipe for this success is a combination of high-quality service with a heavy emphasis on "lean," pushing down costs through "lean operations" and "network optimization and efficiency improvement." Digitalization lowered the cost of deploying its growing fleet of trucks. Further efficiency gains have come from improvements to the firm's automatic sorting capability.

Over half of SF's service products are related to express courier and e-commerce logistics. Although SF began life providing fulfillment services for e-commerce firms Alibaba and JD.com, those customers have steadily reduced their reliance on SF. JD had all along favored doing more in-house. With Alibaba that trend accelerated when in 2017 it took a controlling interest in its logistics subsidiary Cainiao. Given that trend, SF's core activity is now courier logistics at various levels of service – time definite, economy express, general express, and intra-city. The time-definite courier business accounts for 40% of revenues and is growing faster than the rest of the market. But besides the express business, it prides itself on having a well-balanced business with around 35% of its revenues coming from broader supply chain services in China and overseas.[24] Within this segment, it has created a specific focus on cold chain logistics (for food and pharma) where there is unmet market demand and a high bar of entry for competitors.

It is apparent that SF's mercurial rise owes itself at least in part to its clear strategic focus. It has not sought to address all parts of the logistics market. Instead, it has concentrated on areas where it has deep experience and competitive advantage.

SF stands out for its bold moves in acquisitions, alliances, and its heavy investments in aviation. In the domestic market, it has expanded its contract logistics breadth through the 2019 acquisition of the DHL China supply chain business. While DHL continues to perform well in their cross-border courier partnership with Sinotrans, they found it hard to build a profitable domestic China logistics business. Within China, SF has built a strong reputation in cold-chain logistics, whether for food and vegetables or for vaccines and blood plasma. This is a highly specialized business requiring warehousing and transport with multiple levels of controlled temperature. A major move was the acquisition of US firm Havi Food's China cold-chain logistics network. Since the 1980s Havi has been the key supplier of logistics to McDonald's in China. SF is also one of the few logistics firms (along with China Post and YTO) that have their own in-house cold-chain air cargo service within China.

Early on, SF took the decision, as FedEx did, to carve out a niche for itself through owning its own fleet of aircraft. SF Airlines began flying in 2009 and today has over 87 aircraft, 35 of which are B757 200 freighters. Further massive capital investment was made by SF in constructing its own dedicated "professional" freight airport, the first in China – the Ezhou Huahu Airport, in Hubei Province, not far from Wuhan, in the heart of China. SF has plowed US$ 370 MM into the airport itself and US$ 1.7 MM into its aviation distribution center. SF has a 46% share of the airport's equity, the first time in China that a private firm has been permitted to participate in the ownership of an airport. The airport, which opened in 2022, has 2 runways, an apron for 124 aircraft, and 24,000 m^2 of warehousing. It has 10 international and 50 domestic air cargo routes. By 2025, it is expected to handle 2.45 MM tons of cargo per annum. SF has "the ambition to make it the Memphis of China,"[25] a reference to FedEx's key cargo hub in Tennessee, US. It is also similar to what UPS and DHL have in Louisville (Kentucky) and Leipzig (Germany). Looking at SF, one could say that it is emblematic of the scale and muscle of China's private logistics firms which has permitted them to engage in the construction of China's basic transportation infrastructure, something which hitherto only the Chinese state has had the resources to accomplish.

SF's global reach was transformed in 2021 when it spent HK 17.5 BN (US$ 2.25 BN) to take a controlling interest in Hong Kong-based Kerry Logistics. Kerry, which was founded way back in 1981 by a member of the Malaysian Kwok family, brought to SF much-needed international capability. As a top, SF executive put it at the time of the merger. "Frankly, we don't have a global footprint at this moment: we are in about 20% of the countries that DHL and FedEx are in."[26] In 2021, SF and Kerry had revenues of US$ 3.4 BN and 5.3 BN, respectively. Together they formed what was described as the second largest logistics firm in China, after Sinotrans.[27]

SF is well run and well financed. Though it has some way to go to before becoming a global rival to FedEx and UPS, its ambitions to reach that scale and strength seem well-founded and reasonable. Like all of China's large logistics firms, it claims to have a strong reach into the poor 3rd- and 4th-tier cities and the rural areas. But, in many cases, this remains aspirational rather than the current reality. Still, SF's strong reputation is well established. As one Chinese logistics expert put it, "In China, SF has good price, high-quality service and are reliable. They even come to me and put the package in a box for me."[28]

"The Tonglu Gang" of express delivery logistics firm – STO, Yunda, YTO, ZTO

STO Express 申通快递

Established: 1993. *HQ*: Shanghai. *Ownership*: Private. Listed on HKSE and NYSE. Owned by Chen Dejun and his sister Chen Xiaoying. *Market Cap*: RMB 11 BN

Management (Founder Nie Tengfei died in 1998). Chairman: Chen Dejun, CEO: Wang Wenbin.

Revenues (2022): RMB 33 BN. Net Income: RMB 288 MM. Employees: 18,000

Yunda Express 韵达速递

Established: 1999. *HQ*: Shanghai. *Ownership*: Private. Listed on Shenzhen exchange.

Market Cap: RMB 19 BN

Management: CEO and Founder: Nie Tengyun (younger brother of STO's founder)

Revenues (2022): RMB 45 BN. Net Income: RMB 920 MM. Employees: 13,000

YTO Express 圆通速递

Established: 2000. *HQ*: Shanghai. *Ownership*: Private. Listed on HKSE. *Market Cap*: RMB 53 BN

Management: Founder and Chairman: Yu Weijiao

Revenues (2022): RMB 56 BN. Net Income: RMB 3.9 BN. Employees: 17,000

ZTO Express 中通快递

Established: 2002. *HQ*: Shanghai. *Ownership*: Private. Listed on HKSE and NYSE. *Market Cap*: HK$ 111 BN

Management: Founder, Chairman and CEO: Lai Meisong

Revenues (2022): RMB 38 BN. Net Income: RMB 0.99 BN. Employees: 17,000

These four firms are often referred to as the "Three tong and one da" *(Santong Yida)* which refers to three Chinese express delivery firms that have "tong" (as in 'link') in their Chinese names (STO, YTO, ZTO) and one, Yunda, with "da" (as in "reach there"). They are known collectively as this for a good reason. Though today they are today all based in Shanghai, their founders all come from one rural county, Tonglu County, Zhejiang Province, 270 km from Shanghai and 85 km inland from Hangzhou. Given their identical provenance, these four firms are also referred to "China's express [logistics] Tonglu Gang." The term "gang" here is used affectionately. As one Chinese commentator put it, with these four firms, in China's express logistics, "went from a blank piece of paper to the world number one" and represented a victory for China's "ordinary folks," who started with nothing.[29]

These four were established in the period 1993–2002 during the period when the Chinese entered its major growth spurt. First, there was STO Express, established in 1993 by Nie Tengfei. Then came Yunda Express formed by Nie Tengfei's younger brother Nie Tengyun (1998), followed by YTO setup by Yu Weijiao and his wife Zhang Xiaojuan who formerly was close to STO. Finally, Lai Meisong set up ZTO (2002).

In 2022, their revenues ranged from RMB 33 BN and 38 BN (STO and ZTO) to 45 BN and 56 BN (Yunda and YTO), making them major players, though far short of the RMB 137 BN chalked up by JDL.

Our readers are likely justifiably curious about why out China's 2,854 county-level administrative divisions, these four firms came to have their birthplace in Tonglu County. A number of factors can help suggest an answer.

We should not underestimate the degree to which the Zhejiang Provincial Government has over the years been supportive of entrepreneurs. Its relatively relaxed posture towards private enterprises permitted those firms to grow smoothly with the minimum of interference, in contrast to many other parts of China. Being located in a rural community far from the capital Beijing also left more room for innovation. That said, early on, all these companies faced pressure from China Post which tried, ultimately without success, to claim a monopoly over the courier business. Initially, these firms' entry into the business was deemed "black" (illegal) and they were forced to operate for a while under the radar. The success of these four firms is celebrated in Tonglu by a series of commemorative monuments including one where carved in stone are words stating boldly that they took on China Post and won!

The second factor is that Tonglu is located strategically close to the major markets of East China (defined as Shanghai, Zhejiang, Jiangsu, and Anhui) with a population of 215 MM (15% of China's total) which is the most productive and wealthy part of the nation.

Thirdly, we can look to the entrepreneurial spirit and shear hard work of the founders of these four firms that propelled them from rags to self-made billionaire status. Today, Tonglu is seen as an attractive rural place for urbanites to visit. But 25 years ago, sitting in the mountains, it was poor and backward. The founders of these firms began life operating tricycles that carried food and everyday products. But they soon found that they could earn more running a courier business, taking documents down to Hangzhou and getting involved in the procedures needed to get products exported.

Nie Tengfei set up STO in his 20s jointly with his wife Chen Xiaoying. She had dropped out of school to work at a printing and dyestuffs factory where she met her future husband. When Nie died in a car crash in 1998, she teamed up with her brother Chen Dejun (now Chairman with a net worth of US\$ 2.3 BN) to take the business forward. She put things on course for success by signing a delivery contract with Jack Ma for Alibaba's Taobao e-commerce business.

When set up in 1998, Yunda had just 17 employees. Today, its founders, Nie Tengfei's younger brother and his wife Chen Liying, have a net worth of US\$ 2 BN and 1.11 BN. Before establishing YTO, its current Chairman Yu Huijiao had started out as a carpenter and then struggled through the bankruptcy of his architectural firm. He set up YTO in 2000 with his wife Zhang Xiaojun, who had been at school with STO's Nie Tengfei. They began with 15 employees, deploying bicycles which Yu himself pedaled. He now has a net worth of US\$ 1.8 BN.

ZTO's founder Lai Meisong was born in 1970 into a farmer's family in Tonglu County. At the age of 14, having failed the exam to get into upper middle school, he began working in a silk factory. At the age of 16, he began harvesting timber from the surrounding forests. The business grew and by 2001 he had accumulated RMB 5 MM. In 2002, he and some friends launched ZTO Express.[30] Today, Lai has a net worth of around US\$ 3.7 BN.

What is also apparent from the above description is the strong friendship and kinship links between the founders of these four firms which is a strong characteristic of many private firms that emerged in China after the economic reforms. They were also bonded by their use of the local version of the Zhejiang dialect. Although today all are headquartered in Shanghai, the four firms are still celebrated in Tonglu County. As private companies, they are mindful of the need to please the authorities through playing a constructive social role. They maintain some tax-paying entities in Tonglu and provide charitable contributions to their old home. In 2023, Lai and ZTO joined other Zhejiang billionaires in expressing strong support for Xi Jinping's post-Covid economic measures.[31]

In the early days, they tapped into these local relationships for investment funds. Later, they turned to the capital markets. In some cases, they enjoyed financial backing from venture capital. Then, in a period of 16 months in 2016–2017, all four firms were listed on various stock exchanges (Shanghai, Hong Kong, and New York).[32] Three of these were back-door listings, whereby new assets were injected into existing listed companies, thus avoiding the time and regulatory complexity of a fresh IPO.

Another major feature of the financial structure of these four firms is the degree to which they are intertwined with Alibaba and its logistics subsidiary Cainiao. In 2018, ZTO, YTO, and Yunda (and one other firm) took a 10% share in Cainiao. Then, in 2020, Alibaba invested in STO, YTO, Yunda, and ZTO bringing their holdings in these firms up to 25%, 23%, 10%, and 10%, respectively. Some commentators view this as a defensive measure to preempt any attempts by these delivery firms to move upstream into their e-commerce space. But as we discussed above, it is also intimately connected to Alibaba's desire to have robust options for transportation and sorting centers beyond its own in-house capability, which can permit operational flexibility during peak periods.

Unlike Cainiao and JDL, neither of them is locked into an upstream e-commerce partner and both have to compete for that business. Downstream, in contrast to JDL, they have chosen not to own and operate the last-mile pickup and delivery part of the business but instead to rely on "local network partners" for this. There is clearly a trade-off in this. While reducing asset-intensity, capital investment, and balance-sheet pressure, it implies more business risk in terms of less control over that quality of that part of the service. The good news is that, through the way these express delivery firms are closely integrated into Cainiao's IT platform, those risks are greatly mitigated.

We can take ZTO as a representative example of how these four firms operate. ZTO claims to have about 20% of China's express parcel delivery market. It has 79 sorting hubs, with 1,920 line-haul routes between the hubs, serviced by 4,400 line-haul trucks. This is the focus of their business. They do not attempt to offer an end-to-end solution of the kind that Cainiao and JDL deliver. When it comes to the last-mile pickup and delivery, ZTO relies heavily on local partners and also on Cainiao. Through its crossholdings with Cainiao, ZTO has access to Cainiao's own last-mile capability. In all, working through third parties, ZTO has 28,900 local pickup and delivery outlets.

These four firms are also investing heavily in international logistics. YTO is a good example. It is building a "global aviation logistics hub" at Jiaxing Airport, in Zhejiang, close to the boundary with Shanghai. This 97 HA development is seen as a key element in linking the Lower Yangzi region with the Belt and Road. YTO is expanding its existing fleet of B757Fs and B637Fs. From this hub, the air cargo will connect to the rest of China through intermodal rail, road, and water. YTO has also invested US$ 150 MM in Yiwu, China's "small commodities capital" in central Zhejiang, including creating dedicated rail routes between Yiwu and Europe.

All four firms appear to be profitable. But the net profit of STO, Yunda, and ZTO is skinny, ranging from 1% to 3%. YTO's at 7% looks healthier. These firms constantly emphasize that they face "cut-throat" competition in China's express delivery industry. Their mantra is that through growing volume and adopting technology for instance to achieve un-manned operations at sorting centers and using algorithms to optimize the optimize operations, they can increase their competitiveness through creating economies of scale and lowering operating costs.

How two Chinese online retailers serving international customers have stormed the market

Shein 希音

Established: 2008 in Nanjing. *HQ*: Recently moved from China to Singapore. *Ownership*: Private. Seeking stock market listing. *Management*: Founder and CEO: Chris Xu (Xu Yangtian)
Revenues (2022): US$ 24 BN. Employees: 11,000

Temu

Established: 2022. *HQ*: Boston USA. *Ownership*: Private. Part of
Shanghai-based ecommerce giant Pinduoduo (PDD).
PDD revenue (2022): RMB 130 BN. *PDD market Cap*: US$ 162 BN.
PDD Management: Co-CEOs: Chen Lei and Zhao Jiazhen (founder
Colin Huang recently left PDD)
Temu revenues: N/A. Employees: 13,000

Shein and Temu are exclusively online retailers that allow thousands of China
vendors to sell and ship directly to global consumers in the US, Europe, Australia,
Latin America, and elsewhere. Shein's growth since it was founded in 2008 has
been phenomenal. Tema's rise since being established in late 2022 has been even
more stunning. In 2023, these two firms had the world's leading shopping apps.
Temu's apps received 338 MM downloads while Shein's got 262 MM. This
compares with 188 MM downloads for Amazon Shopping, their nearest rival.[33]
In 2023, Shein and Temu were shipping 600,000 packages to the US *per day*.[34]
Packages are typically already individual labeled and addressed to the consumer
before they leave China. China-owned ByteDance Tiktok Shop has also recently
also entered the US market.

Although Shein is now based in Singapore, its roots are in China, having been
founded in 2008 by Chris Xu in Nanjing and later moved to Shenzhen. Shein had
sales of US$ 24 BN in 2022 which are projected to grow to US$ 59 BN by 2025.
It is seeking a stock market listing in the US with its market value put as US$
70–90 BN. As the world's largest fashion e-commerce retailer, it not only has
close links with 3,000 suppliers but also gets involved in the design of garments.

Temu, set up in the US in late 2022, is an offshoot of one of China's largest
e-commerce firms, Shanghai-based Pinduoduo (PDD), which has a stock market
value of US$ 162 BN. Temu represents a bold move by PDD to go beyond the
China market and to take on Amazon in its home market, competing on the basis
of being a "faster, cheaper and leaner version of Amazon."[35] Most of it sales
are in the US. It uses sophisticated AI-based logarithmic technology to custom-
ize offers to specific consumers. As it barnstorms global markets, it has already
come into conflict with Shein with numerous suits and countersuits in the US,
UK, and elsewhere.[36]

With regard to its logistics, Shein has invested heavily in warehousing not
only in China for sorting, packaging, and labeling but also in the US, the UK,
and elsewhere. For transport, it relies heavily on air-cargo and has a strategic
alliance with China Southern Airlines Logistics. In the countries into which it
sells, it relies on a wide range of local transport firms. For instance, in the UK,
the delivery to consumers is handled by firms such as EVRI, the Royal Mail,

German-owned DPD, and UPS. PDD is well known for a strictly asset-light approach, preferring to rent its warehousing than own it. Its logistics philosophy for logistics has been described as "mostly outsourced, ephemeral and unenumerated."[37] That said, Temu puts great emphasis on their smart warehousing as a competitive advantage. They have made a large investment in state-of-the-art automated systems for sorting and tracking to "reduce errors and minimize delays."[38]

The unanticipated and massive uptick in the demand for air cargo resulting from Shein and Temu's explosive growth, is "upending the global air cargo industry," driving up the price of air cargo, especially from South China and Hong Kong, and is "squeezing out space for other industries on air freighters."[39]

Manufacturers which operate their own logistics – home appliances and auto

There are good reasons why many Chinese manufacturers have been slow and reluctant to entrust their logistics to a 3PL. In the 1980s, as the centrally planned economy was dismantled, the existing logistics and distribution infrastructure melted away or continued in a dysfunctional or fragmented fashion. Hence, large Chinese manufacturers built up their own in-house transportation and warehousing. These included firms engaged in home appliances (Qingdao Haier and Meiling) consumer electronics (TCL and Konka), food retailing (Hualian and Lianhua), and auto (SAIC). Today, these capabilities are typically used not just for the firm's internal needs but also to service external customers.

Established in 1984 in Qingdao, Shandong, Haier Smart Home (formerly Qingdao Haier) is the world's largest home appliance manufacturer. Its growth has been fueled by a number of acquisitions including that of GE's home appliance business (in 2016). Today, it has revenues of US$ 38 BN. Haier's founder Zhang Ruimin was early in recognizing the power of logistics efficiency to lower costs and drive profitability. He invested heavily in building up his firm's in-house logistics skills. In 2010, the various parts of this capability were consolidated in a new entity called Qingdao Haier Logistics, which serves both Haier itself and also external customers. Haier never totally relied on its own logistics and worked closely with firms such as COSCO Logistics to gain reach into overseas markets, for instance into Southern Europe via COSCO's Piraeus Port. In recent decades, Haier has developed its own proprietary IT platform called COSMOPlat providing comprehensive linkages across the supply chain from suppliers, transportation providers to customers. It provides for Just-in-Time procurement of parts and of outbound shipping (using Vendor Managed Inventory) thus reducing the inventory carrying costs. As one of China's largest 3PLs, they work not just in home appliances but also in auto, FMCG, and consumer electronics. Their external customers include IKEA, Foxconn, Dow, Avaya, and Yili Foods.

Hisense (revenues of US$ 12 BN), another major Chinese home appliance maker also based in Qingdao, chose not to invest heavily in its own logistics assets. However, Hong Kong shipping and logistics firm SITC and its Qingdao Logistics subsidiary Xinfeng took an equity share in Hisense. This linkup provides Hisense with increased overseas reach, especially in Southeast Asia where SITC is very strong. While not investing heavily in logistics assets, Hisense has built its Hisense Logistics Platform, an IT platform, which, like that of Haier, provides connectivity across the entire supply chain.

China's auto firms have also been active in creating their own logistics capability. SAIC (or Shanghai Auto) is the partner in JVs with VW and GM and also has its own assembly facility (producing MGs for example) In 2000, SAIC established a subsidiary called SAIC Anji Logistics which has since then gone on to become one of China's largest 3PLs, serving external customers as well as its parent SAIC. We saw above how firms such as COSCO and Ryder competed for the inbound part of auto logistics that is the logistics associated with components and parts to be assembled by the OEM. In contrast, Anji has focused on outbound auto logistics. Early on, it pioneered the use of specialize trucks to transport cars within China. It has formed a JV with CEVA Logistics to deliver spare parts logistics across China. CEVA (formerly TNT) and now owned by French shipping firm CMA CGM has considerable experience operating in China.

China is ramping up its auto exports which in 2023 reach nearly 4.91 MM vehicles, for the first time ahead of Japan (4.42 MM).[40] It is expected that China's exports will increase rapidly, largely due to the role of electric vehicles (EVs) which while currently a bit less than 30% of the total exports but are expanding their market share in Europe and elsewhere such as in Mexico. Anji is playing a major role in this export drive. Its "ports logistics" business marshals cars at the port, not just through the enormous parking lots but also by preparing the onerous paperwork for different markets. Anji has also branched out heavily into shipping itself and owns 31 RO-RO (roll-off, roll-on) PCC's (Pure Car Carriers). In 2024, it launched its first dual-fuel (the second fuel being LNG) powered PCC with a 7,600 CEU (car equivalent units) capacity. As an indication of Anji's dominance in this area, COSCO formed a JV with them in 2021 in which Anji enjoys equity control (65%). In 2021, COSCO had five PCCs, compared to Anji's then 25 vessels.

China is caught in a situation where, as its exports of autos grow very rapidly, the supply of ships to transport them is tight and costly. As of 2024, China had less than 3% of the world's fleet of PCCs – just 39 vessels with a capacity of 115,000 vehicles. In addition to Anji, Chinese auto makers Chery Group and BYD (China's largest EV maker) are establishing their own fleet of RO-RO vessels. BYD has a number of such vessels on order. Its first one (which is leased) left China in January with 5,000 EVs bound for the Netherlands and Germany. In common with Anji's latest vessel, it has a dual-fuel engine, which can be adapted to run on LNG. The Chinese state press applauds China's growing fleet of PCC vessels as "expediting the new opportunity for 'our own transportation of national vehicles' (*guoche ziyun*)," which feeds into the narrative of reducing China dependence on external factors.[41]

Notes

1 Paul G. Clifford, *Project Notes*, 2000.
2 Paul G. Clifford, *Project Notes*, 2003.
3 Paul G. Clifford, *Project Notes*, 2017.
4 Feng Boming in *2022 Annual Report*, Sinotrans.
5 This person was co-author Paul G. Clifford, then China Country Head for Mercer Management Consulting. The details are from his memory and project notes.
6 China COSCO Shipping Holdings *Annual Report 2022*.
7 Website of China Logistics Group.
8 Wu Youxi, *zhongguo wuliu jituan de fazhan lujing shi shenme?* Financial Sub-Group, China Federation of Logistics & Purchasing, on *Sina* 18 Oct, 2022.
9 Wu Youxi, *zhongguo wuliu jituan de fazhan lujing shi shenme?* Financial Sub-Group, China Federation of Logistics & Purchasing, on *Sina* 18 Oct, 2022.
10 Cainiao-Alibaba Group webpage.
11 Helen Norman, *Extending Cainiao Smart Logistics Network's global reach*, on *Parcel and Postal Technology International*, Apr 5, 2021.
12 Cainiao-Alibaba Group webpage.
13 *Alibaba 2021 Investor Day*, on Cainiao Smart Logistics Network, 2021.
14 *Alibaba Fiscal Year 2023 Annual Report*, Alibaba, 2024.
15 Luke Schiefelbein, *Is JD.Com The Future of Chinese E-commerce?*, on *Forbes*, July 25, 2018.
16 Luke Schiefelbein, *Is JD.Com The Future of Chinese E-commerce?*, on *Forbes*, July 25, 2018.
17 Luke Schiefelbein, *Is JD.Com The Future of Chinese E-commerce?*, on *Forbes*, July 25, 2018.
18 Luke Schiefelbein, *Is JD.Com The Future of Chinese E-commerce?*, on *Forbes*, July 25, 2018.
19 Peter Erisman, *Alibaba's World*, Macmillan, 2015, p. 200.
20 Meemi, *JD Logistics (Part 1) Introducing JD Logistics*, on *Investor Insights Asia*, Mar 7, 2022.
21 *JD.com's JD Logistics Unveils World Largest Intelligent Logistics Park with Integrated Warehousing Warehousing and Sorting Capability*, on *Jingdong corporate blog*, June 14, 2023.
22 Vivian Yang, *JD Logistics and Geopost Announce Strategic Partnership to Strengthen International Express Logistics Services*, on *Jingdong corporate blog*, July 21, 2023.
23 *Everything You Need to Know about the Jingdong Logistics IPO*, quoted on *Protocol*, Feb 19, 2021.
24 *Investor Presentation 2022*, by SF Express.
25 Sun Wu, *Just Opened. A Look at China's Brand-New Ezhou Huahu Airport*, on *Simple Flying*, July 23, 2022.
26 Eric Kulisch, *SF Express Merger with Kerry Logistics Creates Logistics Powerhouse*, on *Freightwaves*, Feb 12, 2021.
27 Eric Kulisch, *SF Express Merger with Kerry Logistics Creates Logistics Powerhouse*, on *Freightwaves*, Feb 12, 2021.

28 Confidential interview with a Chinese logistics expert, Feb, 2024.
29 Ye Shuai, *Zhonguo kuaidi zhi xiang – Tonglu de gushi*, on *iyiou.com*, Sep 13, 2019.
30 On *Billionairesindex.com*.
31 Ryan Mc Morrow and Joe Leahy, *China's Billionaires Back Xi Jinping's Plan to Restore Economy*, on *Financial Times*, July 20, 2023.
32 Gabriel Wildau and Ma Nan, *How One Chinese Rural County Spawned Four Courier Empires*, on *Financial Times*, Apr 13, 2017.
33 Source is *Statistica* cited Ben McPoland, *Is Shein about to IPO on the London Stock Exchange as an Exciting New Growth Stock?*, on *The Motley Fool*, Feb 29, 2024.
34 Arriana McLymore, Casey hall and Lisa Barrington, *Rise of Fast-Fashion Shein, Temu Roils Global Air Cargo Industry*, on *Reuters*, Feb 21, 2024.
35 Dam McCrum, *The Mysterious Rise of the Chinese E-commerce Giant Behind Temu*, in *Financial Times*, Mar 5, 2024.
36 Dam McCrum, *The Mysterious Rise of the Chinese E-commerce Giant Behind Temu*, in *Financial Times*, Mar 5, 2024.
37 Dam McCrum, *The Mysterious Rise of the Chinese E-commerce Giant Behind Temu*, in *Financial Times*, Mar 5, 2024.
38 *Behind the Scenes Look at Temu's Warehouse Operations*, on *Trand on News* (undated).
39 Arriana McLymore, Casey hall and Lisa Barrington, *Rise of Fast-Fashion Shein, Temu Roils Global Air Cargo Industry*, on *Reuters*, Feb 21, 2024. How Shein and Temu Are Upending the Global Air Cargo Industry, on *Businessoffashion.com*, Feb 21, 2024.
40 Qi Xijia, *China Surpasses Japan to be World's Largest Auto Exporter in 2023, Showcasing Economic Momentum*, on *Global Times*, Jan 24, 2024.
41 Wang Feng, Liang Xizhi, *Zhongguo xinnengyuan qiche jiasu chuhai cuisheng "guoche ziyun" xinjiyou*, on *xinhuawang*, Jan 16, 2024.

Chapter 14

How global logistics firms have navigated the China market

It is reasonable to state the companies outside of China created third-party logistics providers (3PL) concept while China came late to the game. But as we highlighted in the previous chapter, China, in the full flood of its economic reforms, embraced these new principles with energy and creativity. This permitted Chinese 3PLs to establish themselves, offering today real competition to their foreign competitors. However, there were a host of other factors that limited the foreign firms from becoming dominant in the China market.

As with the previous chapter on Chinese firms, we do not aim to provide an exhaustive picture of all major players. Instead, we have focused on what we consider to be a highly representative and contrasting sample of foreign firms which have entered the China market, with differing goals, scope, and approaches, and with differing degrees of success.

Why was China slow to welcome foreign logistics firms?

How do we explain why China quickly embraced foreign direct investment (FDI) but was slow to permit it in the logistics arena? In 1979, China promulgated its first law on Sino-foreign equity joint ventures (EJVs). Although China's "open door" to trade and FDI was always only partially open and always driven by national self-interest, China in general viewed FDI very positively. There are a number of reasons for this. FDI filled major gaps in the economy, such as in auto production and consumer products, and provided an influx of technology which rubbed off on the rest of the economy. It provided investment capital at a time when the government coffers were depleted. The government also saw FDI as valuable competition that would force Chinese state-owned firms to take on global "best practices" and become more competitive and sustainable. Once the reforms began, China demonstrated a deep hunger to learn from advanced economies. It could be argued that even as it trumpets that it had "opened up" to foreign investment, China ensured there was never a level playing field so that the environment favored the Chinese side. That said, there is no denying that China did create the

DOI: 10.4324/9781003489115-18

positive conditions, which combined with the huge magnet of Chinese market size and above all potential, that encouraged flows of foreign capital into China.

Nevertheless, it took China's World Trade Organization (WTO) accession in 2001 to finally open up logistics to foreign firms. There are two main reasons behind this reluctance to permit foreign logistics firms to enter the market. First, China's Soviet-trained planners valued engineering and manufacturing over modern management processes and software (in the non-IT sense). It put capital into large-scale industry and into rail transportation but was oblivious to the inefficiency that dysfunctional central planning imposed on logistics. This legacy continued to hamper progress well into the reform period. Second, China viewed transportation and logistics as an area of high risk for national security and was unwilling to permit foreign investors to play a major part in its strategy setting or operations. Even today, with foreign 3PLs given access to the domestic market, the Chinese party-state continues to regulate it tightly and to exercise control over key aspects such as the railways.

Working in partnerships

When in 1979 China first permitted FDI, it was only through JVs with a Chinese partner. It took until 1986 for Chinese law to permit 100% foreign firms. Some sectors such as auto manufacturing and logistics remained subject to partnership requirements until more recently.

Once the so-called WFOEs (wholly foreign-owned enterprises) became legal, most new investors chose that route over the JV one. In some existing investments, the foreign party quickly bought out its Chinese partner to make the firm a WFOE. As WFOEs grew in numbers, the evidence was stark. Even at the admission of Chinese officials, JVs were less well run than WFOEs. The old JV structure proved in many cases to be recipe for disagreement between partners on strategy and operations and usually resulted in weak compromises. Of course, there were outstanding examples of JVs working well. But overall, JVs fell out of favor and for good reason.

Prior to China's accession to the WTO in December 2001, Chinese law and regulations dictated that foreign logistics firms could only gain access to the market through forming an EJV with a Chinese firm, with a 50% cap on the foreign firm's equity share. Under those conditions, it was impossible for a foreign firm to gain full operating control.

As a condition of WTO accession, China agreed to further open logistics to foreign investment. To soften the impact on Chinese firms, this was done in phases: first, the 50% equity cap for the foreign side in JVs was removed and then at the end of 2005, 100% foreign ownership in logistics became legal, four years after China's WTO accession.

As foreign firms make direct investments in China, once they have determined the scale of the market opportunity, the next big question is typically what should be the market entry vehicle. So, by 2005, a foreign logistics firm developing a market entry strategy for the China market was faced with a clear choice of forming a JV or going it alone with a WFOE. The decision was driven by business considerations not by the regulatory environment. The Chinese Federation of Logistics & Purchasing published an article by our co-author on the prospects for foreign logistics firms in China in 2005. He made it clear that while some would quickly opt for WFOE status, others in the logistics space and more so than in manufacturing would prefer to form JVs where they could leverage the extensive network capability and government relationships of its China partner.[1] That proved to be the case.

A good example of a firm that pursued the WFOE option is Kuehne + Nagel (K+N), today the world's largest 3PL (annual turnover of US$ 47 BN). K+N planted their flag in China very early on, with a first representative office there in 1979 which within 10 years had expanded to 18 offices in 15 Chinese cities. These rep offices were only permitted to engage in "liaison" and could not sign business contracts. By the mid-1990s, the China market was reaching take-off point and K+N sought to find new ways to engage. It took an equity share in Singapore logistics firm SembCorp which in turn had partnered with Shenzhen's Shekou Industrial Zone, owned by state firm China Merchants to form a JV called St-Anda. ST-Anda made some inroads in selling services to MNCs operating in China, such as Colgate Palmolive and Johnson & Johnson. But more broadly speaking, ST-Anda's customer base was a poor fit with that of K+N. This was a common issue in China JVs, not just in logistics. The intent of these JVs was for the Chinese side to provide market access and client connections. But too often, the quality of the services or products offered by the Chinese partner did not match what was required by the foreign party's clients. With knowledge of the opening up post-WTO accession, K+N sold its position in SembCorp and decisively went on its own, winning a WFOE logistics license in April 2004, ahead of other firms due to having a Hong Kong domicile. Today, in China, K+N has 3,000 "logistics specialists" and 39 companies, all but two 100% owned by K+N. It has grown in China both organically and through acquisition (such as Apex Logistics in 2021). Tactically, it is prepared to form strategic partnerships, such as the one with China pharma logistics specialist Jointown. But the big picture of K+N in China is one of seeking to be in full control of its business to ensure top-notch delivery and to avoid the risk of reputational damage. China is important to K+N not just through the revenues it generates but also due to the role that the services it provides in China play in rounding out the global capability required by their MNC clients.

In contrast, other foreign firms opted for the JV route into the China market, with mixed results. As mentioned above, the Chinese partner was seen as bringing access to Chinese customers. The problem with that was that Chinese shippers were heavily price-driven and were often unwilling to pay for the services that a foreign 3PL provided. The Chinese firm was also seen as having a strong branch network across China. However, as mentioned earlier with respect to Sinotrans, the network was often a loose coalition of semi-autonomous entities that were hard to utilize in order to deliver an integrated logistics service. What stands out as an unquestionable benefit that the Chinese side could bring were its government relationships at the central and local levels. Even after the JV was established, there was a need to obtain the necessary operating licenses for transportation province-by-province.

Even if on the surface, there was a strong strategic fit between the Chinese and foreign sides, even if there was a shared vision of the services to be delivered, negotiations on partnering often faltered when it came to the question of ownership. The hardest nut to crack was to get the Chinese side to yield equity control and, with that, operating control. A weak Chinese partner might be willing to do so at a price. But for a large, proud Chinese logistics firms, there was little appetite to give up management to the foreign side. That was the case with COSCO Logistics which, as we discuss below, was unable, despite plenty of goodwill and enthusiasm, to imagine itself as the minority partner to the US firm Ryder System in the China market.

A number of foreign logistics firms did form JVs. As discussed below, DHL formed a JV with Sinotrans in 1986 to provide a cross-border express package service. That was and remains an outstanding success, delivering value for both sides in the venture. However, DHL additional JVs with Sinotrans to address the domestic Chinese market failed and were unwound. JVs by UPS (with Sinotrans) and FedEx were both also unwound, with a cost to the foreign side of hundreds of millions of US dollars.

While it is true that in logistics or more broadly, FDI in China is conducted through WFOEs rather than partnerships or JVs, it is a mistake to make a blank assertion that JVs cannot work. There are examples of such collaboration being fruitful and harmonious. Much is down to the creativity of the executives of both sides, the degree to which they can transcend the cultural barriers, and above all shape an outcome which is beneficial to both sides. That positive outcome has been apparent in the history of Shanghai GM, the auto JV. In logistics, it is clearly demonstrated in the longevity and profitability of the DHL JV with Sinotrans on cross-border express business. In 2018, we saw the Havi Group, a global cold-chain logistics provider heavily focused on serving the fast-food chain McDonald's, inject its China logistics business into a JV with China cold-chain specialist SF (Shunfeng), with SF having the majority equity share. Although Havi had operated in China for decades, this decision was an acknowledgment of several things. First, China has a new set of emerging private logistics firms such as SF with strong capabilities. There is a number of factors at play here. These new firms have embraced modern management principles that make them highly competitive against foreign players. They also enjoy the clear benefit (compared to foreign firms) of being a Chinese firm in China, no small thing given the increasingly strident nationalism in China. On top of this, McDonald's

China business is now majority owned by a Chinese entity and presumably for Havi having a Chinese partner was a good way to ensure it maintains that critical relationship in China. But as we discussed earlier, McDonald's has built their reputation in China based on a high level of supply chain integrity and safety. They and Havi were both taking some risks in giving up control in China!

DHL: three businesses and three very different stories in China

DHL represents one of the world's most recognizable logistics brands, with a sprawling global empire spanning over 220 countries, and is segmented into three distinct business units: Express, Forwarding, and Supply Chain. The origins of DHL as a group lie in the cornerstone acquisitions of the express services of DHL Worldwide Express, the forwarding capabilities of Air Express International (AEI) and Danzas, and the contract logistics solutions of Exel. Upon acquisition by Deutsche Post, the formerly state-owned German mail service, these companies were reorganized under the unified DHL brand and supplemented with a series of other smaller acquisitions over time.

These divisions sought entry into the Chinese market with varying degrees of success, each with its own narrative arching over time. This chronicle dissects DHL's foray into China, offering three mini-stories of strategy, execution, and the outcomes they reaped.

DHL Express. Long-term success. DHL Express made its foray into the Chinese market in 1986, capitalizing on the country's newly opening economy and burgeoning growth prospects. Rather than going solo, the unit entered through a strategic JV with state-owned Sinotrans, a decision mandated by China's then-foreign investment regulations. This partnership turned out to be more than just a requirement; it became a cornerstone for DHL Express's future success in China.

In the early years, DHL-Sinotrans worked diligently to establish its presence, particularly in Tier 1 cities like Beijing, Shanghai, and Guangzhou. The company combined its globally recognized DHL Express services with the local advantages provided by Sinotrans. While DHL brought in its global express network and international customer base, Sinotrans reciprocated with regulatory expertise and extensive local express distribution networks. This relationship bypassed many of the hurdles that often challenge foreign entrants, laying a solid foundation for growth.

By the time regulations relaxed, allowing WFOEs in express delivery, DHL opted to maintain its JV with Sinotrans. The partnership had matured into a mutually beneficial relationship, with local insights and ties within the Chinese market and a market-leading global express network. Jerry Hsu, the former President of Greater China Area DHL Express Asia Pacific, attested to the partnership's success in 2006, stating that it had achieved an impressive average annual growth rate of 35%–45%, and had captured a 40% market share.[2]

Fast-forward to the 2020s, DHL-Sinotrans has seen over 35 years of steadfast commitment to the Chinese market. Over these years, DHL has invested more than RMB 10 BN in China for logistics and related infrastructure, successfully establishing an express delivery network that covers 80% of China's population and economic centers. Nearly 8,000 employees work daily to serve customers nationwide. Outpacing international competitors like FedEx and UPS.[3]

While other JVs have foundered or were abandoned in favor of wholly owned structures, DHL's alliance with Sinotrans continues to thrive, a testament to the JV's durability and adaptability. The ongoing success of DHL Express in China serves as a compelling example of how international expertise paired with localized strategy can yield exceptional results in a complex, evolving market.

DHL Forwarding: Underwhelming. Freight forwarding operations for the Deutsche Post DHL Group effectively began in China in the 1990s when it acquired global freight forwarder AEI, including its existing China operations. This provided an initial foothold in the market and was rebranded as DHL Forwarding several years later.

However, over the last three decades, DHL Forwarding has struggled to establish itself as a major player in China's freight forwarding industry compared to its leading position globally. While maintaining a steady presence, it has lagged far behind Chinese state-owned giants and private players.

In the early years, DHL Forwarding focused only on cross-border air and ocean freight, leveraging DHL's global networks while avoiding high competition in domestic transportation. It also targeted sectors like automotive and technology that were seeing rapid growth in 1990s China.

By the 2000s, DHL Forwarding remained a mid-tier player in the market. Industry sources suggest it held less than 2% market share compared to state-owned leaders like Sinotrans with over 15%.

More recently, DHL Forwarding worked to expand in areas like e-commerce and healthcare to capture new opportunities, but the unit is not considered an innovator shaping the landscape of the logistics industry in China.

Ultimately, DHL Forwarding's China story reflects the challenges foreign companies face in gaining scale and market leadership. While a consistent presence for 30 years, its muted impact highlights the difficulty of transferring overseas business models into China's unique environment. Compared with Chinese players, they have found it harder to achieve intimacy with local customers and partners.

DHL Forwarding's China experience contrasts sharply with the Express division's leading market share. This divergence illustrates that global scale alone does not guarantee success in China; that close connection with the local market is essential.

DHL Supply Chain: Graceful exit. In the mid-1980s, Exel Logistics, foreseeing the enormous potential of the Chinese market, entered into a strategic JV with state-owned Sinotrans, the leading logistics company in China. This partnership, focusing primarily on contract logistics services, facilitated Exel's entrance into China's early logistics market. The JV prospered for many years and accelerated in 2005 when DHL acquired Exel Logistics. However, in 2007, DHL decided to purchase the remaining 50% of the Sinotrans-Exel JV in China[4] and transitioned the JV into a WFOE operating under DHL Supply Chain in China.

By 2009, the firm managed a vast operational expanse, managing 60 warehouses spanning 23 key cities, including Hong Kong. These warehouses, covering more than 6 MM square feet, were driven by a dedicated workforce of 4,400 employees.[5] Such figures positioned DHL Supply Chain among the international leaders in the logistics sector in China and Hong Kong. Their operational capabilities were further enabled by the acquisition of pivotal local and national governmental licenses, ensuring their legal operations across the nation. This intricate licensing network, covering everything from regional transportation to specific hygiene standards for food warehousing, set them apart in the logistics arena. Their clientele mirrored their stature, encompassing a range of global heavyweights. Their services catered to a spectrum of sectors: healthcare giants such as Abbott and Johnson & Johnson; tech leaders like Lenovo and Nokia; and automotive OEMs including Honda and Ford. DHL provided diverse offerings: everything from temperature-controlled storage for healthcare products to specialized manufacturing support for tech brands.

Despite the dramatic success in the early 2000s, the 2010s presented significant challenges for DHL Supply Chain. A closer look at the numbers paints a clear picture: In 2007, DHL Supply Chain's China revenues stood at around US$ 400 million[6] — fast-forward to 2017, and the revenue had risen to only US$ 486 million (RMB 3.5 billion),[7] suggesting an annual growth rate of just about 2%, which pales in comparison to the market's 10%–15% annual expansion.

By 2018, DHL Supply Chain needed to adjust its strategy in China – the company announced a significant transaction with SF Express, a leading player in China's logistics landscape. On the surface, DHL described the move as the "transfer its supply chain operations in Mainland China, Hong Kong and Macau," while emphasizing that the transaction was a "supply chain alliance with SF."[8] The press release underscored the mutual benefits, where SF would leverage DHL's global expertise, and DHL would tap into SF's deep domestic market knowledge. Frank Appel, CEO of Deutsche Post DHL Group, painted a picture of a harmonious partnership, aimed at catering to China's "sustainable growth."

However, the real background of this transaction pointed toward a different narrative. The sale of its supply-chain support operations to SF Express for RMB 5.5 BN (US$ 792 MM) was more indicative of DHL Supply Chain's challenges in a rapidly evolving Chinese market. The transaction effectively allowed SF Express to acquire the China supply chain operations of one of the largest global contract logistics players in the region, while in reality, DHL was exiting the world's largest market. Though framed as a partnership, the move was a clear signal of DHL Supply Chain's difficulties in capitalizing on China's booming logistics market.

Ryder System: asset-light in China

Miami-based Ryder System, Inc. (Ryder), with revenues today of around US$ 12 BN, is best known for its truck leasing and renting (without providing drivers) and its "dedicated" truck services (with drivers included). But it also has a successful logistics business called Supply Chain Solutions (SCS) which provides outsourced 3PL services and supply chain consulting. In 2000, SCS already had a footprint in the US, Canada, the UK, and Latin America. That year it entered the Asia market through acquiring Singapore-based Ascend Logistics and began exploring an entry into China's logistics. Its growth in China and its mastery of the complexities there is a positive story. It is about how a foreign firm not only grew an asset-light business but also served China customers.

A key question Ryder had to address in China was the kind of market entry vehicle, what kind of entity, it wanted to set up in China. In 2000, Chinese foreign investment regulations meant that to set up a fully operating logistics company, it was necessary to establish an EJV. As mentioned above, the foreign party to the EJV could not hold more than 50% of the equity. Early on, the Chinese firm Tonghui Logistics expressed interest in forming a JV with Ryder. Later on, COSCO Logistics also showed strong interest in a JV. But Ryder resisted that temptation. That was a wise move. Other firms, such as UPS and FedEx, were to spend hundreds of millions of US dollars to extricate themselves from ill-considered JVs in China. Ryder determined that, under those conditions, the Chinese side would essentially exercise management control, making it hard to deliver the services according to Ryder's standards. Moreover, Ryder felt that entering into such a JV they would be "training a competitor."[9]

Ryder decided instead to test the water in China by establishing a small consulting firm in Shanghai. Since GM was SCS's largest global customer, they tried to support Shanghai GM through teaming up with Tonghui. They also sought to do some pre-export kitting to support HP's printer manufacturing in Shenzhen. But this proved complicated given Ryder's lack of a Chinese business license to operate as a logistics firm and the need for delicate negotiations with the local authorities to get anything done.[10]

In December 2001, China acceded to the WTO During the accession negotiations, there had been pressure from the US to further open up FDI in China, for instance in insurance and in logistics. The final accession agreement laid out a phased-in approach to the loosening of regulations governing foreign 3PLs entering China, Initially, they were permitted to have majority foreign equity control in a JV and later gained the right to establish a WFOE, in which the foreign firm has 100% ownership. Ryder networked tirelessly with the Chinese government to get itself at the front of the queue for a WFOE license and in April 2006 was awarded one. They invested US$ 5 MM, the registered capital legal minimum for a foreign 3PL WFOE in China. It started business in Shanghai with around six employees.

The burden of regulatory complexity continued. Further approvals were needed from various government ministries and agencies. The WFOE's full licensing came in stages, first logistics consulting, then warehousing and finally trucking. To get the trucking license, the WFOE was forced to own some trucks (it bought three box trucks) despite its plan to be asset-light (or asset-free). Beyond the national trucking license, the firm had to secure provincial-level trucking permits. The firm had its registered office in one location with a couple of staff and its servers for data storage, while the rest of the firm operated from a quite separate place. Rules on taxation were opaque. The regulatory environment had many gray areas. For Ryder, it was "constant dance."[11]

Ryder found it essential to have a strong government advocate to help get things done. The WFOE forged strong links with district governments in Shanghai, first in Pudong's Jinqiao zone where it was first located and later in Luwan District (now merged with Huangpu District) in old Shanghai, where they later moved. The district governments were willing to assist since they were competing for the firm's tax revenues.[12]

SCS is organized by industry verticals. The WFOE chose to focus on certain areas such as inbound auto, consumer durables, and specialty chemicals. They stayed clear of cold-chain logistics given the fragility and risks of providing services in this area. They noted that it was then common in China for refrigerated cargo to be compromised since it would be trucked to a location where it was transferred to a non-refrigerated truck for the line haul and put back on a refrigerated truck near the end of the journey.

In terms of its customer selection, they initially targeted their large global Fortune 100 MNC clients. But they found that these firms were not confident about the capabilities of the start-up WFOE. In the early stages, when an MNC client came into town, it was better to invite them out for a meal rather than show them around the operations which were just in their infancy and not that impressive.

While the WFOE did work closely with COSCO Logistics to support Daimler Chrysler in Beijing, more broadly speaking it was decided within six months to make a strategic shift toward smaller MNCs and Chinese manufacturers. An excellent example of the smaller MNCs was the Italian firm Merloni TermoSanitori, a producer of water heaters which had a fast-growing production facility in Suzhou, Jiangsu. In later 2007, the Ryder WFOE signed a multi-year contract with Merloni, which had 200 wholesale customers in China, whereby Ryder would consolidate 18 distribution points into one centralized facility and ten smaller regional warehouses. Ryder's Warehouse Management Systems were deployed.[13]

Ryder's China head took to the road in China, addressing countless local logistics conferences many in the remote locations (such as Wuhan) where he was often the only foreigner. The brand-building paid dividends. Its largest Chinese client was Qingdao Haier, the nation's leading producer of white goods, such as refrigerators and washing machines. In Shanghai, Ryder established and staffed a half-million-square-foot warehouse for Haier.

Many foreign 3PLs entered China with the goal of mainly doing cross-border import-export business. Ryder did do some of this kind of business, for instance in the auto industry. But its focus was essentially on the intra-China business, that is within China. This was pioneering work, which contributed strongly to the improvement of China's supply chain.

In China, Ryder's value proposition to their clients was that they offered a level of logistics expertise that local 3PLs could not provide. This was based on Ryder's network analysis. Ryder knew how to identify the data packages needed and to process that data to achieve network optimization. At that time, the Chinese 3PLs could not do this.

Another aspect of Ryder's boldness was a strong focus from the outset on being asset-light or (except for the three trucks we mentioned before) asset-free. To do this, they formed numerous alliance agreements, involving long leases, with Chinese warehousing firms. Ryder staffed and operated these warehouses but did not own them. With regard to trucking, they did shorter term contracts with Chinese providers but avoided spot transactions. One of the most fruitful collaborations Ryder had with Chinese logistics firms to gain access to transportation assets was with COSCO Logistics, led by their excellent CEO Ye Weilong, as mentioned earlier.[14]

The asset-light approach came with its challenges. Notable is the fact that with this model, the bulk, say 40%–50%, of the pricing is labor. Since Chinese labor costs were so low (maybe 10% of the level in the US), the corresponding margin was relatively low compared to the US. The competition with Chinese 3PLs, many of which were state-owned enterprises (SOEs) and not that preoccupied with profitability, made it impossible for Ryder to price-up based on the value they offered. In turn, Chinese shippers were often willing to go with the cheapest, the lowest bid, thus disregarding the risks that a rock-bottom price might imply. So, Ryder typically was forced to accept pricing that was discounted compared to what the firm earned globally. But it was a mixed picture. Some well-run modernized Chinese shippers such as Qingdao Haier were more sophisticated and less price sensitive since they were aware of the price/service quality trade-off. The WFOE's profitability was also adversely affected by the licensing of its IT systems, the global compliance and accounting costs. But Ryder was more focused on growth rather than on profitability at this early stage. They saw their China business as a "beachhead" which ultimately would open up the "billion person" market.[15]

Ryder staffed most of the warehouses it leased. They would send managers with a two-year experience to watch over the operations in smaller facilities. The leased warehousing often was sub-standard. During the Chinese Lunar

New Year, an unusually heavy snowfall in Shanghai resulted in the roofs of the warehousing for Haier collapsing. Chinese insurer Ping An was reluctant to pay up and Ryder ended up in litigation with them. In one warehouse, there were ventilation holes at the base of the walls through which goods were being stolen. These had to be filled in. In some warehousing facilities, there was pressure to provide accommodation for workers under the principle of the "iron rice bowl," a legacy from the period before the reforms.

The firm did create dual-language English-Chinese versions of its IT systems. But efforts to use a local Transportation Management System (TMS) were not productive. Ryder did find one local warehouse management system. But when the Ryder head office examined the software, the verdict was that it had been pirated by a Chinese firm. IT systems were a cost burden for this small WFOE. Back then, IT was not delivered through Software as a Service (SaaS). Typically, you had to pay not only for a license but also for software implementation.

In China, Ryder determined that while the East-West rail links in China were poor, the North-South network was adequate. But still they lacked confidence in the ability of the railways to handle goods efficiently and safely. Also, the railways did not provide a Less-than-Truck Load service. Ryder relied exclusively on road transportation.

Ryder saw their logistics growth following China's development and moving into the interior. But at that time, while they did extend beyond the coastal plains around Beijing, the Lower Yangtze, and South China, this meant only to places such as Dalian in Northeast China. "Wuhan [way inland in Hubei] was an outlier." They did not have reach into centers such as Chongqing in Western China.

Only a couple of the WFOE staff were foreigners (from the US or Singapore). Attracting and retaining local Chinese talent for the firm was a critically important mission. Ryder formed cooperation programs with Shanghai's Tongji and Fudan universities, from which each year they brought in interns. When local staff were hired and trained, there was the constant challenge of them being poached by Chinese firms. Ryder's head office staff were startled to see the "techish" and "cool space" at the Shanghai office, created consciously to retain the talent.

The rapid growth of the business in China meant that the Shanghai office had to be moved twice. Workspace overflowed into the conference room and when it was needed for an event or a client meeting, staff, with their computers, were sent out to the local Starbucks.

In addition to serving clients in China, the China operations also began providing outsourced services (Business Process Outsourcing or BPO) for global clients through offices such as in Shanghai, Suzhou, and Nanjing, where there was a strong cadre of English-speaking staff. This began to generate a valuable and profitable revenue stream.

Ryder's close and passionate engagement in China endeared it to China's logistics industry which in turn heaped praise on the firm. In 2007, the Shenzhen

Logistics Association honored them as an Excellent Foreign Logistics Company, stating;

> "Ryder has done a great job of providing world-class supply chain services worldwide and in China. We are confident that Ryder will continue to bring state-of-the-art supply chain practices and know-how to the Shenzhen market and help local manufacturers improve their efficiency and reduce logistics costs."[16]

In 2008, the Wuhan International Logistics Committee gave Ryder the Golden Service Enterprise Award.[17]

At its peak around 2013, Ryder's China business had grown to a significant scale. In China, it had 8 offices, 250 employees, 700,000 square feet of leased warehousing, and 200 "transport corridors." It had a core customer base in China of eight to ten long-term clients and generated revenues of around US$ 50 MM.

The end to Ryder's voyage into the China market came principally as a result of global financial pressures on the Ryder parent company. There was a pullback of the SCS business to just North America (US, Canada, and Mexico). First SCS quit Brazil and Argentina. Then it got out of Asia, first China in 2014 and then Singapore in 2019. They hung on in Singapore longer than in China since the accounts there were tied to key global customers.

The Ryder story in China is unusual in the way it focused on the intra-China market and provided world-class services to Chinese shippers. Though Ryder's presence in China lasted less than 15 years, its rapid growth and accomplishments stand out. It is also undeniable that, although it balked at a full JV with Chinese logistics players, its impact, through the alliances it formed with them, undoubtably contributed to the refinement and skills creation in firms such as COSCO Logistics.

The Havi Group – and their customer in China – McDonald's[18]

On April 23, 1992, the US fast-food chain McDonald's opened its first store in Beijing, a two-story building on the corner of Chang'an Boulevard and Wang-fujing. Technically, their first store on China's Mainland was in Shenzhen, but that was essentially an offshoot of and fully supported by their franchise just across the border in Hong Kong. The Beijing store really was the breakthrough. It was the largest McDonald's in the world, with a line of 29 cash registers, seats for 700, staff of around 1,000 which on that first day served 40,000 customers. Three decades later, in late 2023, McDonald's had 5,500 stores in Mainland China, with a target of 10,000 for 2028.

In China, the extraordinary success of McDonald's was in no small way the result of the quite extraordinary performance of The Havi Group, a global logistics provider to the firm, which was instrumental in facilitating its entry into

China. Today, Havi, while having gone through a long development in China including ownership changes, remains the sole logistics provider for McDonald's in that market.

Chicago-based Perlman-Rocque, the predecessor to Havi, took its name from its two founders. Ted Pearlman, a charming and inspirational leader, built their business around providing the logistics for food and packaging to McDonald's, based in Oak Brook, just outside of Chicago. He later changed the name to the Havi Group, (representing the names of the wives of the two founders). In the 1980s, McDonald's established strong franchises in both Hong Kong and in Taiwan, where they partnered with local entrepreneurs. In Hong Kong, their partner was the mercurial and far-sighted Daniel Ng, who was able to demonstrate that Chinese people enjoy eating beef patties. Through smart management of real estate costs, the biggest cost element in Hong Kong, he was also able to keep the hamburger price low enough to generate a mass market. This learning process in Hong Kong (and in Taiwan) provided a strong foundation and justification for McDonald's strategy to enter Mainland China. Havi was already entrenched in Hong Kong, with large box trucks, each with three compartments (one for frozen, one for chilled, and one for ambient temperature) which delivered all the food and packaging to the numerous stores around Hong Kong. It should be stressed that the Hong Kong supply chain was relatively simple, involving products arriving on ships in refrigerated containers which were then dispatched to storage and distribution points in Hong Kong. The only locally sourced products were sesame buns (from the Garden Bakery) and dairy. When it came to entering Mainland China, it became essential to source all the products locally. Firms such as Tyson (chicken) OSI and Keystone (beef), Bimbo (bakery), and producers of kitchen equipment all followed McDonald's into China. Despite its long-standing policy against investing directly in the supply chain, in China, McDonald's was forced to establish its own JV in Beijing to provide dairy products at an acceptable quality and safety level.

A key to understanding McDonald's attitude to its suppliers and logistics providers that made the supply possible is their laser focus on food safety and cleanliness, which in turn became a foundation of the market reputation and trust it enjoyed. As one former McDonald's executive in China put it:

> The McDonald's brand name represented trust. The operating model was exceptionally detailed. I told our people in China, if you don't know, ask. Call this number.[19]
> There was no room for cutting corners.

In their approach to their China market entry, McDonald's was careful and cautious, not speedy. They were very conservative: "everything by the book." Their China strategy contrasted starkly with that of the chicken fast-food chain KFC. Led in China for 26 years by an energetic and visionary entrepreneur called Sam Su, KFC opened their first store in Beijing in 1987 five years before McDonald's. By the time, McDonald's planted their flag, KFC was pulling away in terms of store numbers. KFC also opened their Pizza Hut business in China. KFC seemed oblivious to the risks it was taking on and, in so doing, gained a cost advantage over McDonald's and was able to win a larger footprint in China. It took risks on real estate land titles and on construction costs. And above all, it took risks in its supply chain. For a number of years, KFC China suffered from reputation-damaging food safety issues. There was the use of carcinogenic Red Dye No. 3 (erythrosine) in its China chicken products (2005), growth hormones and antiviral drugs (2012), and the OSI expired-beef scandal (2014). Despite all this, KFC was still able to grow speedily and today has around 8,000 stores[20] in China compared to McDonald's 5,500.

Despite its higher quality standards, McDonald's did also get caught up peripherally in the OSI beef scandal. The Chinese government made an example of McDonald's. But the subsequent investigations showed that McDonald's had no culpability. Overall, McDonald's accepted slower growth as the cost of an uncompromised supply chain with a focus on food safety.

Havi worked extremely closely with McDonald's on its growth in China. Their relationship was "symbiotic." There was "mutual understanding," with open book accounting (Havi shared its entire cost structure with McDonald's, as was common practice for any supplier wanting to work with McDonald's), with agreed profit margins for Havi. To ensure supply chain safety in China, McDonald's initially permitted Havi very good profitability. But gradually, market pressures led MacDonald's to demand lower logistics costs. To offset that, and to allow Havi to gain economies of scale, around 2010 they permitted Havi to go after other fast-food chains in China such as Burger King and Subway. The problem was that Havi offered a "five-star" service and those others were only ready to pay for a three-star service.

The logistics requirements for McDonald's in China were very onerous. There had to be everything that is on the menu – "could never be out of product." Also, there was careful management of inventory. There could not be too big of a buffer stock, but no sell-out was permitted. "The key was to keep an inventory where the product is fresh. [McDonald's China] had the lowest average inventory I have ever encountered. Nothing less. Very fresh."[21]

Havi's value proposition to McDonald's has been and remains "added value, value based, reduce inventory, not just cost-per-unit." As they put it "we tried to tell the story of the total cost of logistics, direct and indirect."[22] This was classic solution selling.

In China, Havi adopted a moderately asset-light approach. It has been willing to rent the warehousing and distribution centers across China but plays a hands-on role when it comes to the warehouse operations including the systems' interface. Havi prefers to have total control over the trucks that ply between the factories, distribution centers, and stores. As with the warehousing, this has to do with Havi's emphasis on food safety and the deployment of innovative cold-chain technology to achieve that. "For Havi the key was to invest in food safety. You could not get sick from McDonald's. If it [the supply chain] got broken there were big issues." So back to "McDonald's brand name is Trust." "Havi provides an overarching benefit, maintaining McDonald's reputation and trust in McDonald's standards."[23]

This "trust" extends beyond just food safety to hygiene. McDonald's China has led the way in proving clean toilets. Even though during the SARS pandemic (2002–2003), McDonald's sales in China declined by up to 50%, customers still preferred to go to their stores since they had confidence in the way McDonald's disinfected the stores and recycled the air in the ventilation systems.

Cold-chain resilience lies at the heart of Havi's logistics in China. As one former Havi executive put it; "cold chain has been an issue in China for 35 years and China is still dealing with that."[24] Today McDonald's in China states that two factors have transformed their logistics. First the transportation infrastructure, the super-highway system that permits Havi's trucks to efficiently link the regions, factories, and stores. Second is technology – "our key solution is digital."[25] Using the internet, suppliers and restaurants are connected. It provides greater efficiency in terms of reducing unnecessary inventory, that is increasing the stock turnover rate. On the back of this, the Internet of Things (IoT), using the internet as the platform, is deployed for real-time temperature control and traceability on trucks and in warehousing. It is also used for real-time adjustment to route planning. But the core reason for this monitoring is food safety rather than efficiency or TMS.

In China, both Havi and McDonald's have gone through some significant transformations. In 2018, China's SF (Shunfeng) Holding formed a JV with Havi Group in China with the goal of creating the nation's largest cold-chain logistics provider.[26] Today, McDonald's still relies for 100% of its China logistics on this re-constituted "new Havi." Havi continues to provide, independently from SF, the skills and experience of the old Havi. But SF, through their controlling equity share in the new venture, brings new corporate and financial backing to Havi. More than that, McDonald's stresses that SF has a very strong digital capability, which adds to their overall "digital logistics eco-system."[27]

The new Havi and muscle will be vitally important for McDonald's China which has embarked on a growth spurt. The background to this is that in 2017, McDonald's sold a 20-year franchise of 80% of their China Mainland and Hong Kong business for US$ 2 BN to China-owned CITIC Capital (with a controlling interest of 52%) and the Carlyle Group (28%).[28] In late 2023, McDonald's reaffirmed its commitment to the China market by re-acquiring Carlyle's share.[29] CITIC Capital, which remain in control, needs to work swiftly to recoup their investment over 20 years. They have set the target of going from 5,500 stores in 2023 to 10,000 in 2028.

As an indication of the new impetus and capital being brought to bear, after three years of construction, the McDonald's Supply Chain Smart Industry Park has opened in Xiaogan City, close to Wuhan in the heart of China's "mid-west." McDonald's China, Havi (logistics), Tyson (protein), Bimbo (bakery), and Zidan (packaging) have contributed around US$ 230 MM to establish this combined production and logistics center covering 300,000 m².[30] McDonald's intends to use the Park to supply not just Wuhan but also Chengdu and Chongqing, a region where they expect to double the number of stores.

The McDonald's US parent is worried about this enormous growth in China which it sees as a gamble that might entail a greater risk tolerance, for instance in terms of food safety. Under this pressure stemming from McDonald's concerns, the new owner reportedly hung fire during 2022, but then in early 2023 announced 600 new stores. Observers also express concern that when the 20-year franchise gets close to its end, the new owner will not be willing to continue to "refresh" or upgrade the stores.

Putting aside these potential risks, the Havi story in China clearly illustrates how a foreign logistics firm, now most significantly coupled with a vigorous private Chinese partner, can build and operate a complex cold-chain system in China, and in so doing have set a very high standard which other local firms will likely emulate. It is also an excellent example of how private sector activity in logistics neatly dovetails with the Chinese government's planning objectives on logistics specialization.

Notes

1 Paul G. Clifford, *2004 nian de zhongguo wuliu: huigu yu zhanwang*, China Federation of Logistics & Purchasing, Dec 24, 2004.
2 *DHL The Long-Time China Player*, on *Forbes*, October 2006.
3 *DHL Express Celebrates 35 Years of Commitment to Chinese Market*, on *Global Times*, Dec 15, 2021.
4 *DHL Confirms Sinotrans-Exel Deal*, on *IAA PortNews*, Dec 14, 2007.
5 Armstrong & Associates, DHL Supply Chain site visit, Nov 9, 2009, by Richard Armstrong.
6 Armstrong & Associates, DHL Supply Chain site visit, Nov 9, 2009, by Richard Armstrong.
7 Takashi Kawakami, *DHL Sells China Supply-Chain Units to Top Local Courier*, on *NikkeiAsia*, Oct 27, 2018.
8 *Deutsche Post DHL Group and SF Holding Conclude Landmark Supply Chain Deal*, company press release, Feb 18, 2019.
9 Confidential interview by Clifford, Sep 27, 2023.
10 Wong Joon San, *Ryder Expands Its China Logistics Infrastructure*, on *Payload Asia*, June 1, 2007.
11 Confidential interview by Clifford, Sep 27, 2023.
12 Confidential interview by Clifford, Sep 27, 2023.
13 *Italy's Merloni TermoSanitari Selects Ryder to Manage Supply Chain Operations in China*, press release by Ryder, Sep 4, 2007.
14 Ye Weilong went on to be a main board member at COSCO Shipping. He died from cancer relatively young.
15 Confidential interview by Clifford, Sep 27, 2023.

16 *Ryder Hailed as Logistics Provider in China*, on *Fleetowner*, Apr 1, 2007.

17 Edward Rifenburg, Lisa Brumfield Hagen, *Ryder Honored for Logistics Leadership in China*, on *CNN Money*, Mar 5, 2008.

18 This section on Havi relies in part on a series of confidential interviews carried out with contacts with close and detailed knowledge of Havi and McDonalds, conducted on Aug 20, Aug 30 and Sep 4, 2023.

19 This section on Havi relies in part on a series of confidential interviews carried out with contacts with close and detailed knowledge of Havi and McDonalds, conducted on Aug 20, Aug 30 and Sep 4, 2023.

20 This section on Havi relies in part on a series of confidential interviews carried out with contacts with close and detailed knowledge of Havi and McDonalds, conducted on Aug 20, Aug 30 and Sep 4, 2023.

21 This section on Havi relies in part on a series of confidential interviews carried out with contacts with close and detailed knowledge of Havi and McDonalds, conducted on Aug 20, Aug 30 and Sep 4, 2023.

22 This section on Havi relies in part on a series of confidential interviews carried out with contacts with close and detailed knowledge of Havi and McDonalds, conducted on Aug 20, Aug 30 and Sep 4, 2023.

23 This section on Havi relies in part on a series of confidential interviews carried out with contacts with close and detailed knowledge of Havi and McDonalds, conducted on Aug 20, Aug 30 and Sep 4, 2023.

24 This section on Havi relies in part on a series of confidential interviews carried out with contacts with close and detailed knowledge of Havi and McDonalds, conducted on Aug 20, Aug 30 and Sep 4, 2023.

25 This section on Havi relies in part on a series of confidential interviews carried out with contacts with close and detailed knowledge of Havi and McDonalds, conducted on Aug 20, Aug 30 and Sep 4, 2023.

26 Liao Shumin, *SF Express Parent, HAVI to Set Up Cold Chain Logistics JV in China*, on *Yicai*, Mar 13, 2018.

27 This section on Havi relies in part on a series of confidential interviews carried out with contacts close to Havi and McDonald's, conducted on Aug 20, Aug 30 and Sep 4, 2003.

28 Jethro Mullen, *McDonald's Gives Up Control of Its China Business in $ 2 Billion Deal*, on *CNN MoneyInvest*, Jan 9, 2018.

29 *McDonald's to Acquire Carlyle's Stake in McDonald's China*, press release by Carlyle, Nov 20, 2023.

30 *CFLD introduces McDonald's Smart Supply Chain to Central China's Hubei*, on *Global Times*, Dec 23, 2020.

Section 4

Conclusions

Chapter 15

Conclusions

Scenarios and strategic implications

Having drilled deeply down into the history, evolution, and current situation in China's logistics, the time has come to take stock of what this all means in the big picture. Here we become forward-looking, considering the scenarios, trends that will drive the development of China's logistics and the strategic implications of all this. Forecasting economic and business trends is a risky and often unrewarding game. Nonetheless, we owe it to our readers to use the foundation of our knowledge of how China's logistics have emerged in recent decades as a basis for providing some guidance on where this may lead and why it matters.

In doing this, we shall focus on aspects of China's logistics that stand out to us as highly significant and in some cases counter-intuitive. What elements of our narrative of China's logistics were not anticipated or perhaps initially underestimated? In the course of the research and analysis, what has emerged as of the highest strategic significance? What comes as a revelation – both to us and to our readers?

Assessing the scenarios

The future of China's logistics is intimately linked to macro-economic and geo-political scenarios. Recent economic and political trends and developments have thrown into question the notion of a sustained upward straight line, unbridled growth, with regard to China whether internally or in overseas markets. Predictability has now been replaced by uncertainty. The future of China's domestic market and of China's role in the global economy are both, in the jargon of scenario planning, "critical uncertainties." That said, the former is in our estimation less of a risk than the latter.

As we documented in Chapter 12, a crisis over Taiwan would have an immediate and potentially catastrophic impact on the global economy and world trade, and with it, on China's logistics internationally. While China's domestic market would continue to function, the slowdown in world trade would also have a ripple effect through China's economy and logistics. The hope is that sane minds and smart thinking on both sides can avoid this kind of crisis. While we need

DOI: 10.4324/9781003489115-20

to avoid complacency and blind stupidity that leads to us sleepwalking into this scenario, it may be reasonable to view the all-out war between the US and China over Taiwan as having a very high impact but a relatively low probability. That said, there are numerous other scenarios with regard to Taiwan, such as an accidental incident, a stand-off, or a blockade, which fall short of this but would still have a dramatic impact on world trade and logistics.

There are numerous serious weaknesses in the Chinese domestic economy, be it the real-estate overhang, local government debt, an aging population, and youth unemployment. On top of this, it can be argued that the party-state has chosen to play an increasingly strong role in the economy, especially the state sector but also with private firms, even at the cost of some economic growth. But there is no hint of the Chinese economy "collapsing" in the near or mid-term. On the contrary, the experience of the last 40 years suggests that the government is pragmatic and flexible enough to weather these storms and to come out still with continued, if lower, growth. Much is made of the cold winds and lack of vitality that pervades much of Chinese industry and commerce. But another story that is not told enough is that countless China's small firms and many larger ones, often benefiting from the nurturing side of the party-state, are innovating across a wide range of technologies. This will continue to propel China's economic thrust and its transition to higher quality growth. On top of this, one-third of the economy remains to be urbanized. All of this sets the scene whereby China underperforms in some respects and likely does not speedily overtake the US in economic size or quality, while at the same time does continue to grow steadily overall and, in some sectors, such as e-commerce, to grow more rapidly. China has a scale much like that of the US. And just like it would be foolish to bet against the US, we are justified in saying the same about China. This bodes well for the progress of China's logistics industry in its domestic market. Moreover, that progress will surely be underpinned and enhanced by the Chinese government which accurately perceives the economic uplift, green dividend, and social impact from a more efficient logistics performance.

The critical uncertainty for the Chinese economy and its logistics posed by the external scene is more troublesome. On the international front, we first need to take careful stock of the Taiwan issue, not just the apocalyptic all-out war scenario but also severe types of disruption which fall short of that.

Beyond Taiwan, we are left with two broad scenarios, sustained globalization, or a decoupling and a bifurcation of the world economy. In some respects, the latter scenario is already playing out and competing in real time with the incumbent globalized economy. There are of course many sub-scenarios that we could get into. But these two capture the fundamental choices faced by the world and especially by two nations, the US and China, both of which think it is "exceptional," itself a problem in terms of attitude.

We should acknowledge that how these two scenarios play out is extremely complicated and defies simple generalizations. In some sectors and product areas, globalization will continue unabated and China will continue to be at the heart of these logistics systems. In other areas, there will be a trend toward bifurcation of the supply chain and with that the logistics system and ecosystems. These two scenarios will likely coexist and thus China's logistics will need to plan and cater for both.

The decoupling or bifurcation scenario comprises a further serious deterioration of relations between the US and China over a wide range of issues including Taiwan, further restrictions on technology sales, trade-related issues such as government subsidies and also on human rights. In this scenario, the US and other foreign businesses decouple or separate themselves economically from China on a major scale, rethinking the globalization, supply chain, and logistics that make it work, and reshoring or nearshoring (bringing industry back home or to places such as Mexico). This scenario also strongly implies a global bifurcation when it comes to technology and related standards: one technology sphere of the world dominated by the US and some European nations and another where China is the predominant supplier of technology from cellular infrastructure and mobile phones to industrial automation driven by AI. Within this decoupling, the West would wean itself off China-made home appliances, or of other products such as solar cells and in the near future also electric vehicles (EVs), which now face punitive tariffs from the US. Under this scenario, efforts to get round these tariffs by building factories in the US or Europe will also likely meet strong resistance, on national security grounds but also for protectionist reasons. This curtailing of the export of Chinese products into developed countries will surely dampen demand for logistics that make goods flow. But it would be a mistake to overestimate the impact of this scenario on China's logistics firms. Much of the logistics for foreign firms currently sourcing or manufacturing in China will continue to be handled by their global third-party logistics providers (3PLs) not by Chinese firms.

Moreover, this major decoupling scenario would have little or no impact on China's trade flows with developing countries through the Belt and Road Initiative (BRI) and other channels. With other markets cut off by decoupling, China would surely put greater emphasis on this alternative. This is already happening. In this area, China's logistics firms would continue to dominate and grow.

Additionally, while much emphasis is put on the degree to which China's trade with the US and EU may be a risk, it is worth noting the large scale of Japan and South Korea's trade with and investment in China which will likely continue to create strong demand for cross-border logistics.

In the context of rising geopolitical tensions, we also note that China's logistics and related technology will find themselves vulnerable and exposed. We have documented how dock cranes and autonomous truck technology have come under scrutiny over US national security concerns. It is to be expected that other elements of this industry will find themselves in the crosshairs.

The second scenario, continued globalization, is that despite all the saber-rattling by the US, the severe restrictions on chip sales and the pressure on firms to disengage from China, the decoupling does not amount to that much, perhaps 10%, and where it happens, it is more about shifting investment and source from China to SE Asia than back to the US. The global supply chain, and the logistics at the heart of it, was built painstakingly over decades. It takes a perception of very high risk to persuade foreign firms to stop sourcing from China. Moreover, many firms not only source from China but are in China to take advantage of future growth – something exemplified by Apple who says they are "in China, for China." Business leaders work to a longer timeframe than most political leaders. If there is any guarantee that the current political pressure to decouple will not yield the expected results, it is because those running MNCs push back. US semiconductor firms may follow the US regulations to the letter. But one of their overriding goals is to maintain their trade relations with China. The same goes for Taiwan chip manufacturer TSMC. While under this scenario, trade flows between China and the world may seem some drop-off as firms do some limited "de-risking" away from China, the fundamental upward growth trend in international logistics will be sustained. While much of these trade flows may be handled by foreign logistics firms, there are, assuming the tariff barriers are not too fierce, major trade flows in which Chinese 3PLs and shipping lines will handle (in some cases, using specialized vessels) the export of wind turbines, solar panels, EVs, and batteries.

Which of those two broad scenarios prevail is hard to predict. Much will depend on political intentions and reactions to events on both sides which can at times appear irrational, or be driven by internal politics or a lack of vision. Some political efforts at decoupling will be more noise than action. The argument that decoupling will be less than it is talked up to be carries considerable weight, not least because business leaders would rather not make that leap into the unknown. Moreover, there is abundant evidence that the Chinese government, while, on the one hand, hedging its bets through fostering that idea that it can rely on itself and on relationships with the developing nations through the BRI is firmly opposed to decoupling with the developed nations and deeply wishes to take its rightful place as a true global player.

The linkage to the broader economy

China's logistics will continue to mirror the Chinese economy. But the predictability of the past is replaced by uncertainty. Logistics is closely linked to the pace and cadence of economic development. That is why analysts dissect the financials of UPS as a way of reading the economic tea leaves. If we had been writing this book 15 years ago, we would have described the inexorable growth of China's GDP, starting from the inflexion point around 1992. Although the percentage growth slowed from double to single digits, that was predictable since the total pie had grown exponentially. There were hiccups resulting from global recession, internal political events (Beijing 1989), with stop-start cycles from overheating to deflation, to stimulus measures to prop up growth. But most felt that the Chinese "economic miracle" was sustainable and unstoppable. Today, a positive future for China's economic future looks far from assured. It should be stressed that there is little to suggest that China is about to collapse. Judging by early experience, it has a strong ability to ride out the storms and to adjust as needed. But what is becoming apparent is that China is not going to overtake the US economically any time soon, whether it is in terms of GDP quantity or quality. China has not bounced back from Covid-19 as it had hoped to. There are geopolitical pressures, especially from the US which seek to "contain" China's rise. The real estate market, which is the source of most Chinese citizen's wealth, is in crisis. Its stock markets are dangerously volatile. The government has been forced to deploy its strong financial reserves to launch new stimulus spending. Coupled with this is Xi Jinping's new political approach since 2012, whereby he has chosen to put the highest emphasis on strengthening Party rule at all levels and all sectors, even though this will likely negatively affect economic performance. But the story is not all doom and gloom. China's bets placed through investment in high technology from semiconductors to AI are in part paying off. Still, it is undeniable that a dark cloud hangs over China's economy and with that inevitably will put pressure on China's logistics firms, many of which have invested heavily in future growth which may come slower than anticipated.

The new transportation infrastructure helps China's logistics catch up

China's transportation development will continue to enable the growth in logistics. Little could be done about China's geography which is less kindly than that of the US when it comes to permitting an integrated logistics system. But the transportation system was another matter. As China entered the period of economic reforms, its transportation infrastructure was extremely weak – a railway system that was utterly unresponsive to economic needs and a road network unsuited to long-haul trucks. Today China boasts the largest super-highway network in the world. The railways have finally been brought into the modern age. China has some of the largest and most efficient seaports in the world and is exporting that expertise to other nations.

Gaps and major gaps and weaknesses in transportation are being addressed. A glaring example of the remaining weaknesses is the slow development of China's rail intermodal transportation network. But this will continue to receive large-scale investment, for instance in raising tunnel heights to permit the double-stacking of containers. China will ultimately match the US's preeminence in rail freight.

The government is also driving change in terms of China's transportation mix. The flourishing of China's superhighways has resulted in much of long-haul being done by trucks. We expect to see further action by the government to switch to more environment-friendly freight trains. Likewise, high-speed freight trains have recently been introduced as an alternative to the air cargo used by China's e-commerce and express logistics providers. Government at all levels will continue to lead the upgrading and adjustment of transportation, as the bedrock for commercial logistics activities.

From backward to leapfrogging the rest of the world

Much of China's logistics still lag behind the rest of the world. This book celebrates the massive progress China has made in effectively adopting modern integrated logistics since the reforms began in 1978. More than that, it is out-innovating the rest of the world in e-commerce and express logistics. But the legacy from the previous period of rigid and dysfunctional central planning still leaves a serious hangover. China's logistics have improved but remain still only half as efficient as those in the US, based on their proportion of GDP they represent. As the Chinese government candidly said in late 2021, China's logistics are "large but not strong." Behind this statement are a host of weaknesses that still plague China's logistics. Much of the trucking is fragmented, inefficient, and small scale. There is the poor intermodal rail system that we mentioned. Much of the legacy warehousing is damp, insecure, and not fit for use. Despite some consolidation, much of it driven by the government, there remains a dearth of large Chinese firms delivering modern integrated logistics. The market is highly price-focused making it difficult to make a profit delivering premium services. China's realization of the significance of logistics was rather belated. Many of the issues we identified 25 years ago when we did a survey of China's 3PL market still remain today. The narrative for the future will likely continue to be one of extremes – a remarkably strong performance in some key sectors of the logistics market coupled with a continuing effort to escape from the shadow of the pre-reform era.

China continues to lag the world in outsourcing of logistics to 3PLs. The legacy of weak logistics that was historically dealt to China manufacturers led them to build their own logistics capability and to avoid entrusting this vital function to others. There is continued resistance by manufacturers to outsource to 3PLs due to the poor quality of services offered. Today, it is typically the small factories that outsource their logistics. Major Chinese industrial players have mostly built their own in-house logistics capability and often then have spun it out (as we saw with Qingdao Haier). When these large-scale industrial concerns do seek outside logistics support, it is often not a complete outsourcing to a 3PL but through a half-way house whereby they invest in taking partial ownership of a suitable logistics firm, ensuring that they have a degree of control over the service delivered.

But as the government and the industry itself address the "fragmented and scattered" aspect of China's logistics, so we shall see China's factories more willing to reduce their own in-house trucking and warehousing and put their faith in 3PLs which they deem to be efficient, reliable and secure.

Heavily price-driven competition in logistics continues to hamper progress. A key feature of modern integrated logistics is that the outsourcing to 3PLs is done on a contract basis (over one year) which permits the 3PL to demonstrate efficiency improvement over time and thus being able to command a premium price based on quality of service and cost reduction. In much of China's logistics market that business model remains elusive. A large proportion of the logistics services provided are still on a spot (non-contract) basis and are undifferentiated in terms of quality and accordingly heavily price-based. The result is that Chinese 3PLs who seek to offer higher quality differentiated services find themselves unable to achieve the price that their level of service deserves. Profit margins, even for China's largest players, are skinny compared to the global market. This in turn reduces the funds that can be reinvested for technology and service transformation. This makes the intra-China market tough for foreign 3PLs to operate in and also hampers the growth of local players. The solution ultimately is to reduce the fragmented nature of service provision in this industry through more company consolidation, to nurture the up-tiering of the capability of smaller firms, and by more regulation and standardization (so that bad actors cannot gain advantage). The Chinese government plays a key role in driving this process. In the meantime, cut-throat price-based competition will continue to plague the market.

Although the asset-intensive business model continues to dominate in China, new technology can facilitate an asset-lighter one. As elsewhere in the world, China debates whether it is necessary for 3PLs to be asset-heavy, that is to own their own transportation and warehousing, or to be asset-light, that is to outsource those capabilities. Being asset-intensive means greater capital investment, likely higher balance sheet leverage and a reduction in financial flexibility. In China, it has long been generally accepted that a relatively high degree of asset intensity is vital to ensure the quality of service and the security of goods in what is a highly fragmented and unruly logistics marketplace.

Recently Chinese e-commerce and express delivery firms have begun shaking things up and challenging the notion that is best to have a high degree of ownership down to the basic level. The reason is that the highly sophisticated IT platforms adopted by these emerging new players permit the 3PL to have a real-time view of how subcontracted providers are performing, thus making ownership of the assets less relevant. JD Logistics chose the asset-intensive route and may be paying the financial price of this. In contrast, Alibaba's Cainiao operates through the large delivery firms in which it has made minority investments and through countless smaller firms, all of which are seamlessly integrated into Cainiao's IT platform, permitting a high degree of transparency and control end-to-end through the logistics process.

The vital and exemplary role of the Chinese government in shaping China's logistics

A key finding in this book is the positive role that China's government, the party-state, has played in nurturing, supporting, and investing in China logistics in multiple ways. As we have mentioned, there has also been a negative side to this in terms of heightened interference in Chinese firms. But the evidence strongly indicates that overall this government intervention has and will continue to play an essential and valuable role in the development of China's logistics. As we acknowledge the fundamental part that the Chinese government plays in this field, we also suggest that other nations might do well by learning from China.

Even with likely economic headwinds, logistics are a high priority for China and could outperform other sectors. As we have observed, the Chinese government has recently woken up to two key facts: firstly, the nation's logistics are backward and, secondly, fixing logistics is an obvious opportunity that can greatly enhance GDP performance while at the same time contributing to reducing greenhouse emissions. Under this situation, it is apparent that even in a period where economic growth may be faltering, China's logistics will be nurtured and supported by the Chinese government. This support will come in many forms: not just transportation infrastructure, but also in government development of logistics parks and hubs and access to financing for large Chinese logistics firms which are leading the way in consolidating the fragmented logistics market. Given the high priority ascribed to logistics, this support will be accorded to both private firms as well as state-owned enterprises (SOEs). As this likely scenario of government engagement plays out, China's logistics industry may well see growth beyond that achieved by the economy as a whole.

When it comes to logistics the Chinese government exhibits welcome candor not hubris. In the early days of China's reforms, the nation's logistics were appalling, whether it was warehousing with leaking roofs, rat infestation, and prone to theft or a transportation system characterized by railways where you had to bribe to get goods loaded or by road haulage dominated by overloaded, underpowered trucks with the goods covered by a tarpaulin. What is extraordinary is not only that four decades later China's logistics remain backward in some respects, but also that the Chinese government, which is often given to hubris, is extremely candid about the deficiencies of the nation's logistics. This candor may come as something of a surprise to some. It should be welcomed. We also note that this is consistent with the fact that the Chinese party-state is perfectly capable of doing the right thing to improve the economy and the lot of the people, since in so doing, it is underpinning its legitimacy and hold on power. China's five-year plan for logistics is quite explicit and open about the serious weaknesses. These include a residual reluctance to outsource to 3PL, the scattered and fragmented nature of the industry that cries out for consolidation, the gap in the provision of cold chain for food and pharma and the underdeveloped intermodal (road/rail) network, trucking where empty backhauls continue to sap efficiency, and the greenhouse gas emissions caused by logistics. What we can learn from this is that in China today, where the discussion of some subjects is heavily constrained, logistics is not viewed as politically sensitive. It is an area where there is an open, bold, and constructive public discourse. It is obvious that recognizing the problems is a vital first step to addressing them. That does not always happen as a matter of course under China's form of governance. But in this case, things are well aligned for future government-led intervention to push logistics forward.

The Chinese government will continue to play a central role in the development of the nation's logistics. Even since the dismantling of the centrally planned economy, the Chinese government has continued to shape and guide its economy through a series of five-year plans, the current one being the 14th running 2021–2025. Dovetailing with the overall plan has been further plans on key elements so the economy, such as transportation, but extraordinarily, until very recently not on logistics. It is true that over the years, there were a series of planning directives on logistics but there was not an overarching logistics plan, representing a stark and highly significant gap. So, the announcement on December 15, 2021 of China's first national logistics development plan was truly a milestone. Through this plan and the numerous detailed sub-plans within it, the Chinese government has signaled that it places the highest priority on radically improving China logistics as a path to increasing efficiency and thus reducing the burden it places on the GDP (twice as much as in the US) and in so doing contributing to de-carbonization and the "green" agenda.

Given the strong role of the party-state across the economy and society as a while, one can have confidence that the government will continue to play a pivotal role in the development of China's logistics. While in the US and other developed nations, the government is active in investing in the transportation infrastructure, in China the government role extends much further. China's central government sets the pace, through planning, regulations, and investment while much concrete support comes from local provincial and city government. Emblematic of the part that the Chinese government is playing in fostering innovation in logistics is the investment it is making in the Jiuquan-Mingshui Autonomous Highway pilot project in Gansu where the new smart and intelligent infrastructure enables the efficient functioning of driverless or autonomous trucking. On this kind of sound foundation, business firms (SOEs and private) then take on the commercial role. These elements pull together efficiently and creatively. This is a clear representation of China' economic hybrid economic model which is characterized by a close integration of government and commercial interests, and within the commercial side a mixture of private and state ownership.

China's logistics will continue to drive the further integration of China economy and nation. The objective of using economic integration as a tool to enhance national unity has long been a key goal of China's leaders. Given the ironic weakness of the pre-1978, centrally planned economy in accomplishing efficient planning most regions and urban centers could not rely on the national logistics network and so resorted to making sure that they were as far as possible self-sufficient locally. Hence as China entered the period of economic reforms, this legacy left China with highly regional markets, with local policies which favored local firms and, as a result, a poorly integrated national economy. What we have seen is that as China's logistics have improved in leaps and bounds in the last three decades, so the Chinese economy has been increasingly unified. Where before there were duplicated subscale small factories in each major locality, today we are finding that long-haul transportation and efficient regional distribution centers are enabling the creation of high-quality, large-scale manufacturing bases from which the goods can be distributed nationally. This aligns strongly with the government's social planning objective of not only bringing the regions together but also reducing the differences in wealth and the quality of life, for instance between East China and the Center/West, between Tier 1/2 and Tier 3/4 cities, between urban and rural. Both China's five-year plan for logistics and the nation's China's e-commerce and express logistics firms put great emphasis on bringing the national market to the remote and often relatively impoverished rural areas and smaller cities and townships. This not only achieves the social goal of dealing with social inequality but also dovetails with the efforts to stimulate consumer consumption, as a path to economic growth which serves as an alternative to government investment-led stimulus programs. This is one more reason why logistics is dear to the heart of the Chinese government and will continue to receive its nurture and support.

China's local government has emerged as a key factor in promoting modern logistics. Local government in China, at the city and provincial level, has seized the initiative to encourage the development of logistics. This is driven by a number of factors such as the desire to attract investment, create jobs, stimulate consumption and wealth creation, and to generate fiscal revenue. It manifests itself in the creation of logistics parks and hubs, which in the interior of the nation are often linked into rail routes to Europe and SE Asia. These hubs sit astride the new corridors for cold-chain logistics. They also encompass manufacturing bases and clusters which further enhance their core developmental function.

China is reaping a green dividend from its modern logistics. The Chinese government is using its power and control over the economy to force the pace of the nation's green agenda to decarbonize. Making logistics greener is a key element which can yield quick results. Just as happened with passenger EVs, the government is quickly introducing low-carbon freight vehicles using green hydrogen (produced using from solar and wind). Government policy is focused on moving long-haul transportation from the road to the more efficient and greener railways. To wean e-commerce off of air transport, high-speed freight-only trains have been introduced. The propulsion of China's container ships is moving from polluting bunker oil to less harmful LNG, green methanol, and ultimately thorium molten salt reactors. The rest of the world is fast introducing greener logistics. But China's fast progress in this field is a powerful story which needs to be told and emulated!

China views the transformation of its logistics as a tool for social improvement. The Chinese government clearly articulates the value of modern logistics in bringing benefits to parts of society that have been left out of or not been fully connected to the "economic miracle" so far. These are not just the poorest rural populations in remote mountainous areas but also residents of third or fourth-tier cities and their related market towns. The greater reach of logistics is bringing access to e-commerce products and services which were hitherto unavailable. China's logistics firms will typically describe their coverage as being to "almost" all cities and towns, with "almost" representing a large number of consumers still being left out. In the years to come, we shall see these people finally being incorporated into the national economy. New models for e-commerce delivery and pick-up at the village level are being actively implemented. This fits the government's policy of stimulating consumer demand.

The social purpose of logistics that is promoted heavily by the Chinese government also includes "emergency logistics" which come into play after a natural disaster or pandemic. This is not unique to China. But what is striking about the Chinese approach is that in a post-disaster rescue and rebuilding mission, such as we saw in the Wenchuan Earthquake, commercial firms are closely linked to the government efforts.

Chinese logistics firms surge forward with technology at the core

The adoption of technology will continue to fuel growth and performance improvement in China's logistics. China's largest logistics firms (both state-owned and private) have been extremely successful in harnessing and innovating on the back of the latest wave of the IT revolution that has brought the Internet of Things (IoT) and AI. These IT systems are the heart and brain around which all parts of the logistics process function. Whereas in the past, certain parts of the logistics process were digitalized (for instance in container shipping), today these new and much broader platforms link key functions of the logistics firm seamlessly to the shippers of goods, to the customs at the ports, to the payment processors, to its delivery partners down to the last mile, and to the customer – businesses and consumers. On the back of its predominance in 5G mobile telephony, China has deployed IoT across logistics, permitting real-time tracking of goods, monitoring of trucking, and the management of warehousing. China put a heavy focus on deploying AI across logistics whether for guiding package sorting robots, enhancing transport management and routing, introducing autonomous-driven trucks, permitting more full loads on the truck's back-haul, and anticipating demand and potential bottlenecks. As China's investment and innovation in mobile telephony (6G is on the way) and with AI continue to forge ahead, we shall see China logistics continuing to benefit and improve as a result.

In particular, what stands out is the stellar performance of China's privately owned e-commerce/express delivery logistics firm in technology innovation. This technology adoption will not only continue to be upgraded but will also further permeate the market, through newly emerging logistics firms or most critically to smaller transportation or warehousing providers that can hitch a ride with the big firms through plugging into their IT platforms as "partners."

The Chinese government's own national logistics data platform LOGINK plays an increasing role, aggregating data on freight rates, vessel availability, port facilities, regulations, and documents. This is designed primarily as a way to give a hand-up to China's host of small subscale logistics providers that do not have their own resources to generate such data. However, large Chinese logistics players, while sharing information with this platform, will, for competitive reasons, continue to keep client-specific data confidential within their own proprietary IT platforms.

China's e-commerce and express delivery firms are using a new business model to leap-frog the rest of the world. China's e-commerce is the largest in the world, accounting for 28% of the nation's retail sales. But more than that, it is also the world's most efficient and technologically advanced e-commerce. At the heart of this extraordinary story is the adoption of a new type of business model.

As we entered the digital era, large incumbent logistics firms such as UPS transferred their data from paper to electronic systems. Chinese firms were latecomers to logistics and have been able to exploit this fact by rethinking the entire business model for delivering logistics. They have essentially become huge data collection vehicles. Data is collected electronically at every point in the process and then processed using AI into ways to optimize and streamline the process. This speed and broad scope of the data collection permits the optimization to be determined even before execution of a given step in the process. This is a groundbreaking shift away from the older logistics business models.

As e-commerce has exploded into life in China over the last two decades, China has not only benefitted from imported IT but has also innovated on its own across the whole industry, through entire integrated platforms down to smart and highly automated warehousing and sorting centers and to the last mile delivery. Using IoT, China's ecommerce giants have created a seamless network connecting manufacturers, customers, and those carrying out the fulfillment whether in transportation or storage. AI is used to select the optimal outsourced transportation provider or to guide the goods real time on the optimal routes. The Chinese providers are taking the digital integration to a new level, permitting them to leapfrog the rest of the world in both the sheer numbers of items processed and in the quality of service provided.

China will continue to catch up with regard to specialization in logistics. In the developed world, logistics specialization is taken for granted. However, much of China's logistics is plain vanilla, one-size-fits-all. As a logistics laggard, China has come rather later to the game when it comes to specialization. But, driven by both market needs and a strong push from the government, we see strong momentum to rectify this weakness. China's auto industry was relatively quick to focus on auto logistics, whether inbound components, outbound finished vehicles, or after-market parts service. Now in the last decade, we have seen in particular attention being focused on building a cold-chain logistics network throughout the nation, something that remains inadequate. Government investment in cold-chain parks and refrigerated railcars is complemented massively by the bold efforts of firms such as SF (Shunfeng) to invest heavily in cold-chain warehousing, trucking, air cargo, and through teaming with the foreign firm that provides cold chain for McDonald's in China. Foreign firms specializing in truck and container refrigeration have invested in China-based production.

This has enormous implications for the Chinese economy and the Chinese consumer. It further drives the integration of the Chinese economy, so that chilled or frozen products can be shipped far from the production location. Chinese farmers in remote areas will find it easier to get their produce to market. There will be less wastage of food and produce and, critically, it can help ensure food safety. Cold-chain is also vital for the build-out of a nationwide pharma supply chain, whether for vaccines, blood supplies, and other products requiring a controlled temperature environment. We have confidence that the construction of a resilient cold-chain logistics capability will see continued progress and yield significant social benefits for the Chinese people.

China's largest state-owned logistics firms will continue to benefit from government patronage and support. It is a good time to be a SOE in China. The Chinese Communist Party (CCP) has all along set its sights on making "socialism" work and a core element of that is the SOE part of the economy. Among these, Sinotrans has successfully transformed itself from a freight forwarder under the centrally planned economy to now China's largest 3PL – a highly focused and well-organized provider of contract logistics. The creation of China Logistics Group (CLG) brought together many legacy storage and transportation assets that had lingered, fragmented, after the reforms. Among the large SOE logistics firms, there are two contrasting models: firstly, sheer scale but no guarantee of quality, as exemplified by CLG, and, secondly operational excellence, as with Sinotrans. Even though these firms have successfully won contracts for foreign firms for the intra-China market, their core customer base will likely remain Chinese manufacturers whether in China or for the global supply chain. They are also highly focused on more traditional logistics business and are finding it hard to break into the e-commerce sphere which is dominated by more agile, newly emerged private Chinese firms.

There is little doubt that, in the current political climate that we expect to persist into the medium term, Chinese SOE logistics firms will experience significant Party control whether in day-to-day operations or in their overall strategic trajectory, something which may have an impact of how fleet-footed or adaptable to market conditions they are. But on the upside, there is no doubting the support they will receive from the government and the state banks. This serves to strongly indicate that these SOE firms will continue to play a powerful role in China's logistics market.

Given their strategic role in the nation's economic development, we expect China's private logistics firm to avoid severe political headwinds. There is little doubt about the China party-state's preference for the state-owned sector of the economy since it helps define China's version of "socialism" and is an area where the Party can exercise close control. At the same time, there have recently been numerous examples of private firms, such as Alibaba, that have been targeted for "rectification and clean up." This is partly because these firms operate in new areas which need regulation. But it is also because some of these private entrepreneurs with enormous wealth behind them (and much of it offshore) were speaking out of turn, upstaging the nation's political leaders and not showing fealty to the party-state. In clipping their wings, the authorities revealed a degree of animus toward private enterprises which is deep in the CCP's DNA. But the party-state is also pragmatic and smart. It also acknowledges that, compared to state firms, the private sector is more profitable, innovative, and creates more jobs. Therefore, while clamping down of some private firms to send a signal about what lines may not be crossed, the government pledges its fulsome support for private firms, just as long as they accept party "guidance." When we look at China's private e-commerce firms, their captive logistics arms or other private firms that provide their delivery or fulfillment capability, it is obvious that they play a critical and innovative social role in bringing products and services to China's citizen right down to the poorest villages. Therefore, it seems implausible that they would face blatant discrimination by dint of their private ownership. That does not mean that their billionaire founders may not become caught up in the never-ending anti-corruption campaigns. They will also face pressure to contribute to "society," to make investments in state firms, to plow funds into logistics hubs such as Alibaba's Cainiao is doing in Hainan Island. But their role is so established and essential that our assessment is that the chances of them being seriously interfered with are low.

While there is space for clearly differentiated foreign logistics firms to grow and succeed within China, market leadership or dominance may be elusive. There are a number of reasons why foreign players will struggle in the intra-China logistics market. Chinese competitors have strong home advantage when it comes to gaining licenses and other approvals from local government. Profitability is also elusive for foreign firms since they have a higher cost base and find it hard to match the cutthroat pricing that is typical across the intra-China market. They have to work harder and differently to succeed in the China market which nonetheless still represents large scale and in many areas unmet needs. We have documented how foreign firm Havi specializing in cold-chain logistics for fast food firms has been able to achieve sustained profitable growth in China. But even with that specialized edge, the key aspect was that it was focused on serving McDonald's in China. Following one's global clients into China can work for foreign logistics firms.

But broadly speaking the area where foreign logistics players enjoy more of a level playing field and can operate successfully is in cross-border business, handing imports and exports, and again for their global customers. They are already intimately linked to the IT systems of these global customers. Moreover, these customers have traditionally been willing to pay a premium for the services of their trusted global providers. However, as Chinese firms are upping their game, even that element is being challenged.

Once the foreign logistics firm determines there is an addressable and profitable market in China the question then becomes what vehicle to use for the market entry. The idea of finding a Chinese partner to form a joint venture has proven to be increasingly unworkable. Any half-decent Chinese partner expects to have operating control over the JV. Chinese firms willing to accept playing a backseat role are typically weak, bring little to the table and may turn out to be troublesome. There is the option to enter or grow in the Chinese market through acquiring a local logistics player. Apart from having to pay heavily for this, the main risk is that unlike acquiring a manufacturing company which has fixed assets, when it comes to such a service company the core of the value is human assets, the team that runs the 3PL. There is no guarantee they will stay around after the acquisition. Moreover, the existing customers of the Chinese firm being acquired will most likely not be willing to pay more for premium services. While forming rigid equity ventures may be out of favor and making acquisitions may be risky, there may well be benefit in forming lose alliances whereby a strong Chinese player gains assistance from the foreign firm in global markets, in return to providing transport and storage for the foreign firm within the Chinese market.

So, while foreign logistics firms will rightly be extremely wary about seeking to compete with Chinese firms in the intra-China market, there is significant potential for them to play in the cross-border market, working of their global customers and possibly relying on the local infrastructure of Chinese providers.

With a few striking exceptions, Chinese logistics firms are not yet storming the world market. If you look at Chinese manufacturing, there are numerous sectors where, on the back of large scale and efficiency within China, they are now having a major impact of world markets. The obvious examples are in telecommunications infrastructure, household appliances/white goods, consumer electronics, solar panels, batteries, and EVs. The same large-scale push into global markets is also happening with engineering (roads, bridges, seaports, railways). But why are China's logistics firms so far not making that kind of impact worldwide?

China's logistics are of course intimately connected to much of this global thrust, supporting Chinese manufacturers for instance through major logistics hubs in Europe. They participate heavily in the BRI which can be viewed as fundamentally facilitating this flow of goods from China into global markets. We have documented the major move by SF, "China's FedEx" which acquired a major holding in Kerry Logistics, thus greatly beefing up their international reach, especially in SE Asia. China's e-commerce firms and the logistics firms that they own or which support them are establishing warehousing in Europe and elsewhere overseas to handle products sourced overseas (especially luxury and fashion goods). But what we have not seen yet is major Chinese logistics firms making a full-frontal challenge to global logistics firms (with the striking exception of two Chinese e-commerce firms bringing Chinese products to US consumers, as discussed below). We saw how Sinotrans and COSCO Shipping have increased their footprint in Europe through making acquisitions of local firms. While some have to do with transportation, most of this is warehousing. Chinese logistics firms find operating internationally challenging and risky. Much in the same way as foreign firms struggle with the regulatory environment and local behavior in China, so Chinese logistics firm overseas face similar challenges and a steep path of learning. Outside China, they also face the added dimension of labor unions which play a powerful role in trucking.

When it comes to e-commerce, we observe that Chinese e-commerce is not clearly connected to international e-commerce. Part of this is down to the Great Fire Wall, imposed by China to restrict and control internet communications. But more important is the very specific nature of China's e-commerce, driven by the Chinese language and customs. China's e-commerce has led China to leap-frog the credit card era and go straight to e-payments, But Alipay or WePay have emerged quite separately from PayPal. On top of this, more than 30% of China remains to be urbanized, thus presenting e-commerce with much future growth in the domestic markets and making global markets less essential.

Notwithstanding, the barriers described above, China's domestic e-commerce is witnessing a fast-growing flow of luxury products from Europe much of it carried by air cargo. But the late-breaking news of the last few years has been the extraordinary growth of two Chinese e-commerce firms, Shein and Temu, that ship Chinese garments and other products from China to the US and Europe and, in so doing, are taking on and exceeding the performance of Amazon. This trend looks likely to continue to grow. It has already sparked a huge uptick in demand for air cargo from China to the US.

Closely linked to the world

China's BRI's fundamental role is to support the flow of goods and not something more sinister. Some argue that the BRI is essentially China's master plan to curry favor internationally, to use debt-diplomacy to create dependence, and to project its political and ultimately military might across the world. However, the evidence is that to date, the BRI is fundamentally an economic program to deploy internationally the products, skills, and investment funds generated in its internal market. China's ports investment in Piraeus (Greece) and elsewhere are designed to facilitate the flow of Chinese goods into the world. Of course, the BRI does often bring with it a degree of political and financial dependence on China. But it is a mistake to underestimate the benefits of the BRI to participating nations.

If, down the road, the scenario of the severe decline of globalization were to materialize, the BRI would assume much more significance as the alternative to the trade flows with, in particular, the US. It would truly be China and the "global South" linking up to form a quite new international economic order. We do not regard that scenario as the most likely one and expect the BRI to coexist alongside more traditional trade relations.

We also should pay attention to the degree to which China is mindful of the pitfalls of being overextended in the BRI, including the risk of overlending to nations that cannot repay. We expect China to continue to learn from the mistakes made in the first decades of BRI and to adjust accordingly. The BRI will be refined and grow. It represents an entirely new system of trade and investment centered around China. As Xi Jinping himself has pointed out, the BRI in many respects boils down to logistics, the flow of goods. Chinese logistics firms will grow at the heart of the BRI.

We should not underestimate the strategic significance of the China-Europe railway land bridge. Experts are divided on the significance of the multiple freight rail lines that cross central Asia connecting Europe and China. Some, while correctly noting that container ships sea routes are the most cost-efficient way to transport goods, then move on to cast doubt on whether the rail routes will ever amount to much. One key fact that emerges from our research is that the railways across the land bridge are already achieving considerable scale and, while they will likely never eclipse the ocean routes for most goods, seem likely to grow rapidly based on a series of strategic factors.

These rail links from China to Europe via Russia and Kazakhstan are not ideal. They may be quicker than ships but still face the complexity of transfer between different rail gauges. They can never match the capacity of container ships. Since the Ukraine War, passing through Russia is not acceptable for some shippers, to the extent that one line includes a leg using ships to carry the containers across the Caspian Sea, so as to avoid Russia. The Asia-Europe rail lines are not yet electrified. Meanwhile, ocean shipping is reducing its negative environment impact through adopting new forms of propulsion.

But it is apparent that China views the land bridge as a highly strategic alternative to ocean routes and is investing heavily to help make them function smoothly. The ocean routes from China (and for that matter from South Korea and Japan) to Europe face a raft of geopolitical threats whether in the Taiwan

Straits or in the Red Sea. Maersk and China's COSCO Shipping have already been routing their vessels around the Cape in response to the Red Sea crisis. Some European exporters such as automakers shipping auto components to their plants in China have also taken to the rail links.

Chinese firms, with strong government support, are investing heavily in a fast-growing infrastructure for handing containers at multiple railway border crossings such as Khorgos on the border with Kazakhstan. China's major logistics firm are ramping up the number of scheduled rail services to Europe and the UK. At a large terminal at the inland port of Duisburg in Germany, every week dozens of freight trains arrive from China. A perfect example of this is the trains which travel 11,000 km from China's "capital of small commodity capital" Yiwu, in Zhejiang, to Duisburg in 15 days, carrying toys, clothing, tools, home decorations, and furniture. They return to China carrying whisky, wine, expensive textiles from Italy, high-end kitchen utensils, and baby food. Given the right type of product, there is a strong business argument for these rail links over ocean shipping. If we add in the strategic importance of China having alternatives in case of sea route disruption, then the land bridge is certainly of great strategic and business significance and is only likely to grow more so.

China's promotion of the BRI and trade with the global South does not imply that China intends to back out of the broader economic order and trade flows. Even though China is hedging its bets by forging new trade relations through the BRI and numerous free trade agreements, the evidence strongly suggests that China has no intention of pulling away from the global economic order. It would like to see the WTO revitalized, as an alternative to bilateral action from the US. And now, as a fast-rising, major actor on the world stage, it will continue to push for some reform of the post-WW2 "rules-based order," created by the US, even though that will inevitably create geopolitical friction. It is clear that China has no intention of abandoning the broader global order and will not voluntarily shrink into its apparently more compliant but maybe ultimately less reliable trade partnerships. Based on this analysis, and also on the continued strong reliance of the US firms, especially the retail industry, on Chinese products, our expectations are that logistics flows, that some predict are at risk, especially the ones most sensitive to geopolitics such as trans-Pacific, will continue to hold up quite strongly.

Concluding on an uplifting note

In final conclusion, the story of China logistics remains one of stark contrasts, of both extraordinary innovation and residual backwardness, and of both extraordinary government support and constraints brought by geopolitical tensions. The progress China's logistics have made over recent decades is an astonishing story of catch-up with the rest of the world. But this inspiring story goes beyond just becoming world class. With regard to e-commerce logistics, we have seen China leapfrogging the world in creating radical new technology-centric business models driven by IoT and AI. In stark contrast, at the same time much of China's logistics are still struggling to overcome the legacy it inherited from the centrally planned economy. This continues to be a drag on economic and social development. Fortunately, this weakness is amply recognized and is being addressed in multiple ways.

What stands about China's logistics development in recent decades is the core role that government has played in a myriad of ways, from the planning and investment emanating from the central government, to the inspirational impact of local city and provincial government in fostering and building logistics hubs across the nation.

Another striking key feature of China's logistics is the uncertainties around the future of global trade. The headwinds coming from multiple forms geopolitical tensions have already forced some limited adjustment to the global supply chain and may bring much yet greater threats to trade and international logistics.

The story of China's logistics, from its history of underachievement to its flourishing in recent decades is one of epic proportions. It encompasses the destiny that is geography, the transportation system that was upgraded so rapidly, the strong role of the Chinese government, and then the state firms and private entrepreneurs that have taken up the baton and run with it. They have done this within the domestic market, integrating the Chinese economy (and with it the nation) in a way never seen before. China's logistics have stepped up to the plate and delivered on the international scene, especially along the trade routes of the BRI. The story of China's modern integrated logistics exemplifies the Chinese people's hunger and perseverance, a passion to learn and innovate, as the path to "revitalize the nation" (*zhenhua*). It is a heroic story of how the Chinese have fully grasped the new technologies to improve economic efficiency, help meet targets for environmental sustainability, and, not least, improve the lot of the nation's citizens.

About the authors

Dr. Paul G. Clifford is a nonresident Senior Fellow at Harvard's Kennedy School of Government. He is the President of the management consultants Paul G. Clifford & Associates, LLC. He is also an Honorary Fellow of the Foreign Policy Association and External Associate, Lau China Institute, King's College London.

He first lived in China as a student in 1973–1974. After that he worked in China as a corporate banker with The First National Bank of Chicago (now JP Morgan Chase), with strategy consultants Oliver Wyman and with US technology firm Cisco Systems where he was driving strategy in China on smart and connected cities, through a strategic alliance with China Development Bank.

He has deep experience in China's logistics. He led consulting teams that advised a number of China's largest state-owned logistics firms on their restructuring and strategic planning. He has also advised foreign logistics providers on their China market entry strategy. He has supported foreign investors in China on their supply chain issues across a wide range of sectors. He has also consulted to foreign and Chinese clients on China's railways, intermodal transportation, shipping, and public urban transportation.

He was elected as Executive Director of the China Federation of Logistics & Purchasing.

He is the author of the book *The China Paradox. At the Front Line of Economic Transformation,* which profiles the 40 years of China's economic reforms.

He studied at the School of Oriental and African Studies, University of London, where he received a Ph.D. in modern Chinese history, and at Peking University. He has taught at universities in Mexico, the UK, and the US. He is fluent in Chinese.

Christopher Logan is the President of LOGISTEED International and Chief International Business Officer of LOGISTEED Ltd, which was formerly Hitachi Transport System. Based in Singapore, he leads the contract logistics and freight forwarding business outside the home market of Japan, driving strategic growth in Asia Pacific, Europe, and the Americas.

Previous leadership positions included Managing Director, Freight and Logistics Lead for Asia, Middle East, and Africa at Accenture based in Singapore; Chief Strategy and Marketing Officer at Agility Logistics, based in Hong Kong; and Principal at Oliver Wyman where he lived in Beijing and advised logistics clients in China. This blend of experience offers him a comprehensive view of the logistics sector, from operational challenges to strategic planning.

As an active World Economic Forum Young Global Leader, he collaborates with global stakeholders to tackle pressing challenges in logistics. His international work experience encompasses the US, China, Hong Kong, Indonesia, South Africa, and Canada, providing him with a broad, cross-cultural perspective.

He is an alumnus of Ivey Business School at Western University and has completed executive education programs at the Harvard Kennedy School, the Yale Jackson School of Global Affairs, and the Lee Kuan Yew School of Public Policy.

Index

Note: *Italic* page numbers refer to figures.

Printed in the United States
by Baker & Taylor Publisher Services